building culture

procurement of UK arts construction

Bridget Sawyers & Walter Menteth

Project
Compass

CONTENTS

context

conclusions

methodology

appendices

Available digitally under separate cover at:

projectcompass.co.uk/wp-content/uploads/2021/04/Building-Culture_APPENDICES_210405_R4.pdf

Donald Hyslop is an urbanist working on the regeneration, reinvention, economic and social development of cities and communities.

His work begins with people, a human scale, and is shaped by a value and principles-based thinking and practice. Partnerships and active participation are central, and Donald is a long-term advocate and practitioner of the importance of public and open spaces, heritage, diversity, circularity, and co-production.

Long term leadership roles at Tate Modern, Borough Market and Better Bankside BID has enabled the meshing of community, culture, and business which he believes are fundamental elements in vibrant communities, bringing balance to our cities and towns.

He acts as an advisor and consultant to cities across the world on innovative social development. Expanding and exploring thinking and practice as a broadcaster, curator, public speaker, and writer.

As Chair of Creative and Culture Skills UK Donald is determined to ensure that opportunities for creative skills, education and employment are available to all. In these important times of recovery and change putting the voices of young people centre stage will be a priority.

I Foreword

As a shy but inquisitive ten-year-old I was taken by a neighbour to my local museum in the town of Dumfries in Scotland. Climbing the stairs of the tower of the museum we passed the treasures of archaeology, natural history and antiquities which were to become the basis of many future visits. However, the purpose of the journey that day, lay atop a spiral staircase, where a secret door unlocked a room in the roof of the tower. It was here that the curator of the museum, Alfred Truckle, would when the weather permitted reveal in real time, through the world's oldest operating camera obscura, the life and happenings of the town and its people around us.

Upon reflection, this experience of refraction, was formative in helping ignite a lifelong interest in history, buildings, and the power of culture. Shaping a way of thinking and practice in how these can affect and bring positive changes to the places we live and the communities we are part of.

building culture is a comprehensive survey and commentary of the processes and power of cultural development and its reach across the United Kingdom. The authors have taken time, consideration, and great attention to detail from which they then present some of the urgent and important challenges and issues of our time. These are expertly framed through a diverse set of exemplar projects as case studies. They have also helpfully situated all of this within the complex (and sometimes confusing) world of planning, policy, and funding regimes. The result will prove an essential resource to students, practitioners and others looking to understand the world of cultural development with all its many challenges and opportunities. It is also important to understand that this is much more than a survey.

The recommendations the authors present to us here are central to a dialogue which is much needed about the values and principles needed for our society in the future.

In the best of times but also in times of crisis and adversity it is from the public and voluntary sectors that innovative and community focused solutions often come. This is particularly true in our built environment and cultural lives. In the UK, and across the world, as we emerge slowly from the Covid pandemic and face the huge social and economic challenges before us it is in these areas we can once look again to creative, innovative, and practical rejuvenation. However, this needs also one feels to be a time where we take the opportunity to move to a clearer sense of and more human approach to how we live, work and play. In environmental language this is a form of social rewilding. The buzzwords of transparency, diversity and co-production need to be made real not least in tackling the institutionalised inward-looking bureaucratic processes that ultimately exclude the very people they proclaim to support.

The time has also come to leave behind the outdated approaches of inflexible master planning and our overdependence on the simplified idea of the visionary creative individual. In an increasingly digitally connected world, we can be both locally rooted and globally known. Thinking and approaches to commissioning and living which are adventurous, decentralise structures and bring a diverse multiplicity of voices to place shaping will perhaps also bring us some reflection and refraction anew.

Donald Hyslop
April 2021

II   Introduction

This book reviews recent UK building culture exploring how construction work in the arts sector has been instigated, implemented, acquired and driven by public funders, commissioners, architects and project teams, from inception. How arts and cultural buildings are procured and built is then analysed, in the context of the processes and procedures which inform their architectural implementation and the quality of their outputs.

The content includes a description of eleven recent UK cultural buildings, illustrated with photos, drawings and data. These insightful case studies, written by architects, clients and competition programmers, uniquely illuminate the reality behind delivering these projects, from commissioning and appointment to completion. The case studies cover a spectrum of building types, art forms and procurements.

Comparative analysis of commissioning practices in the UK arts sector is then provided, with evidence drawn from the case studies alongside evidence from a unique national data set of cultural commissions. Among issues analysed are how projects are funded, by whom, which types, the scales, where and over what time-scales, and how consultants and project teams are appointed, along with the routes and by which the most successful projects have been enabled. The funding, structures, strategies and processes of the main UK arts funders over the period is explained along with the scope and extent of the guidance funders provide to support the processes of implementing projects.

The impacts on the sector of Brexit and the Covid-19 pandemic are also included. The rapidly changing scenario is explored in greatest detail, along with supplementary information on funders, their policy, guidance and programmes, within the appendices and under separate cover.

Building Culture provides better understanding of the methods adopted and the outputs that have been achieved, across a range of contexts and scenarios, typologies, sizes and costs, and the quality of outputs being delivered. Together the content, analysis and recommendations offer unique insights into the sector, and a resource for policy makers, clients, their advisors, construction consultants and arts professionals. By benchmarking recent practices this also provides a means to constructively inform the future, against the historic backdrops of Brexit and the Covid-19 pandemic.

There had been an expectation, on commencing this book, that the arts sector would provide progressive and exemplary built environment patronage in the development of their estates, by clients, commissioners and funders — offering the best of UK practices. From previously sampled evidence, the sector still appeared to provide opportunity for young and emergent architects to gain access to new and creatively challenging projects and innovative work, and doing so by more flexible creative approaches.

This is generally found to be the case, evidentially in this detailed examination, although room for significant advancement remains, particularly compared to some other nations.

Concerns about climate change, sustainability and resilience also raised further research questions — about the effectiveness of the buildings and their outcomes. An intention of this examination was to evidence the practice outcomes within the sector further, against these criteria, and explore those that are exemplary, with the aim of providing models for UK adoption.

Throughout **Building Culture** the definition of arts and cultural buildings applied is '**buildings used for the production, performing and exhibiting of art and heritage**', with culture as 'the ideas, values, and practices of the engaged society', particularly those in it's production and consumption.

The data set that has been collated excludes the creative industries and the following however:
- cultural hubs
- creative workspace and enterprises
- makerspace and shared workshops
- incubator hubs
- community spaces
- archives
- visitor centres
- public art
- bridges
- churches and places of worship
- landscapes and gardens

The focus of this book's research is upon arts facilities provided with support from public funds. Most arts capital projects have an element of public funding which is awarded on the basis that commissioners have to have a transparent public procurement process. It has been found that such funding conditions are generally applied even when the public sectors proportionate contribution falls below the mandatory requirements, or 50% financial contribution.[1] The majority of UK capital arts projects therefore are thought to have been captured within the unique data set constructed for the purpose of this publication.

Philanthropic giving, particularly in the arts, makes a critical contribution, the largest noted being for £11.25m towards Opera North's capital development. In this research, however, the private funding provided, through a range of foundations, organisations, companies and private individuals, has not been evaluated.

———

Building Culture is organised into six sections with it's appendices, under separate cover.

The foreword and introduction, with key recommendations preface the second **section of Ten Case Study Chapters** contributed by eminent architects, competition programmers and a client. These case studies provide substantive detailed insights into eleven specific projects that are sequentially organised according to the four UK nations *(fig. II.1)*. They explore the context in which each project progressed.

Breathing new life into historic buildings, by extending their contemporary use with new facilities, is still seen by some as constraining.

The Royal Academy of Music (RAM) described **by Ian Ritchie and Brian Heron** in Chapter 1 illustrates the calibre and ingenuity offered by an assured architectural strategy and delivery, which has turned complex multiple constraints, imposed by the existing buildings, into opportunities. The programming for this educational institution had to account for RAM's ongoing operation within the listed historic structures. The new works cunningly deliver an additional recital room above the main auditorium, together with a standard of facilities far above what was originally anticipated or briefed.

This is the only case study project that has mainly been privately funded. Nevertheless University College London, RAM's host institute, determined to run a competitive process for re selecting the architect following planning approval. Delivering a project of such quality in these challenging physical circumstances had many intervening procedural and contractual issues.

This description provides a uniquely informative insight into how this complex construction project has been so successfully steered. The extraordinary quality of RAM's new theatre and recital hall has been delivered with technical flair, expertise, craft and a level of invention that displays the professional expertise necessary to guide design of this calibre. RAM have procured a building they are proud of, that upholds their international reputation and achieved this with the highest levels of measurable sustainability. Deservedly it has received many accolades

Wilton's Music Hall described **by Tim Ronalds** in Chapter 2 is a small delicate and complex project that had multiple stage funding. Relative to it's scale and cost the project took considerable time — nine and a half years from start to completion. The project however clearly benefited immeasurably from stakeholder/design team constancy. This allowed a singular and exquisitely well-judged vision to be reliably delivered to an exceptional standard. Wilton's Music Hall is a testament to the stamina, tenacity and dedication of both the client and architect. It manifests uniquely the difference in providing consistent employment, that delivers professionalism and values beyond any measurable or anticipated expectation, and the procedures for appointment that have more recently become ascendant — namely the fragmentary appointment of architects over different work stages.

Aberdeen
Art Gallery

TheTheatre
Royal Glasgow

Edinburgh
Printmakers

The Giant's
Causeway

Walk the Plank

Tŷ Pawb
(Everybody's
House)

Wyeside Arts
Centre

Wilton's
Music Hall

The Oriel
Myrddin Gallery

The Royal
College of
Music

High House
Artists'
Studios

fig. II.1
*Location of the
case studies*

Wilton's Music Hall's delicate listed historic fabric has been addressed by celebrating its archaeology. It has been executed with appreciative self-effacing detailing, delivered with a consistency appropriate to its simple raw spaces and has been done so robustly. It has a sensitivity, subtlety and sensuality which goes far beyond any iconic offering, and should be a must on any London tourist itinerary.

Walk the Plank, described **by Luke Cooper and Sylvia Hebden** in Chapter 3, is particularly illuminating for the importance given to aligning human empathies and social values in the process. The client's progressive creative aims and ambitions led them to engage widely, to deliberately attract young new design talent. The desire to source such talent locally and re-use, what might initially have appeared, an unprepossessing building provides a lesson for a more sustainably regional circular economic strategy. This is the only case study project which fell below the EU threshold values and therefore had no need for a public tender to be issued in OJEU. The project however used a transparent process having a most economically advantageous tender (MEAT) assessment for the selection of the architect. Weighted at 40% this was the lowest found among the case studies. The team nevertheless have delivered a delightful upcycling project offering exceptionally distinctive architectural value on a very tight budget.

A project that also achieved extraordinary value, which was delivered on an exceptionally short time-scale, with a low budget, and for the production of art, and which has many similarities with Walk the Plank, is **High House**. As **Hana Loftus** describes in Chapter 4, this was also **HAT Projects** first commission as a new practice working in the sector. It provides various sizes of artist's studios within a freestanding new building, conceived as an integral part of a regeneration masterplan, in Purfleet, Essex. High House's design economy and lyrically simple execution appear underpinned by a well-conceived and planned commissioning strategy led by robust and supportive public authority project management. This process has translated into an enormously successful, judiciously clever and exceptionally appropriate facility that delivers excellence with flair.

From the client's side, as **Alex Reedijk** describes in Chapter 5 on the **Theatre Royal Glasgow**, the complexity of delivering a well-conceived project is never easy. In a highly competitive environment which had a two stage tender process the main contractor's ability to deliver on their price submission, despite extensive value engineering, placed significant pressure on the project with poor initial site leadership, disruption to progress, issues of workmanship, sub-contracted packages and the final contractual resolution.

Nonetheless, the client team reveal extraordinary capacity and ingenuity in surmounting the challenges. This included deploying their own workshop and staff to deliver a £1m specialist staircase joinery package, which had otherwise failed to attract any viable external tenders. This initiative was a rare and resourceful approach to resolving a pivotally important architectural package within the new building, without which the whole scheme would have been significantly diminished. Despite some exceptional challenges the client team's unswerving commitment and sheer determination to deliver a project of exceptional quality, for Scottish Opera appears remarkable, hugely professional and a great success.

Aberdeen Art Gallery, described by **Chris Coleman-Smith** in Chapter 6 is a project that has gone through a particularly long 12 year gestation. Among the case studies it is the largest project overall at 7,741m^2 and at £34.6m the most expensive, but at a cost of £4,470m^2, was less than four others. The architects selection took roughly 20 months, at a time when the late Gareth Hoskins' practice was only ten years old. This bold vision for rejuvenating the city gallery, as part of a wider area masterplan, has finally now been exquisitely executed.

As **Chris Coleman-Smith** reflects *"An important factor in the success of this project … was that key design decisions were not made until after the original brief, and … ideas tested"* and that there was an *"enlightened client who … understood their own priorities … (ensuring) those priorities were upheld throughout"*

A characteristic of many of the case studies has been the pursuit of a clear and highly creative vision for bringing new life to old buildings. At the listed Aberdeen Gallery, along with the restoration and refurbishment of the existing fabric, the juxtaposition with the old of a dramatic new roof scape / roof top contributes bold originality to the transformation.

While the new V&A Gallery Dundee by Kengo Kuma & Associates attracted significant support and funding from the Scottish

fig. II.2
*Interior of the V&A
Dundee by Kengo
Kuma Associates
© Bridget Sawyers*

Government, Aberdeen Art Gallery didn't *(fig. 1.2)*. This is, perhaps, a tale of two cities because funding the Aberdeen Gallery has taken significant independent prolonged effort and commitment from the City of Aberdeen, National Heritage Lottery Fund, BP and public donations. The confident sense of civic purpose that has driven it, prevailed.

Providing for the creative arts as a key catalyst within cultural led regeneration plans, whether through development of facilities in converted buildings or in new buildings, is a recurrent theme amongst the case studies. This development model gained particular currency after construction of the Guggeheim in Bilbao and led to a number of UK projects such as the Turner Contemporary in Margate by David Chipperfield Architects *(fig. 1.3)*.

This is also the case at **Edinburgh Printmakers** which **Nicola Walls** describes in chapter 7. This existing listed building provides an important new cultural institution within the emerging Fountainbridge area, to the west of Edinburgh's centre. On completion it sat surrounded on two sides by land awaiting development. Similar cultural based regeneration strategies at this scale may be considered less likely for the foreseeable future.

As Nicola Walls discusses, Page \ Park Architects take considerable care evaluating their bidding, the project type, value, requirements for experience and whether there is an incumbent, to ensure that the requirements and conditions applied at the outset make bidding viable. Page \ Park were also architects for the **Theatre Royal Glasgow** and have a strong and well-earned presence in the sector established over many years.

Nevertheless, following a successful competitive bid, Page \ Park went on to design the Edinburgh Printmakers facility, with its new street entrance, galleries, café, shop, airy, generous and well-arranged printmaking studio and creative industries spaces. A delightful, sensitive and contextually appropriate re-visioning of this listed building has been delivered which successfully provides a vital addition to the locality and Edinburgh's cultural offer, at a very competitive price of £2,453m². The contrast between new and old are finely engaged and fully exploited with robust, well executed and considered detailing that conveys its exceptional value.

It might be perceived that there is no more challenging culturally based regeneration programme than the viable conversion of an existing town centre car park into an arts centre — one can imagine, perhaps, the client's initial trepidation, while functionally the structural challenges alone can be significant. At **Tŷ Pawb** in Chapter 8 **Sarah Featherstone** describes successfully delivering this difficult programme which is now, rightly, recognised by Arts Council Wales as an exemplar.

At 4,000m² this building is a beguilingly large mixed use project for the arts, that provides a diversity of integrated facilities. Pro-active consultation and engagement with the local community, in the design solution and in it's production, has been a key to successfully informing the iteration of this creative design. Featherstone Young Architects have delivered something here that is unique, in terms of its vision, the programme, the pro-active engagement, the economy of its execution and its delight. They have done so to an exceptionally high and robustly appropriate quality which is a testament to their resolve.

With a declining high street retail sector and increasing obsolescence of many town centre car parks, the congregational, cultural and social activities offered by this visionary and innovative project clearly delivers a valuable template for the future economic regeneration of other city centres.

In Chapter 9 **the Oriel Myrddin Gallery and Wyeside Arts Centre** are compared by **Angus Morrogh-Ryan** of De Matos Ryan Architects. Work on progressing the Oriel Myrddin Gallery to completion commenced in 2016 from an RIBA Stage 0-2 feasibility undertaken by others. However, complexities arose with land purchases and access, necessitating a strategic reappraisal. The Wyeside Arts Centre was a 2018 award for a RIBA Stage 0-2 commission with DeMatos Ryan Architects appointed as lead consultants of a multi-disciplinary team, with nine other consultants, for a relatively small project. Further commissioned consultancy reports were then also required.

This comparison shows how projects can change, and questions how procurement, resources and consultant services might be allocated better to improve value, with more progressive, iterative and flexible business planning.

The Giant's Causeway described by **Jim Roberts** in Chapter 10 perhaps illustrates the most unusual project. This is the earliest Case Study, commencing in 2003 and opening in 2013 and was procured by a design contest. It is the only project from N. Ireland, was promoted by the N. Ireland Government, is a new building on a world heritage site and unusually combines a gatehouse with a regional exhibition centre.

This site of global stature was Henegan Peng Architects first building commission. Their highly lauded design solution derived from a process that has appropriately delivered a magnificent and distinctive internationally recognised building. It is testament to how individual projects, when well-designed at their conception and using a design contest with effective procedural management, can deliver cultural value well beyond anything anticipated.

In the following section of data analysis information from the cohort of case studies is then analysed, appraised and evaluated in **Case Study Projects — Summary Data,** in Chapter 11. **UK Data Research and Analysis** of a 2013-2018 sample of 421 arts and heritage capital projects across the UK is then appraised, in Chapter 12.

This unique data set, which has been constructed specifically for this publication, offers exceptional insights for evaluation of arts and cultural buildings over the time frame. This chapter includes the locations, national and regional (where available) expenditures, numbers of grants awarded, art forms and building types, notification numbers and types, the procurement route adopted, the basis of how awards have been assessed and to whom, illustrated graphically and highlighting examples of best practice and some less so.

The Context in which UK arts facilities are built is described and reviewed in the subsequent section, **Capital Programme Funding** in Chapters 13 and **Current Guidance**, Chapter 14. The funding ecology and specifically that of the national arts funding bodies, the formations for those providing the infrastructure and resources to realise these projects, along with the conditions applied and guidance offered to arts organisations when instigating development of arts projects is summarily reviewed in these two chapters. This provides an analytical overview, of the structures available to authorities, clients and design teams to communicate the landscape in which public arts and cultural buildings are acquired.

The arts and cultural sector is maintained by a complex funding ecology which is under constant review, change, evaluation and justification. In addition to national arts funding, there is earned income through sales, donations and fundraising initiatives. The impact of this on the capital infrastructure is outlined within this section.

Conclusions are then detailed and reported in Chapter 15.

The **Contributors' Biographies** in Chapter 16, and Chapter 17 the **Research Methodology** follow with a **Glossary of Terms**, and **Index**, in conclusion.

The appendices, under separate cover, investigates **Brexit** and the **Covid-19** pandemic impacts on the sector and responses emerging to the rapidly changing scenario up, to March 2021, along with supplementary information on funders, their policy, guidance and programmes.

Building Culture builds on the approaches and methodologies developed by **Project Compass CIC,** in a series of previous outputs which aim to:
• Improve transparency, access, opportunities and innovation.
• Analyse trends which inform construction and architectural outputs.
• Inform the reform of policy, and support best practice with appropriate guidance.
• Advocate for better procurement as it leads to better design.
Allowing for comparative UK and international:
• Appraisal and analysis
• Benchmarking of processes, procedures, and practices
And all so as to offer resources for expanding capacity and knowledge, in the UK and internationally so that outcomes can be improved.[2]

Since 2009 **Project Compass CIC** has built a unique data set of UK architectural procurement. This provides an unparalleled research resource for interrogation of the construction sectors performance.

The format of the case studies in **Building Culture** match the thirteen case studies in the Project Compass publication, **'Competition Culture in Europe: Voices'** (2018), which alongside the supplementary essays discussing the

fig. II.3
The Turner Contemporary, Margate by David Chipperfield Architects completed 2011 © Walter Menteth

potential opportunities from historic, contemporary and future international competitions allows for comparative analysis with the international and national practices found there.[3]

Analysis of UK construction industry procurement, by Project Compass reported in **'Public Construction Procurement Trends 2009-2014'**, provides a benchmark for scrutinising some of these new findings.[4] Where comparisons are made within **Building Culture,** these are cross referenced. The data set from 2013-19 presented in **Building Culture** is specific to the arts sector, but overlaps the previous reporting period in **'Public Construction Procurement Trends 2009-2014'** by 5 year quarters. Many of the trends found previously can be seen to have continued and others show some marked divergences. These largely reflect well on the arts sector, in relationship to the wider UK context.

Building Culture in part aligns with the programme of knowledge dissemination instigated at the Conference on Competition Culture in Europe (CCIE), 2017.[5] The publication from this conference '**Competition Culture in Europe 2013-2016'**,[6] provides further resources including information on national practices and regulations, portals, organisations engaged in competitions, and their platforms, along with case studies, for comparative analysis across seventeen countries.

———

This book describes and evidences how recent projects progressed, despite the many pitfalls. It provides understanding of — the opportunities offered by projects; their processes and how those have arisen (described in fullest detail in the case studies); of the sectors performance related to objectives, funding and guidance; and of the sector's wider construction outputs, and in comparison to international practices.

Building Culture commenced in 2019 before the impact of Covid-19 on the arts and cultural sector began to be realised. Because many organisations are long-standing institutions which are either buildings (venues, museums etc.) or production companies (orchestras, dance, theatre, etc.), and because of the restrictions on public programmes, huge additional demands are currently being placed on those organisations, public funding and policy.

Together both Brexit and Covid are a potential tsunami, to which the escalating impacts of climate change should be added. Many arts institutions have already been closed, mothballed, or are struggling to survive. It can be assumed that, in the immediate short and medium term, there is unlikely to be a focus on the type of building programmes seen within the past decade. As it continues to emerge this context is addressed.

Building Culture provides resources and insights into the sector, through which a better future may be foreseen and modelled. This can inspire progression, innovation and reform while informing practices, so that in future better UK building culture may be delivered. The lessons that can be learnt here are, for the coming decade's new situation, now more prescient than ever, if adaptation, flexibility and resilience are to be effective and coherent.

References

1   The Public Contracts Regulations 2015 Regulation 2. Definition of "bodies covered by public law" www.legislation.gov.uk/uksi/2015/102/regulation/2/made (accessed 2 July 2020)

2   www.projectcompass.co.uk

3   Menteth W. (ed) Competition Culture in Europe: Voices. Project Compass, London 2018 ISBN 978-0-9931481-5-6. projectcompass.co.uk/index.php/compass/publications/ (accessed 2 July 2020)

4   Menteth W., O'Carroll O., Curtis R., Sawyers B., Public Construction Procurement Trends 2009-2014. Project Compass CIC, London 2014. ISBN 978-0-9931481-0-1 projectcompass.co.uk/index.php/compass/publications/ (accessed 2 July 2020)

5   projectcompass.co.uk/index.php/2017/10/04/ten-steps-to-improve-architectural-competition-culture-in-europe/

6   Competition Culture in Europe 20103-2016 2016 Architectuur Lokaal projectcompass.co.uk/wp-content/uploads/2020/09/R2-Competition-Culture-in-Europe_180314-AL_web_def_comp.pdf (accessed 2 July 2020)

III   Key findings and recommendations

1. KEY FINDINGS

1.1 GENERALLY

1.1.1 **Equality, diversity, inclusion, quality and sustainability performance is generally better in the arts sector, relative to other UK construction sectors.**

Many instances where the sector has evidently been generally out-performing other UK construction sectors in procuring and delivering buildings were found, although far more should still be done.

1.1.2 **Procurement and delivery in the arts and cultural sector offers clear best practice lessons applicable to other sectors.**

1.2 FUNDING DISTRIBUTION AND CULTURAL RECOVERY

1.2.1 **An inequitable distribution of award funding across the UK and within the English regions was found.**

The largest inequity found was the 24.2% of the total UK funding awarded to four London projects. These four projects have advanced at the expense of wider social values, potentially including, amongst others, the ability for new arts initiatives to emerge. This imbalance has been acknowledged since 2000.

1.2.2 **There is an absence of strategic cultural infrastructure planning and few common funding delivery structures and processes.**

1.2.3 **Poor resource staging by funders and clients, and inappropriate project management extend and jeopardise many projects programmes.**

1.2.4 **Cultural led regeneration, when not carefully considered, can create unsustainable infrastructure.**

1.2.5 **Large projects are now less likely to succeed than those that are smaller, local, nimble, mixed use and flexible.**

1.3 FUNDERS AND CLIENT GUIDANCE

1.3.1 **The nations and agencies provide extensive advice, but there is a significant shortfall and a lack of meaningful direction for supporting clients through procurement processes.**

1.4 SUSTAINABILITY

1.4.1 **Outcomes have been more sustainable, because more arts projects reuse existing buildings and most projects target high environmental standards.**

Environmental awareness was found to be well embedded in the sector. Targets have been ambitious and guidance on sustainability is expansive and comprehensive. For new buildings high environmental performance standards appear sought. A large preponderance of capital projects re-used and adapted existing buildings. Sustainable outcomes, arising largely from the conserving embodied energy, were typically found to be exemplary, relative to other UK construction sectors.

1.4.2 **The traditional project management 'time, cost and value' axioms appear to apply less in this sector, unless balanced with sustainability as a fourth measure.**

This offers project managers' lessons on how best to remodel those traditional project management axioms in response to the climate crisis. This aligns, for example, with the London Energy Transformation Initiative (LETI) recommendations for a zero carbon future. With the retail collapse, innovative high street projects, such as Tŷ Pawb, also offer a sustainable exemplar for potential city centre regeneration.

1.5 EQUALITY, DIVERSITY, AND INCLUSION (EDI)

1.5.1 Strategies embedding equality, diversity and inclusion (EDI) are successfully delivering highly valued, good quality outputs.

1.5.2 Many arts organisations have focused upon engaging with equality, diversity and inclusion in their revenue funding programmes, but far less so in their capital programming.

Relative to other UK construction sectors the arts sector was however found to be exemplary in some respects. For example, from the outset of lottery funding, in 1995, consideration was given to ensuring disabled access is provided and this was embedded in capital lottery programmes. So accessible buildings are expected, although delivery can be variable.

1.5.3 The sector offers the best opportunities to access and win contracts for Micro and SME businesses (MSMEs) and female empowered consultancies, because of it's better inclusivity.

In procurement, unusually, access by MSME business consultancies to design commissions remains particularly high and the distribution of work across the sector better reflects the available talent pool. The case study sampling also suggests that design consultancies led by women are achieving higher than average engagement. This inclusion is delivering innovative high-quality outputs and contributing towards making a more vibrant and creatively innovative culture.

1.5.4 In the arts capital programming little specific data could be found reporting BAME inclusion for people working on project commissioning and delivery, or the diversity of the audiences to whom the projects are targeted.

From the findings on the national distribution of award funding what is notable and related, is how much funding is allocated to specific geographic regions, large projects and traditional art forms.

1.6 QUALITY OF OUTPUTS

1.6.1 Value, cost, and quality are different things, but because they interrelate they can become confused. Evaluating their inter-relationships requires clear objectives and understanding.

The budget, procurement route, contracts, programme, design quality, and values all interrelate.

In early Lottery funded projects design and construction quality was entrenched in an exemplary way within the funding guidance and criteria. There is now far less guidance, criteria are less assertive and funding bodies guidance on procurement routes is variable, if featured at all. This is possibly because of a mistaken assumption that quality expectations have become a given requirement.

1.6.2 As the case studies testify, the sector is returning more creative outputs that deliver higher design quality, and better value, appropriately, with consistent social benefits.

1.7 USE OF PROCUREMENT ROUTES & PROCEDURES

1.7.1 More flexible, effective and efficient procedures, specific to individual projects, have been used.

1.7.2 Procurement and tendering procedures remain frequently inappropriate and poor.

The procedures being used in the arts sector are appropriately project specific. Very few appointments have been made from frameworks, by a call off.

1.7.3 The appointment of design consultants 'called off' from frameworks remains extremely rare, in the arts sector.

The use of frameworks for the appointment of consultants is not recommended for cultural buildings, other than possibly for larger institutions having multiple sites and or requiring a prolonged programme of cyclical maintenance and repairs.

1.7.4 The open and restricted procedures are the only two types of procedure being used, of the seven that are available.

1.8 SELECTION AND ASSESSMENT VALUES

1.8.1 Selection criteria and assessment methods have been relatively well considered and appropriately tailored to outputs.

Too many selection evaluations were still found weighting bid prices too high relative to quality and value. Only two projects were found having a 100% quality and value assessment. Both of these had specific and well considered competitive procedures to enable this, and required the assessment of drawn submissions, with peer reviewed evaluation.[1]

1.8.2 No funder guidance was found for embedding social value distinctly.

Assessment of this emerging criteria needs considered guidance by funders, so it doesn't impinge upon qualitative values — if it is to be distinctly evaluated. On criteria and their evaluation Government provides clear guidance stating that, *'price and value should focus on value over cost'* and furthermore *'paying more for higher quality maybe justified if the whole life cost is advantageous'*.[2]

1.9 TRANSPARENCY

1.9.1 Lack of transparency is growing, with many instances where there were no records reporting the results of procurements.

It is critical that post Brexit the processes and the digital infra-structure, including the tender portals that sustain procurement, can deliver transparency and address the potential for corruption.

1.9.2 Digital infrastructure remains fragmentary, inadequate and there is no single pre-eminent national portal for issuing procurement notices, documents and processes.

The government appear committed to addressing these transparency issues, migrating towards open data standards for all and building more suitable digital infra structure, which is to be welcomed.[3]

2. RECOMMENDATIONS

2.1 COVID-19

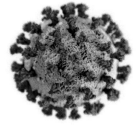

(Covid-19 responses, to March 2021, are tracked and described in Appendix H)

What seems clear in 2021 is that:

- Post Covid-19, there will be less money in arts cultural funding and less in people's pockets.
- Many building based organisations are, or will be, at risk from associated loss of revenue, limited or non-existent reserves, and Local Authority austerity cuts, with increasing pressure on maintenance and renewal costs.
- During any Covid-19 recovery economic pressures will be compounded by the impact of Brexit.
- There will be a loss of those who come with greater burdens and cannot survive. This tragedy in the making will see a survival of the fittest and have deep impacts on, among others, communities, young people, and cultural diversity.

It is probable that without suitable arts' policy reform the combined impacts of Covid-19 and Brexit, as described, will deliver long term damage to the sector from now until beyond 2030.

2.1.1 **In anticipation of long term Covid-19 and Brexit impacts appropriate measures should be taken to provide the best possible support for sustaining the vitality and diversity of UK culture.**

2.1.2 **The key principles underpinning cultural support should be EDI, flexibility, and giving opportunity to new emerging working and creative practices.**

2.1.3 **In anticipation of a period of recovery from the pandemic, there should be a strategic shift in the allocation of funding resources. This should be towards seasonally based external activities, those occupying mixed use facilities, having more self contained users in well ventilated manageable spaces and digital media— rather than single use facilities for mass gatherings.**

2.1.4 **To sustain the widest possible arts base forward, project size will now become more critical than ever and this should be at an appropriate and smaller scale.**

2.2 FUNDING DISTRIBUTION AND CULTURAL RECOVERY

2.2.1 **As part of any Covid-19 cultural recovery the inequitable distribution of award funding across the UK and within the English regions needs to be addressed with an urgent national strategic infrastructure review.** *(NB. Prior to the pandemic Creative Scotland had undertaken a national strategic review).*

There is now an opportunity to holistically review the national capital portfolios in light of funding constraints, additional operating costs, continued reduced revenue and spatial future proofing, and encourage more creative thinking for the asset management and community wealth building. This might require local authorities to creatively consider interdependencies, how arts / cultural and community organisations can align interests to address social, health and wealth equalities, and collaboratively address the climate emergency.

2.3 FUNDERS' AND CLIENT GUIDANCE

2.3.1 **To ensure better value and outcomes funders' and clients need more effective assistance and better guidance to support navigating the procurement, design, construction or refurbishment process for cultural buildings.**

2.3.2 **A revised and updated version of the Creating Excellent Buildings, A Guide for Clients should be produced.[4]**

2.4 SUSTAINABILITY

2.4.1 **More curation of existing assets can deliver advantages for sustainability, from flexibility and in project programme phasing.**

2.4.2 **As climate crisis, Covid-19 and Brexit impact, the arts sector should anticipate driving sustainability further, with greater ambitions and better targeted policy and guidance.**

2.5 EQUALITY, DIVERSITY, AND INCLUSION

2.5.1 Arts funders should develop strategic EDI policies for the requirements sought from their capital projects, the procurement and the standards to be expected from those who are funded, to align better to the standards applied to their revenue funding.

2.5.2 There should be better data gathering to support improving BAME inclusion through procurement commissioning and delivery.

2.6 DESIGN QUALITY

2.6.1 Clients need to be fully supported in their understanding of how the best design quality can be achieved through the process.

2.6.2 Design quality, procurement route, budget, contracts, and programme are interrelated and the associations need to be aligned and monitored through the processes, for decision making and to ensure design quality.

Given the lengthy time-scales of project gestation and delivery the procurement route for arts buildings clearly needs careful consideration if quality is to be sustained.

2.6.3 Investment in good briefing and feasibility studies are essential to ensure that funding, expectations and budgets are aligned.

2.6.4 A clear strategy should be put in place to ensure control over the design is maintained through the design and construction stages.

Design principles agreed during the early design stages should not be lost after RIBA Stage 3, during technical design or later.

2.6.5 From RIBA Stage 2, clients should seek to minimise risks to design quality by contracting the same design team through all subsequent RIBA Work Stages.

This sustains a 'golden thread' over a projects progression. Break clauses can easily be provided in standard consultancy contracts, allowing employment to be concluded if works do not proceed. Break clauses are a faster, cheaper and far better option than multiple staged appointments.

2.6.6 When a Design and Build process must be used, the design consultancies should either be novated to the contractor or retained by the client and empowered with a watching brief, only after RIBA Stage 4A.

2.7 PROCUREMENT ROUTES

2.7.1 Greater use of design contests should be encouraged in funders guidance.

This competitive procedure is versatile and flexible, may be most appropriate, takes no longer than a two stage restricted procedure, is used frequently internationally and offers the cultural sector significant benefits.

2.8 SELECTION CRITERIA AND ASSESSMENT

2.8.1 Where it is appropriate 100% qualitative assessments are recommended.

In an open or restricted procedure this may be done by specification of a fixed price (or ranged budgetary prices). In a design contest it is done by a fee negotiation after the resulting award, with any unsuccessful negotiation(s) passed over in order of the winner ranking.

2.8.2 If selections need to be based upon price and quality assessments, then price should be no greater than 30%.

2.8.3 If selections need to be based upon price, quality and social value assessments, then price should be reduced in proportion to the extent of the social value being assessed, and without reducing the quality being assessed.

2.8.4 In mixed price and quality assessments, bidders should pass a quality threshold before their price bids should be considered.

Known as a 'double envelope system', this precludes those who can not reach a minimum threshold standard being able to win a bid.

2.8.5 The 'mean average' price rather than lowest price fees bid, should be used as the basis of assessment.

Price bids based on the mean narrow average methodology are better at ensuring projects are adequately resourced, are lower risk and offer best social and economic value.

Best value does not mean lowest price. Lowest price can lead to lower quality of design, supervision and construction, and, in many cases, to higher risks, lower whole life and sustainable values with adversarial attitudes and greater downstream maintenance and repairs cost.

2.8.6 Those who commission should consider carefully how best they construct and balance their methods of selection and evaluation to attract the most appropriate consultants to their project.

2.8.7 They should be open to selection and evaluation of measurable values and those that appear less tangible or measurable.

2.9 FEES

2.9.1 For smaller contracts it is preferable to reveal the budgeted fee.

If the budget is known it will be easier for the client to compare the design service bids like for like, offers a clearer indication of the resources provided, the quality and is a fairer and more transparent approach. For bidders this provides them with greater clarity to provide a more realistic allocation of days/fees. Or to decide not to tender on that occasion.

2.9.2 Where the budget is not revealed then the brief needs to be clear and precise with sufficient detail and have no, or little, anticipated future change in order for the design team to provide an accurately costed quote.

2.9.3 The client should break down how a bidder allocates cost and resource into project stages when a project has multiple future stages.

2.9.4 The client should also structure how bidders complete their cost and resource allocation across different disciplines, so that an assessment of the relative allocation can be made when a project includes sub-consultants working under the lead consultant.

2.10 INSURANCE

2.10.1 The insurable quantum and purpose of cover levels required under a contract, should be specified in tender invites, rather than the type of cover.

This opens opportunity for the use of single project insurance (SPI) and integrated project insurance (IPI) while better protecting clients and suppliers against insurance market risks.

2.10.2 Insurance should always be as low as proportionately possible.

High insurance values impose economic costs and can exclude MSME's from bidding. The Transport for London - Mayor of London's Architecture design and Urbanism Panel (ADUP)Framework Agreement sets an example of more reasonable insurance levels (at 2021):
- Professional Indemnity Insurance   £2m
- Employer's (Compulsory) Liability Insurance   £5m
- Public Liability Insurance   £10m

2.11 COMPETITIVE PRINCIPLES

2.11.1 The principles of collaboration and co-operation should be given fuller consideration in reforming procurement processes and practices.

Competitive principles currently preclude rewarding the human capital invested by stakeholding participants when pro-actively supporting development. It can also preclude their further engagement. This is particularly applicable to small community based initiatives at their inception and bottom up development. Better facilitation for bottom up development should be enabled, rather than relying only on the principle of competition.

2.12 TRANSPARENCY

2.12.1 The adoption of open data standards across all application, guidance and procurement processes should be accelerated further by governments and all public authorities.

2.12.2 The publication of all notices, including award notices and framework call offs, should be mandated by all public bodies as a condition of the award of capital grant funding.

References

1   The Giants Causeway and the Whiteworth, Art Gallery, Manchester

2   The Construction Playbook. Government Guidance on sourcing and contracting public works projects and programmes. HMG. v.1 Dec. 2020 p.56 Value based procurement

3   'Transforming public procurement' CO. Government consultation paper Dec.2020

4   Creating Excellent Buildings, A Guide for Clients. CABE 2003 webarchive.nationalarchives.gov. uk/20110118110750/http://www.cabe.org.uk/files/creating-excellent-buildings.pdf (accessed 24 March 2021)

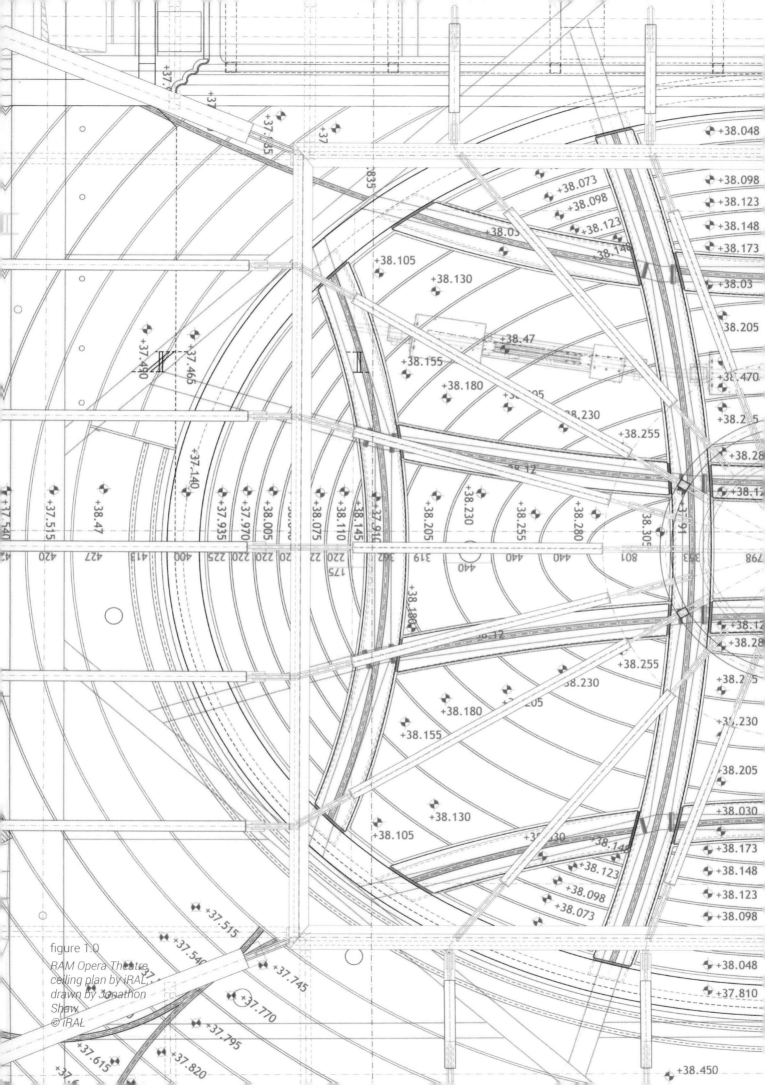

figure 10
*RAM Opera Theatre
ceiling plan by iRAL,
drawn by Jonathon
Shaw
© iRAL*

case studies

1 Royal Academy of Music: New Theatre and Recital Hall

Ian Ritchie and Brian Heron

Ian Ritchie Architects Ltd. (iRAL), England

The Royal Academy of Music's theatre and recital hall project has created two distinct new performance spaces for Britain's oldest conservatoire while new circulation improves connectivity within the academy. The overall concept seamlessly integrates these two exceptional performance spaces within the historic context of the academy site. The theatre, designed for both opera and musical theatre, now forms the heart of the academy, and was realised within the gutted shell of a 1970s fan-shaped auditorium and stage. Above the theatre, the 100-seat recital hall skilfully exploits the last major area into which the academy could expand, providing 230m² of additional space for student rehearsal, performance, public events and recording.

Objective and Vision

We were tasked with designing a theatre for students and the public's enjoyment of performances, while delivering the ambiance, aesthetics and environmental credentials befitting the academy's status as one of the world's première musical academies.

We subsequently developed the potential to create new rooftop spaces over the theatre, incorporating a new 100-seat recital hall and an additional recording facility.

Appointment

Based on our track record in theatre design, Ian Ritchie Architects Ltd. (iRAL) were invited and appointed directly to undertake a feasibility study through competitive interview by the Principal of the Royal Academy of Music in summer 2010 (We do not know which other companies were interviewed). The feasibility study investigated three options for a fee of £26,000 (excl. VAT):

1. A minimum scheme with capital expenditure c. £3m – basic upgrade of auditorium + backstage improvements

2. A full redesign of the theatre and backstage including creating a wing, enlarging the orchestra pit, and a fly tower.
3. A full redesign and rotation of the theatre 90 degrees – stage to the north and entry from main building south.

Composition of Project Team

The client set up a theatre management group comprising members of their board, academic staff and estates team. For the initial feasibility study an integrated core project team with a very direct client relationship was formed at the outset. This included the theatre management group, iRAL, cost consultant (Equals), structural engineer (WSP), services consultant (King Shaw Associates) and acoustic consultant (Arup).

The team produced two feasibilities for internal and external consultations with the theatre users group and local interest groups in order to develop a sensitive approach to urban integration and building operations. Extensive detailed consultations were undertaken with statutory stakeholders and wider 'community interest' groups including: English Heritage, Westminster City Council, Crown Estate, Howard de Walden Estate, St Marylebone Society, Marylebone Association and the Church Street Neighbourhood Group.

Planning and listed building consent was received in Feb 2012 with the consultees' full support, at the first attempt, and with only very minor conditions.

Appointments (Post-Planning)

In April 2014, following two years of fundraising and when the project was given the go-ahead to recommence, RAM appointed Sweett Group as project managers and each member of the consultant team was requested to re-tender their services, as required by the University of London.

fig. 1.1
Royal Academy of Music recital room
© Adam Scott

Each team member was appointed using an OJEU compliant process with project specific selection criteria. Following our submissions and interview process, iRAL were appointed as architect and lead consultant on a RIBA Standard Agreement 2010 (2012 revision) with amendments.

iRAL then also participated in the selection of the engineers, cost managers and other specialist consultants.

Fortunately, iRAL, Equals, WSP and Arup, who had worked on the project up to planning, were able to continue as a team, although King Shaw were unable to continue, due to restructuring, and Atelier Ten were appointed as the new services consultant. In such a complex project, this continuity and the close collaboration from everyone involved proved to be key.

As the project progressed, monthly meetings were held with the theatre management group enabling the client to review the developing design, provide feedback and formalise key design decisions. These continued during the delivery phase, providing the client with the opportunity to closely follow progress on site.

Early engagement with specialist subcontractors

With regards to possible contractors and subcontractors, all levels of suppliers were considered – particularly specialist packages.

We knew the theatre and recital hall would be entirely wood-lined spaces and that the joinery package would be crucial to the success of the project, both in terms of quality of finish and acoustics. So shortly after commencing work on Stage E information (equivalent to RIBA Stage 4), we set about finding the most appropriate UK specialist joinery company, and met with four in the process. James Johnson & Co Ltd. were exceptional from the outset. They were instrumental in providing the specialist input on fabrication, sequencing and finishing required to help inform and develop our tender information details and enhance our vision.

An excellent example of this is the design of the balcony front which plays a key role in creating an embrace between the audience and the performers with the horizontal sweep of the balcony enveloping the stage and pit. We wanted to accentuate the horizontal movement of the balcony and avoid any vertical joints between the prefabricated sections.

James Johnson suggested prefabricating the 3 - bay balcony front assemblies in their workshop and installing the 25 x 12mm cherry slats at the end of each module on site so that the balcony front would be stitched together to read as a single assembly.

Curved in both plan and section the complex prefabrication of the 3-bay balcony modules was also required to integrate services for ventilation and theatre electrics, while in addition the balcony front provides an important acoustic and visual surface.

The exact curvature of the balcony front, including the precise dimensions of a quirk detail, was the subject of Arup's detailed input, as each surface is graduated with cherry slats carefully angled and finished to improve the acoustics and create a completely immersive audience experience.

The details which had been developed in collaboration with James Johnson then formed part of the tender package. And as they were familiar with the requirements of the job they provided a very good value detailed quotation with very few exclusions or caveats.

At this stage, despite James Johnson & Co Ltd. being an integral part of the team having helped develop the design, the project managers wanted to competitively tender this package to 4 or 5 specialist joinery contractors. This risked losing an excellent, talented and committed subcontractor along with all their knowledge, expertise and the evident quality of finish they were capable of delivering.

Rather than going out to competitive tender, iRAL insisted that the project managers should accept James Johnson's quotation. After prolonged efforts, they were eventually persuaded.

When the main contractor was appointed James Johnson & Co Ltd. therefore became embedded as named sub-contractors. Our initial professional opinion of James Johnson & Co Ltd. was well-grounded as both spaces have been finished to an exceptionally high quality, contributing pivotally to the project's success, and they were an absolute joy to work with.

Continuity of Project Team

Unusually, perhaps, on a project lasting almost 9 years from start to finish, both the client and the design team had a very high degree of personnel continuity. Unfortunately the same was not true on the contractor's side.

Osborne were appointed on a 2 stage tender, and as is frequently the case, the promises made in the 1st stage fell away in the 2nd stage. Senior personnel left the Osborne team and were either not replaced or their replacements were not of equivalent competence, contrary to what had been promised at interview. This pattern was also repeated with many of the sub-contractors.

So from the outset the job experienced delays, requiring the client to act by requesting that the construction manager be replaced. Luckily, Lawrence Wilson, the replacement, was exceptional and although some delay was still experienced, the high standard of delivery would not have been achieved without his committed contribution and expertise.

Omission of Acoustic Specification

The original contractor had been asked to price the JCT contract documents on tendering,

fig. 1.2
Royal Academy of Music theatre
© Adam Scott

which included some contractor's designed portions (CDPs).

In their tender submission, however, Osborne only priced selectively and provided an extensive list of exclusions which, for example, covered the acoustic consultant's performance specification (180 pages plus) and associated costs.

As iRAL were to be administering the contract, we repeatedly highlighted the need for inclusion of the priced acoustic specification in the formal contract sum. Unfortunately the project managers and quantity surveyor accepted the contractor's proposition that a priced acoustic specification could be excluded from their contract. Contractually the result became very messy and involved a significant number of costly variations and additional work, which could easily have been avoided if the contractor had been required to properly price the full scope of tendered works.

Extended Contract Duration

The original contract duration was extended from 78 weeks (Feb 2017) to 102 weeks due to the following:
- Delayed start on site due to the project managers not having put in place the Landlords Licences in time
- Installation of tower crane delayed due to adverse weather

- Working with the existing building and dealing with unexpected site discoveries
- Steelwork delays
- Scope changes:
Additional intrusive surveys which had not been deemed feasible prior to works commencing, because it was a live teaching environment and occupied by students and staff.
Items previously excluded by the contractor
Acoustic enhancements to finishes
Acoustic enhancements to services
Additional winches for theatre fly-tower
Additional refurbishment and A/C to basement level practise rooms
Works relating to Crown Estate Licence and Crown Estate Pavement Commission

A change control process was implemented to sign off design changes.

Reflections

1. Trust your Architect:
The client-architect relationship is key to the success of any project and delivering a building as complex as this was only possible with the huge level of trust and unwavering support shown by RAM and the Theatre Management Group, through difficult times and in challenging circumstances. The client's commitment shows in the finished building and the quality produced, which exceeded everyone's expectations. Without this level of trust, the

fig. 1.3
Royal Academy of Music exterior
© Adam Scott

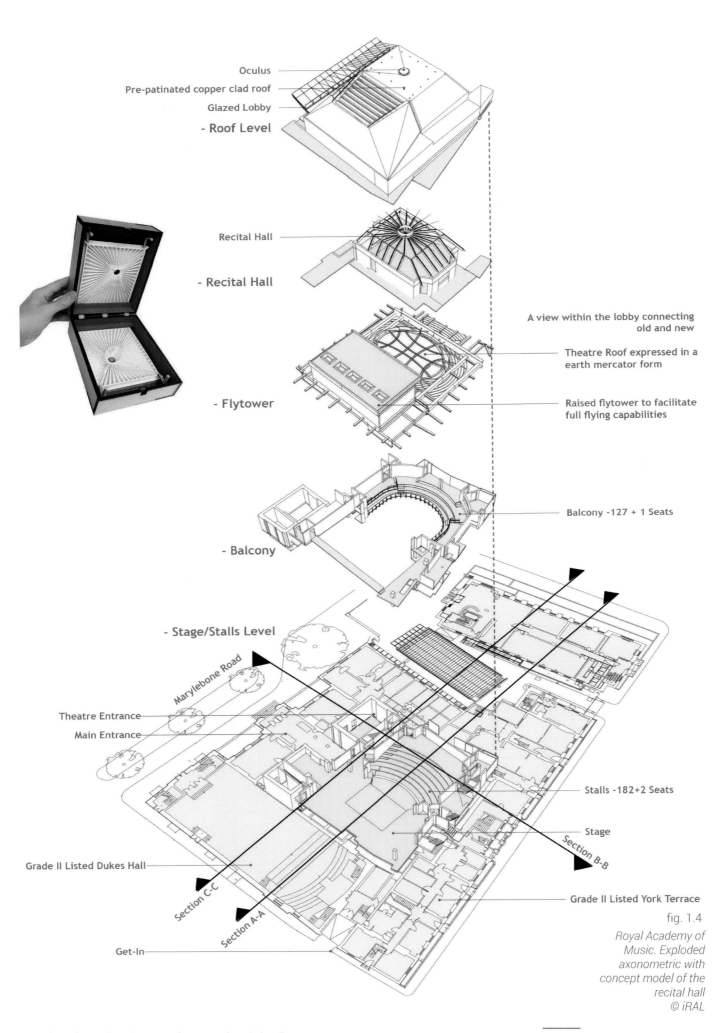

Oculus
Pre-patinated copper clad roof
Glazed Lobby
- Roof Level

Recital Hall
- Recital Hall

A view within the lobby connecting old and new

Theatre Roof expressed in a earth mercator form

- Flytower

Raised flytower to facilitate full flying capabilities

Balcony -127 + 1 Seats

- Balcony

- Stage/Stalls Level

Marylebone Road

Theatre Entrance
Main Entrance

Stalls -182+2 Seats

Stage

Section B-B

Grade II Listed Dukes Hall

Section C-C

Section A-A

Grade II Listed York Terrace

fig. 1.4
Royal Academy of Music. Exploded axonometric with concept model of the recital hall
© iRAL

Get-In

resulting built quality would have been greatly diminished.

2. Early input from specialist subcontractors is vital

We first started working with James Johnson in November 2014, on commencing production of the tender information. James Johnson were instrumental in providing specialist input on prefabrication methodologies, site assembly, detailing and finishes, as required to make the clear design vision a reality. They brought invaluable expertise to the process, and the project's success is largely thanks to their quality of workmanship and commitment.

3. Importance of pre-construction investigations

Undertaking pre-construction investigations is always time well spent, and especially with existing buildings. The more opening-up that can be undertaken prior to agreement of the contract documents and construction commencement, the less risk there is to the client that a contractor can later seize on-site discoveries as an opportunity for claiming delay and/or loss and expense.

As the majority of spaces at RAM were in constant use right up until July 2015, there was insufficient time allowed in the project manager's programme to undertake meaningful intrusive investigations prior to commencement.

fig. 1.5

Royal Academy of Music section A-A
© iRAL

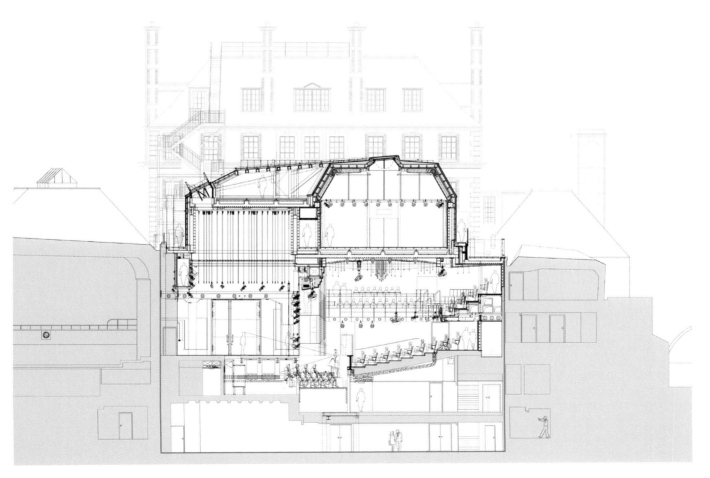

This exposed the client to increased cost risks as findings could not be fed into the contract documents prior to their assignation.

4. Contract
Given the scale of interventions within an existing occupied building and the importance of the sub-contracts, IRAL recommended construction management as the most appropriate contractual form, rather than a traditional one. However, the project manager Sweett Group had been appointed prior to the appointment of the architect (an error in itself) and were set against construction management as a procurement route.

5. Beware of Contractor exclusions
The contractor was asked to tender a price for the contract documents, including the contractor's designed portions, yet priced it with an extensive list of exclusions including the acoustic consultant's specification and all associated costs. To our consternation this met with the project manager and quantity surveyor's agreement.

A significant amount of the scoped detail that would otherwise have been included was detrimentally impacted, resulting in significant additional costs, and detailed design and inputs from the design team.

On receipt of tenders a better approach might have been to ask the contractor to price the excluded scope and the risk, as a design & build contract (or sub-contract), to factor in the cost of all exclusions and any associated risk that they deemed necessary.

RAM would then have had more foresight into exactly what was being offered, rather than being faced with the adverse cost and programme impacts resulting from the omitted items.

fig. 1.6
Royal Academy of Music. Recital hall (above) with lobby (below)
© Adam Scott

fig. 1.7

*Royal Academy of
Music Violin detail
(left), Oculus cable
detail (right)
© iRAL*

PROJECT DATA

Name	**ROYAL ACADEMY OF MUSIC: New Theatre and Recital Hall**
Location	Marylebone Road, London NW1 5HT
Country	ENGLAND
Year	2010

PROJECT DESCRIPTION

Type	New 309 seat theatre for Opera and Musical Theatre, 100 seat Recital Hall, as well as 14 refurbished practice and dressing rooms, five new percussion studios, a large refurbished jazz room and a new control suite for the Academy's audiovisual recordings department retrofitted into an existing conglomerate of various adapted historic buildings originally acquired incrementally by the clients. The complex works programme was undertaken within an operational educational institute
Size	3,389 m^2
Budget Cost	£20m (GBP) (€22.47m)

COMPETITION DESCRIPTION

Client	**Royal Academy of Music (RAM).**
	RAM, Britain's oldest conservatoire, and now part of the University of London, was established in 1822 and granted a Royal Charter in 1830. The Academy is a registered charity and a registered company, governed by trustees. The works lie hidden behind the listed façade of the Royal Academy of Music's Edwardian premises, surrounded by Grade I and Grade II listed buildings and is located within the Regent's Park conservation area The project was privately funded by donations
Programmer/Agent	Sweett Group (now Currie Brown), who were appointed the project managers post planning to completion
Public/Private	Public (Higher Education)
Procedure	A restricted competition procedure, with the contract notice having 3 consultants lots
Procedure Reference	Directive 2004/18/EC. Art. 28 *(Directive 2014/24/EU Art.28 nearest equivalence)*
Stages	2 with a competitive interview (see below)
Project Intention	The competition was called for all post-planning stages to completion. The architects had been previously appointed to undertake the feasibility and planning application stages
Conditions Applied	A project specific selection with criteria authored by Sweet Group. Quality was weighted 75, to cost weighted 25. (Approach & methodology 30, understanding of key issues 20, team & resources 25, fee proposal 25)

COMPETITION FACTS

Timescale	Competition call:	17 December 2013
	PQQ submission:	January 2014
	ITT call:	Febuary 2014
	Interview:	March 2014
Submission Required	Stage 1: Unknown.	
	Stage 2: Unknown	
	A competitive interview	
Announcement	14 April 2014	
Number of Entries	Unreported in Contract Award Notice 2014/S 077-134119	

"The Client-Architect relationship is key to the success of any project and delivering a building as complex as this was only possible with the huge level of trust and unwavering support shown ... through difficult times and in challenging circumstances. The Client's commitment shows in the finished building and the quality produced"

ASSESSMENT & SELECTION

Jury Numbers	7
Jury Composition	RAM Chair of the committee
	RAM Principal, Professor Jonathan Freeman-Attwood CBE
	RAM Head of Finance
	RAM Head of Estates
	RAM Trustee
	RAM Trustee (Construction advisor)
	Project Manager
Number Shortlisted	Unknown
Winner	Ian Ritchie Architects Ltd., with consultants WSP Group (structural engineers) Atelier Ten (services engineers) and cost consultants (Equals) appointed under separate lots, with acoustic engineering by Arup
Runners Up	Unknown
Prizes & Awards	None
Conclusion of Process	Construction design commission
Construction Contract(s)	JCT Standard Building Contract Without Quantities 2005 (Rev 1 2007) – SBC/XQ. After the Stage 1 tender submission and contractor interviews, a Pre-Construction Services Agreement (PCSA) was entered into with Osbourne
Project Completion	January 2018

FURTHER INFORMATION

Ian Ritchie Architects: www.ianritchiearchitects.co.uk/projects/ram/
Royal Academy of Music: www.ram.ac.uk
RIBA National Award and Best London Building Award 2018; AJ Retrofit of the Year Award 2018; AJ Higher Education building of the year 2018; . RICS Tourism and Leisure Award 2018
UK's Royal Academy of Music renovated with £30m in donations. FT 11 March 2018.
Ian Ritchie Architects have undertaken a number of arts projects including: The Crystal Palace Concert Platform, London; Plymouth Theatre Royal – TR2; RSC Courtyard Theatre, Stratford-upon-Avon; RSC The Other Place, London.

fig. 1.9
Royal Academy of Music. Site model
© iRAL

2 Wilton's Music Hall with associated arts spaces

Tim Ronalds

Tim Ronalds Architects, England

We won the project to undertake a feasibility study and, in conjunction with John Earl, a conservation management plan for Wilton's Music Hall in 2006. It was that success which led to our undertaking the design and construction phases of the restoration and conversion of the hall and houses that make up the complex known as Wilton's Music Hall. It took a long time.

The project proved tricky to fund and much of our work in the years from 2006-12 was devoted to planning phased programmes of minor works, and helping with funding applications. But major funding was eventually achieved and the building contract for works to the hall was let in July 2012 and the contract for the works to the houses in June 2014. The final phase of works was completed in September 2015.

We were lucky. Wilton's Artistic Director, Frances Mayhew was at the helm throughout the decade, and we worked very well together. Had there been a change in personnel over that period it might have been a different story — we have found on many projects that a change at the top heralds a reselection of architect and design team. But we stuck with the project and Wilton's stuck with us.

The study we completed in 2006 was the foundation for the project. This is the case for so many arts projects. Architects put in far more work than they are paid for or that clients envisage in trying to set a project off on the right foot and produce a quality report. In other words architects make an investment in the future of the project. And this is where we were lucky again.

There was no demand at Wilton's for the architect to be reselected as the project progressed to RIBA Stage C and beyond.

Our investment paid off. But this is not the case with the procurement of many arts projects. So often, a feasibility study is commissioned (with careful consideration of an architect appropriate to the commission) at the outset because that seems the best way to get started or because funding regimes demand one — but public funding requires an OJEU selection process for later phases, when project managers/procurement agents step in and apply selection criteria which may mean the original architect does not get the job and/ or many practices wasting their time in making time-consuming submissions for a job that is already 'spoken for'.

Arts projects have certain peculiarities:
- They take a long time.
- They are almost always begun before funding is in place (and funding criteria can change over the course of a project: the type of project the Heritage Lottery Fund [HLF] were prepared to fund differed markedly from when we were appointed).
- They involve collaboration with many design team and arts business consultants.
- They benefit from close collaboration on many levels and in our experience are not suited to the 'arms-length collaboration' that project managers when involved try to impose.

Briefing is key. Starting off with a feasibility study seems the right approach, but a reselection after that study is completed does not.

At Wilton's there was no procurement issue with the funding of the works to the Hall by the SITA Trust as the monies were private, not public. With HLF funding the work to the Houses it was a different matter, as HLF operate strict rules on design team procurement. And again we were lucky. Frances Mayhew fought hard

fig. 2.1
Wilton's Music Hall
© Helene Binet

to retain us and HLF accepted that our original selection satisfied their regulations.

They were less happy with the selection of the design team, but agreed that as the design team consultants had been appointed as our sub-consultants for the original feasibility study and because we could demonstrate that we had held our own 'selection process' before asking them to be part of our team, that their appointments also satisfied the regulations.

It is hard to know whether the team would have survived intact without a strong and supportive client. One hopes too that it must have helped that by the time the HLF application was made we had been the architects at Wilton's for several years.

fig. 2.2
Wilton's Music Hall.
© Hélène Binet

fig. 2.3
Wilton's Music Hall.
© Hélène Binet

fig. 2.4
Wilton's Music Hall.
© Helene Binet

PROJECT DATA

Name	**WILTON'S MUSIC HALL: Music hall & associated arts and support spaces**
Location	Graces Alley, off Ensign Street, London E1 8JB
Country	ENGLAND
Year	2006
PROJECT DESCRIPTION	
Type	**Restoration of a music hall and houses that make up a Grade II* listed building**
Size	1,500 m²
Budget Cost	£3m (GBP) (€3.51m)
COMPETITION DESCRIPTION	
Client	Wilton's Music Hall Trust (a charity), with capital funding provided for works to the Music Hall by the SITA Trust, and the Wilton's houses by the Heritage Lottery Fund (HLF).
Programmer/Agent	Jura Consultants
Public/Private	Private (with public HLF funding)
Procedure	An invited competitive selection process
Procedure Reference	N/A
Stages	1 (see below).
Project Intention	To use the feasibility study and conservation management plan to secure the funding required to stabilise and restore the premises.
Conditions Applied	Not known
COMPETITION FACTS	
Timescale	Brief issued 9 May 2006 Competition period: to 29 May 2006
Submission Required	**Stage 1:** A review and response to the brief, approach, proposed design team, programme and fee proposal **Stage 2:** Interview and fee negotiation
Announcement	June 2006
Number of Entries	7

fig. 2.5

*Wilton's Music
Hall. Location plan,
ground floor plan
& sections L-R*

*© Tim Ronalds
Architects*

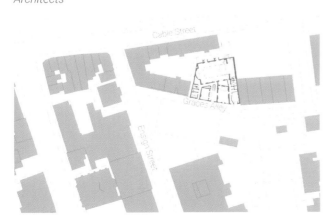

KEY
1. Foyer
2. John Wilton Room
3. Mahogany Bar
4. Kitchen
5. Auditorium

"The most important surviving early music hall to be seen anywhere... It is of outstanding architectural and archaeological significance" – The Theatres Trust. It's history extends back to the 1690s. The buildings that now house the box office, bars, offices and rehearsal space began as houses, shops and a pub.

ASSESSMENT & SELECTION

Jury Numbers	Not known
Jury Composition	Wilton's Music Hall's Artistic Director Frances Mayhew Wilton's Music Hall's Trustees Jura Consultants Project Manager
Number Shortlisted	6
Winner	Tim Ronalds Architects with John Earl
Runners Up	Not known
Prizes & Awards	None
Conclusion of Process	The award Initially led to completion of a feasibility study and a conservation management plan This lead to a design commission – a minor project to underpin the Bar Floor in February 2012 Major works to the Hall began in July 2012 Work to the houses followed, commencing in June 2014
Construction Contract(s)	Bar Floor - JCT Minor Works Hall and houses - JCT Standard Form of Building Contract
Project Completion	September 2015

FURTHER INFORMATION

Tim Ronalds Architects: www.timronalds.co.uk
Wilton's Music Hall: www.wiltons.org.uk
Tim Ronalds Architects have undertaken a number of arts projects including: Hackney Empire; the Landmark, Ilfracombe; Chequer Mead Arts Centre, East Grinstead; Clarendon Muse, Watford Music Centre; Colyer-Fergusson Building at the University of Kent; and Hastings Stade for Hastings Borough Council.

fig. 2.6
*Wilton's Music Hall.
from Graces Alley*
©Hélène Binet

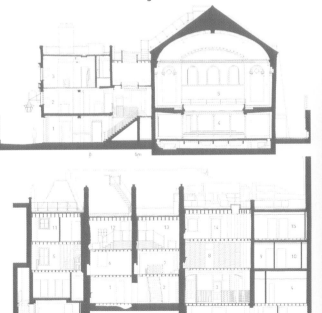

3   Walk the Plank

Luke Cooper and Sylvia Hebden

Architectural Emporium Ltd., and Through and Around, England

Walk the Plank (WTP) is a theatre company originally based on the Fitzcarraldo, a small ship, which for sixteen years toured from Salford to locations such as Orkney, Grimsby and the Channel Islands. WTP established their reputation taking innovative works to new audiences beyond traditional performance confines, undertaking work making large-scale public performance and theatrical productions along with mentoring, training and working with disadvantaged groups to create theatre.

After the loss of the Fitzcarraldo the company was dispersed across various sites, but they wanted a single location to reunite the administration of their delivery, maker and management teams along with space to work intimately with people and a variety of workshops to accommodate their range of productions.

With only a small budget they found their new Cobden Street, Salford site in a harsh industrial area beside a 5m high railway viaduct on the Manchester to Preston line. The site had previously been owned by a steel manufacturer occupying an industrial building with four workshop bays. These structures have been reused and extended to provide WTP's new facilities.

The project was commissioned by WTP and supported by Salford City Council, with capital funding and support from WTP, Arts Council England and additional funding from GHK Charities Ltd, Garfield Weston Foundation, Oglesby Charitable Trust and the Stavros Niarchos Foundation.

The procurement process

As artistic producers WTP's core values include 'nurturing raw talent' and 'positive risk taking' along with 'innovative, alternate, equilibrium-spoiling ways of thinking' so from the start they were keen to seek out young emergent design talent to add value.[1]

The design work was considered of regional interest, and because the value was below the European thresholds there was no need to advertise in the European Journal. So, a strategy was developed to encourage engagement from small local architectural practices. This involved working with the RIBA Northwest office to identify listings of firms based within the north west, targeting practices, mail shots and then visiting firms before the tender call to encourage them to bid, while testing the assessment criteria so that it would not exclude appropriate firms, as part of a pre-market engagement exercise. The bid was then advertised on the WTP and Place North West websites.[2]

The Bid documentation was structured on the principles of an above threshold restricted procedure but made as simple, viable and easy as possible for practices to apply. The financial criteria were carefully considered, bidders were permitted to submit bank references in lieu of three years of accounts to allow new practices the opportunity to bid, only proportionate professional indemnity insurance was requested upon assignation of the contract, while experience sought over the previous five years was broad and the response length of the submissions limited. A full appointment was provided for with specified break clauses at RIBA work stages to secure the clients risk, in the event the project did not proceed for whatever reason.

The client was also keen to ensure that there would be an empathetic relationship with the design team, so at ITT stage 10% of the assessment was by interview, although 60% of the score was based on price. Practices were only requested to deliver early design thoughts and approaches at ITT stage (fig. 4.14).

fig. 3.1
*Walk the Plank
Entrance*
© Simon Buckley

fig. 3.2

Section
© Architectural
Emporium

fig. 3.3

Site location
© google

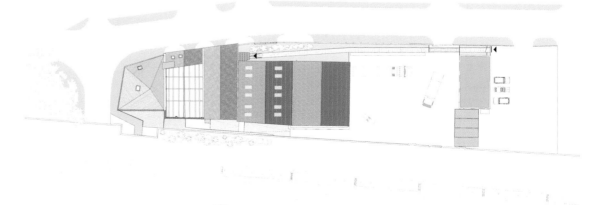

fig. 3.4

Site plan
© Architectural
Emporium

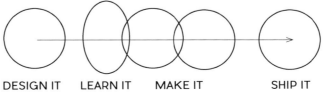

DESIGN IT   LEARN IT   MAKE IT   SHIP IT

*"a strategy was developed to encourage ... small local
... practices ... targeting ... mail shots ... visiting firms
... to encourage them to bid, while testing ... criteria so
that it would not exclude appropriate firms"*

The Project

Initial architectural studies led to the development of a site strategy based on process and production — Design it, Learn it, Make it, Ship it. The offices have been located in a new extension on land left to the North West. This allows unencumbered use of and access to the existing warehouse bays, for production and transportation.

To provide external community space, sheltered from the noisy and unsightly industrial surrounds, the shell has been stripped off the end warehouse bay, much to the client's initial surprise. This now provides a well-used and delightfully sunny courtyard while allowing natural lighting and ventilation to the neighbouring studio and offices.

The irregular plan of the two office storeys under a steep pyramidical roof maximises use of the available site. This provides a dynamic form marking this approach towards WTP. Internally the leaning column that supports the roof apex references WTP's nautical roots on the Fitzcarraldo.

In the offices and public interiors, a considered use of distinctive colour, materials, textures and detailing provide welcoming highlights in this otherwise robustly measured refurbishment.

To improve its performance the buildings envelope has been carefully renewed and upgraded with a sparkling sinusoidal metal cladding which unifies the external appearance. This subtly elevates the building and uniquely distinguishes it from its harsh context.

The project took three years to develop and complete and opened in 2017. It provides an internal floor area of 1,062m^2 at a construction cost of £879k (£827m^2) which the funders consider has delivered extremely good value.

Reflections

Through and Around consider that most architectural procurements are based on an incorrect risk analysis of cost, quality and programme. Appropriate emergent talent is most frequently precluded by disproportionate and onerous procurement processes, their conditions, requirements and assessments. Projects also require long term collaboration

fig. 3.5 *(left)*
Entrance corridor
© Simon Buckley

fig. 3.6 *(right)*
stair and meeting area
© Simon Buckley

"it is ... important to consider how best to develop human ... social values ... empathies ... engagement of ... stakeholders, for efficiency, effectiveness and quality because better value and higher quality is delivered most successfully by maintaining team continuity over all project work stages"

so it is important to consider how best to develop human and social values, team empathies and the best engagement of all the stakeholders for efficiency, effectiveness and quality, because better value and higher quality is delivered most successfully by maintaining team continuity through all project work stages.

In their view WTP's procurement was overly heavy, and it could be even simpler, more accessible and with greater emphasis on quality over price, if done today.

Architectural Emporium worked brilliantly with their design team and the project was delivered with care, collaboration and quality by Skyline, the main contractors. This project has provided a vibrant cultural gem in the heart of a Salford industrial estate. This however is largely because WTP had the ambition and ethos to perceive the site's possibilities, and to successfully engage local talent.

References:

1   WTP, PQQ Tender Documents. Appendix A, The Project Brief
2   PlacesNorthWest www.placenorthwest.co.uk)

fig. 3.7
Courtyard
© Architectural Emporium

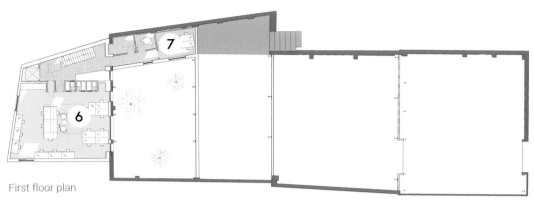

First floor plan

KEY
1. Creative hub/Social space
2. Courtyard
3. Training spaces
4. Clean workshop
5. Dirty workshop
6. Main office
7. Office

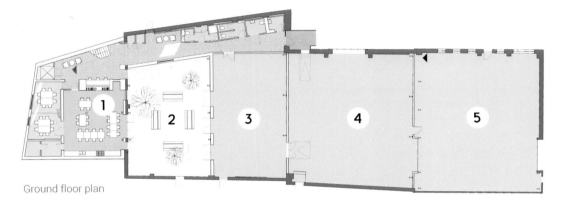

Ground floor plan

fig. 3.11
WTP plans
© Architectural
Emporium

fig. 3.8 *(left)*
Creative hub

fig. 3.9 *(bottom left)*
Production workshop

fig. 3.10 *(below)*
Training studio
all © Architectural
Emporium

PROJECT DATA

Name	**WALK THE PLANK**
Location	Cobden Works, 37-41 Cobden Street, Salford
Country	ENGLAND
Year	2014

PROJECT DESCRIPTION

Type	The workshops, training, education, outreach and administrative base of a theatre and production company
Size	1,062 m²
Budget Cost	£879,178 (GBP) (€971,800) construction

COMPETITION DESCRIPTION

Client	**Walk the Plank**. Project capital funding was provided by Arts Council England with additional funding from WTP, GHK Charities Ltd, Garfield Weston Foundation, Oglesby Charitable Trust and the Stavros Niarchos Foundation
Programmer/Agent	Sylvia Hebden, Through and Around
Public/Private	Public
Procedure	A procedure below the EU Thresholds
Procedure Reference	N/A
Stages	2 and an interview (see below)
Project Intention	The appointment was for full services to completion
Conditions Applied	This below threshold procedure followed the in principle procedures of a restricted competition. ITT bid assessment: - quality 30, cost 60 and interview 10

COMPETITION FACTS

Timescale	Competition call:	6 October 2014
	PQQ submission:	20 October 2014
	ITT submission:	21 November 2014
	Interview:	2 December 2014

Submission Required	**Stage 1:** PQQ (Pre-qualification questionnaire) Probity questions, statutory compliance confirmations, with the questions on relevant and appropriate experience of the architect and lead consultants
	Stage 2: An ITT (invitation to tender) a resource schedule, an indicative fee and an approach was outlined using diagrams and text, and presented at interview
	Interview: A competitive interview.

Announcement	Award:	5 December 2014
Number of Entries	6	

fig. 3.12 *(left)*
Laundry Street

fig. 3.13 *(right)*
Work cabins
© *Simon Buckley*

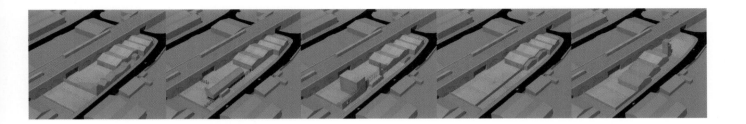

fig. 3.14
*Walk the Plank
process models done
for the ITT & interview
© Architectural
Emporium*

ASSESSMENT & SELECTION

Jury Numbers	4
Jury Composition	John Wassell, WTP Creative Producer & Co-founder
	Andy Stratford, WTP Executive Director
	Sylvia Hebden, Through & Around
	John Clarke, GVA Acuity representative
Number Shortlisted	4
Winner	Architectural Emporium Ltd with a sub-consultant team comprising: - Structural Engineers Elliot Bond, Mechanical & Electrical Engineers, Waterman Building Services, and CDM co-ordinators Rawlings RCS
	Project manager, Sylvia Hebden of Through & Around and QS's Modero were appointed separately by WTP, with Landscape Architect Serena Finzel at a later date
Runners Up	Civic Engineers, Manchester
Prizes & Awards	None
Conclusion of Process	The award lead to a RIBA Stage A-B feasibility study, and subsequently to the construction design commission with services provided up to and including RIBA Stage L
	Following tendering Skyline Property Solutions Ltd. were appointed the main contractors.
Construction Contract(s)	JCT Intermediate form of contract 2011
Project Completion	August 2017

FURTHER INFORMATION

Architectural Emporium Ltd: www.architectural-emporium.co.uk
RIBA North West Emerging Practice of the Year 2018,
Through & Around: www.throughandaround.co.uk
Walk the Plank: https://walktheplank.co.uk
RIBA North West Client of the Year 2018

4　High House Artists' Studios

Hana Loftus

HAT Projects, England

HAT Projects won the commission to design High House Artists Studios in 2011 as a relatively newly formed practice. It was our first successful commission achieved through an open public sector tender conducted under OJEU regulations.

The brief was very clear – to develop cost effective and practical studio space as part of High House Production Park in Purfleet, Essex, which would be managed by the charity Acme Studios as affordable artist and maker workspace. There was a clear link in the business model for the project between construction cost and the affordability of the spaces to artists – the lower the construction cost, the lower the rents could be. The project was funded by Arts Council England and Thurrock Council as a response to the great need for affordable studio space and the benefits of co-location on the Production Park alongside anchor tenants such as the Royal Opera House.

The tender process was clear and transparent, with a 30% weighting to the cost component and a 70% weighting to quality. What was key in allowing us to successfully compete for the project, was that the quality evaluation did not require us to demonstrate prior experience in the specific building typology of the brief – we could evidence high quality work on any kind of building. As a relatively new practice this allowed us to present our experience on a wide range of different building types and demonstrate how they were relevant to the brief. Past experience did not count for a disproportionate amount of the quality scoring – more emphasis was placed on the methodology we proposed for delivering the brief, including our project management and quality management proposals.

We were fairly confident that we would not lose the tender on pricing when weighed against quality, as the brief was extremely clear about the requirements. This was due to the expertise of Acme Studios who were already on board and had completed a demand study and a business plan for the project, as well as holding many decades experience of building and managing studio buildings.

We have had other experiences where a less clear brief has allowed some tenderers to interpret the requirements differently, submitting very low fee proposals which effectively outweighed any quality marking. We have in fact been told by other practices that they deliberately do so and then claim for large quantities of 'extra' fees during the process, exploiting any weakness in the brief. As a practice we have never opted to take this approach, and prefer to quote for the scope of services we believe is genuinely required to deliver the brief, but it is clear that many public sector bodies do not understand how to describe the scope of their requirements accurately enough to allow for a genuine like for like comparison of the cost element of proposals.

The tender asked for a full design team contracted through a lead consultant. This is an effective way of ensuring a single point of responsibility and that the consultant team have good working relationships. We could propose a full team with whom we had worked previously and therefore had confidence in their ability to share our design ethos and work towards the aims of the brief in a creative and efficient way.

We were very fortunate that the client partnership included an experienced studio operator in Acme, alongside the High House Production Park and Thurrock Council team who were clear and effective project managers, but did not try to exceed their knowledge of either the brief for studio accommodation, or the design and construction process. In other words, we

fig. 4.1
*High House Artists'
Studio stair*
© Hugo Glendinning

fig. 4.2
fig. 4.3
*High House Artists'
exteriors*
© Hugo Glendinning

were allowed to work freely with the end operator, building on their extensive research and knowledge of the sector, and develop innovative design responses, appropriately market tested. So long as we kept on time and within budgets, we did not have to go through extensive governance or 'design by committee' processes which can slow down delivery and result in a less effective design solution. It was in many ways an exemplary client partnership which used the skills and expertise of the different team members to the maximum.

The project was completed on time and under budget, and exceeded the expectations of the client in this regard. On the design front, it won a RIBA Award and contributed to the client being awarded regional Client of the Year in the RIBA awards also. It has been published extensively as a case study of how to create efficient, purposeful and well-designed studio space at a low cost. The building was fully let from completion and has had excellent feedback from occupiers, proving to be flexible and adaptable to a range of different users as well as requiring little management and maintenance.

fig. 4.4
*High House Artists'
Studio*
© Hugo Glendinning

"... key in allowing us to successfully compete for the project, was that the quality evaluation did not require us to demonstrate prior experience in the specific building typology of the brief – we could evidence high quality work on any kind of building"

PROJECT DATA

Name	**High House Artists' Studios**
Location	High House Production Park, Purfleet, Essex
Country	ENGLAND
Year	2011
PROJECT DESCRIPTION	
Type	New build affordable creative workspace
Size	2,151m² (GIFA)
Budget Cost	£1.8m (GBP) (€1.99m)
COMPETITION DESCRIPTION	
Client	**High House Production Park/Acme Studios** and part-funded by Arts Council England's capital fund and Thurrock Council
Programmer/Agent	Thurrock Council
Public/Private	Public
Procedure	Open Procedure
Procedure Reference	Directive 2004/18/EC. Art. 28 *(Directive 2014/24/EU Art.28 nearest equivalence)*
Stages	1 with an interview of shortlisted teams
Project Intention	There was an intention to build.
Conditions Applied	Quality was weighted 70, with price weighted 30
COMPETITION FACTS	
Timescale	Competition call: 23 September 2011 Submission: October 2011 Award: November 2011
Submission Required	Detailed project plan, resource breakdown, client and project references, audited accounts, evidence of delivering high quality work in the specification, planning and design of buildings on time and to budget, evidence of relevant knowledge, skills and experience of the team, quality plan, financial tender
Announcement	November 2011
Number of Entries	9
ASSESSMENT & SELECTION	
Jury Numbers	unreported
Jury Composition	N/A
Number Shortlisted	unknown
Winner	HAT Projects
Runners Up	unknown
Prizes & Awards	NONE
Conclusion of Process	Full design commission. HAT Projects architects were appointed in 2011 by Thurrock Council with Skelly & Couch, (Building Services), Momentum (Structural Engineers).
Construction Contract(s)	JCT Intermediate
Project Completion	Construction completed October 2013
FURTHER INFORMATION	
	HAT Projects www.hatprojects.com RIBA East Award 2014, winner RIBA East Emerging Architect of the Year 2014, winner, and RIBA East Client of the Year 2014 was awarded to Thurrock Council.

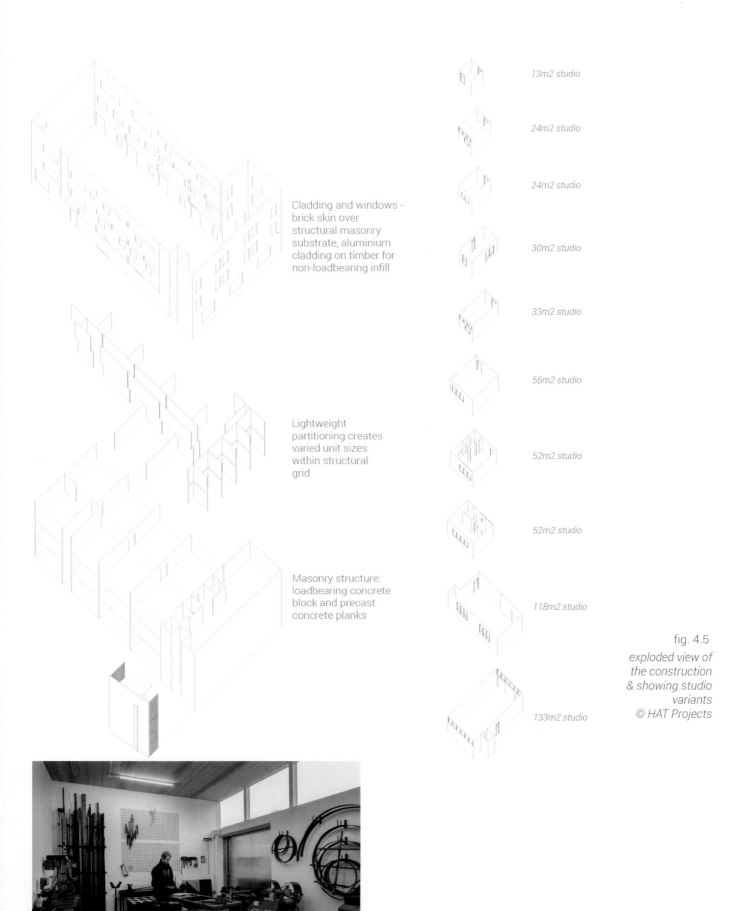

Cladding and windows - brick skin over structural masonry substrate, aluminium cladding on timber for non-loadbearing infill

Lightweight partitioning creates varied unit sizes within structural grid

Masonry structure: loadbearing concrete block and precast concrete planks

13m2 studio

24m2 studio

24m2 studio

30m2 studio

33m2 studio

56m2 studio

52m2 studio

52m2 studio

118m2 studio

133m2 studio

fig. 4.5
exploded view of the construction & showing studio variants
© HAT Projects

fig. 4.6
High House ground floor artists' studio
© Hugo Glendinning

High House Artists' Studios

5 The Theatre Royal Glasgow

Alex Reedijk

Scottish Opera

The Theatre Royal as a building has a fascinating history. First built in 1867 by James Bayliss, as the Royal Colosseum and Opera House, the theatre has survived three fires, two world wars, and a conversion in 1957 into a TV studio. Following the first fire in 1897 the theatre was rebuilt by architect Charles Phipps and remains one of the finest examples of his work. It reverted into a theatre again in 1974 when it was sold to Scottish Opera, becoming the Glasgow home for Scottish opera and Scottish Ballet after a significant renovation.

The Project Vision

There was further restoration of the auditorium and orchestra pit in 1997. An adjacent gap site was purchased in 2009 enabling plans to be developed to extend the theatre's cramped public spaces.

The brief was to provide new front of house facilities, including full disabled access, bars and a café, additional front of house offices and WCs, hosting, and educational space in a new extension directly linked to the historic Category 'A' listed theatre. Our vision was for spacious, accessible foyers that could easily cope with 1,500 people during an interval, as well as providing daytime use for relaxation and a top floor which would boast Glasgow's only publicly accessible roof terrace.

The procurement process

We appointed Page \ Park Architects in 2010 following a two-stage competitive procedure. Prior to the main project to develop the new foyers Page \ Park had been instructed to prepare an initial Conservation Statement which included a Statement of Significance. This informed the decision to demolish the part of the building at the top of Hope Street thus creating the opportunity to create a landmark corner.

The other Design Team members' fees sat below the OJEU threshold for services. These individually held appointments were the subject of competitive fee bids and all appointments were done in line with Scottish Opera's internal procurement procedures.

To ensure that a well-balanced and harmonious team was selected for the project, the architect was invited to contribute to the selection process of the other team members. In the main we were very happy with these professional appointments given the complexity of the building. In the main, coordination of the design between the design team members was excellent however there were one or two areas where the interfaces between architectural and M&E elements could have been tighter and better dealt with in the sub-contracted work packages.

Heritage Lottery Fund (HLF) also provided, as a monitor, a very experienced quantity surveyor who was exceptionally supportive through all stages of HLF involvement in the project. He was introduced into the project about a year in and made a huge difference as the bridge between Heritage Lottery Fund and Scottish Opera.

The procurement processes for the main contractor and sub-contractors was led by the client's project manager, with the client and architect involved closely in the main contractor's appointment.

Reflections on the competitive process

The procurement of the main contractor was a classic mixed OJEU journey of price versus quality, with an assessment of confidence on our part that the contractors could build to the design. There were subsequent and inevitable tensions of available budget versus

fig. 5.1
*The Theatre Royal
from Cowcaddens
Road*
© *Andrew Lee*

unexpectedly high tender returns leading to extensive value engineering (VE).

It was a two-stage procurement exercise and the list of sub-contractors to tender each work package was agreed between architect and other members of the design team and the main contractor.

We believe the successful main contractor, Sir Robert McAlpine & Sons (SRM), submitted an exceptionally keen price to help maintain momentum for their teams in Glasgow.

The complexity of the very exacting in-situ concrete frame package was underestimated resulting in a difficulty for SRM in obtaining competitive tenders; they agreed to (more or less had to) do it themselves — unsuccessfully at the outset due to quality control issues.

The main contractor and the external cladding contractors also significantly under-estimated the lack of repetition in the external cladding and windows, leading to major delays to the programme.

The bespoke staircase, a specialist joinery package worth roughly £1m, failed to attract any viable tender returns due to the complexity of the job and the lack of locally available skills. So as the clients we decided to deliver this package outside the main contract through our own workshops that are more used to creating scenery than buildings. Doing this blurred the lines between client and contractor, and at the time felt like a real risk, but the quality of the finished building is testament to the workshop's talents and the transferability of skills.

Our project manager's experience is that some main contractors will suffer a little to land a project either for cashflow or for reasons of prestige and may then seek to exploit a claims process to offset a low bid should difficulties be encountered. On this project we don't think it was cashflow but company pride and prestige. SRM had carried out the 1970s-80s, refurbishment of the Theatre Royal and always like to demonstrate repeat clients. However, in this situation we believe that they were— so to speak — in so deep before they realised the complexity of the job and their losses were so significant that they had to get very aggressive. In order to obtain the settlement that they wanted they started to build a case, throwing in everything including the kitchen sink, knowing that it would be vigorously contested. Ultimately, we doubt that SRM covered their costs.

Upon reflection, in any future OJEU process, we would try and consider a means of assessing and balancing price versus quality to a greater extent.

As part of the procurement process we interviewed the main contractor's project manager. This leadership role is pivotal in delivering a good building, developing the construction methodology and ensuring a safe and efficient site. From the outset, we felt he was not up to the task, but were reluctant to force a change.

However, history ultimately proved we were correct so, in future, I would trust my instincts and act upon them immediately. We believe that the first project manager was one of the reasons the main contractor appeared to lose control of the earlier part of the job but ultimately, when he was replaced and with other changes made to the team, work quality and pace generally improved.

However, it is worthy of note that despite many setbacks and the occasional dispute, ultimately the main contractor did successfully build the building we wanted and achieved a high standard of finish. A major achievement,

fig. 5.2
Corner view of the Theatre Royal
© Andrew Lee

fig. 5.3
Foyer and stair
© Andrew Lee

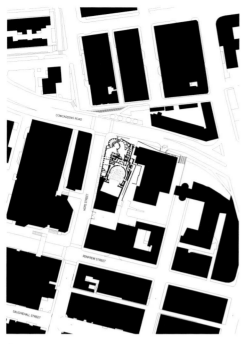

fig. 5.4
Location plan
© Page \ Park
architects

fig. 5.5
fig. 5.6
Theatre Royal Foyer
© Andrew Lee

given all the challenges of design, engineering and quality.

We love the building Page / Park and the team have created for us. Since the foyers opened, we've been delighted by how graciously and effortlessly they are able to host a full-house audience.

They also provide space that invites people to gather, and the café and box office have been well used since. People naturally gravitate to the window bays, looking out on their own Glasgow postcard view. Many choose to linger on the staircase, seeing and being seen, which has always been one of the pleasures of theatre-going.

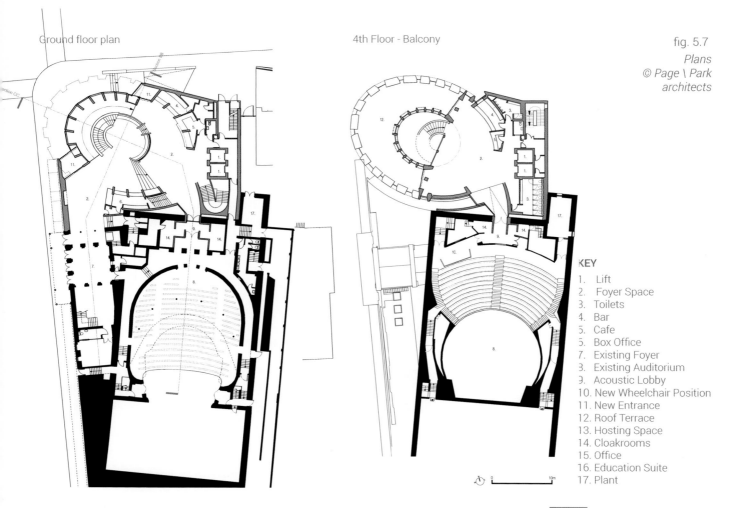

Ground floor plan

4th Floor - Balcony

fig. 5.7

Plans
© Page \ Park
architects

KEY
1. Lift
2. Foyer Space
3. Toilets
4. Bar
5. Cafe
5. Box Office
7. Existing Foyer
3. Existing Auditorium
9. Acoustic Lobby
10. New Wheelchair Position
11. New Entrance
12. Roof Terrace
13. Hosting Space
14. Cloakrooms
15. Office
16. Education Suite
17. Plant

PROJECT DATA

Name	**Extension to the Theatre Royal Glasgow**
Location	282 Hope Street, Glasgow G2 3QA
Country	SCOTLAND
Year	2008

PROJECT DESCRIPTION

Type	The development of new foyers to the Grade A Listed Victorian Theatre to provide universal access to all levels of the theatre
Size	2,727 m² new plus 714 m² within the existing theatre
Budget Cost	£18.5m (GBP) (€20.4m), Construction Cost £13m

COMPETITION DESCRIPTION

Client	**Scottish Opera**, with capital funding provided by the Heritage Lottery Fund
Programmer/Agent	Harry Wood, tX-2 Project Management
Public/Private	Public
Procedure	Restricted competition procedure issued through OJEU and Public Contracts Scotland.
Procedure Reference	Directive 2004/18/EC. Art. 28 *(near equivalent: Directive 2014/24/EU Art.27)*
Stages	2 plus an interview
Project Intention	A feasibility and business appraisal with options had been prepared by AshSakula Architects and Bop Consulting (to RIBA Stage 0). The project intention was for a feasibility design study to be developed up to and including submission of a planning application (to RIBA Stage 3)
Conditions Applied	The 2nd stage was conducted in line with recommendations in the Advice Document on Architectural Competitions provided by RIAS Quality was weighted 75, price 25

COMPETITION FACTS

Timescale	Competition call:	25 September 2009
	PQQ submission:	4 November 2009
	ITT Call:	13 November 2009
	Interview:	13/14 January 2010
Submission Required	**Stage 1**: After expressing Interest, bidders were provided a brief, method of value assessment, & required to respond to a PQQ on probity questions, statutory compliance confirmations, professional team composition & relevant experience. **Stage 2:** A CD containing information & a pre-interview questionnaire was then issued to those shortlisted, inviting submission of 2 x A1 boards outlining an understanding of the brief, site complexities & responses **Interview:**	
Announcement	16 February 2010	
Number of Entries	49 (107 expressions of interest were received)	

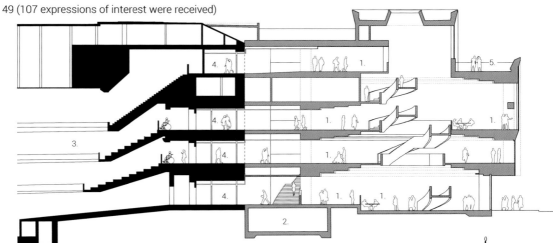

fig. 5.8

Section C - C
©Page \ Park
Architects

KEY
1. Foyer Space
2. Toilets
3. Auditorium
4. Acoustic Lobby
5. Roof Terrace

"This is a building to linger in. And while it engages solidly with the existing structure ... and with the neighbourhood in ... how it mirrors the opposing corner...it also revels in the art of showing off."
AJ 29 May 2015

ASSESSMENT & SELECTION

Jury Numbers	5 for the 1st stage jury and 6 for the 2nd stage
Jury Composition	**With a deliberative role:** Scottish Opera General Director Scottish Opera Board Vice Chair *(2nd Stage Jury only)* Scottish Opera Technical Director Theatre Royal Board Chair (a wholly owned subsidiary of Scottish Opera) *(2nd Stage Jury only)* The Project Manager *(1st Stage Jury only)* An independent architect An independent architect
Number Shortlisted	5
Winner	Page \ Park Architects Structural Engineers, Arup Scotland; M&E and lighting design Consultants, Max Fordham; QSs Capita; Acousticians, Sandy Brown Associates; Fire Consultants, Atelier 10; Access Consultants, Adapt; and CDM Scotland were appointed separately
Runners Up	Tim Ronalds Architects and three others (unreported)
Prizes & Awards	£2,500 honorariums were awarded to each of the four unsuccessful shortlisted architects
Conclusion of Process Construction Contract(s)	The award led directly to commission and work started immediately SBCC Standard Building Contract with Quantities 2011 for use in Scotland, used with a two-stage tender process Sir Robert McAlpine & Sons were appointed the main contractors
Project Completion	December 2014

FURTHER INFORMATION

Scottish Opera www.scottishopera.org.uk
The Theatre Royal www.glasgowtheatreroyal.org.uk
Page \ Park Architects https://pagepark.co.uk/
Architects Journal 29 May 2015 pp 26-40
RIAS Award 2015
RICS Award 2015, Leisure Category
Scottish Design Awards 2015, Leisure/Culture Building Category
GIA Award 2015, Leisure Category
The staircase was nominated for a UK Tekla Award.
The Scottish Opera Project Manager was also involved in the appointment of an Architect and a Contractor for the Design of a new £10m Headquarters for Scottish Ballet in 2007, alongside extensive renovations for the Royal Conservatoire of Scotland, and more recently the rebuilding of the Citizens Theatre.

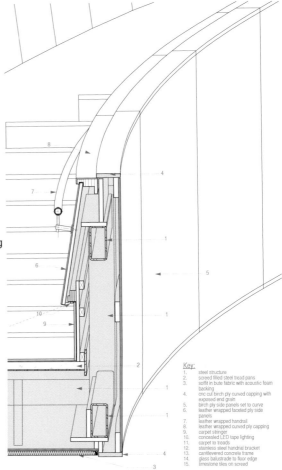

fig. 5.9
*Stair detail
©Page \ Park architects*

Key:
1. steel structure
2. screed filled steel tread pans
3. soffit in bute fabric with acoustic foam backing
4. cnc cut birch ply curved capping with exposed end grain
5. birch ply side panels set to curve
6. leather wrapped faceted ply side panels
7. leather wrapped handrail
8. leather wrapped curved ply capping
9. carpet stringer
10. concealed LED tape lighting
11. carpet to treads
12. stainless steel handrial bracket
13. cantilevered concrete frame
14. glass balustrade to floor edge
15. limestone tiles on screed

6 Aberdeen Art Gallery

Chris Coleman-Smith

Hoskins Architects, Scotland

Hoskins Architects was appointed in 2009, by Aberdeen City Council, to provide building design consultancy services for the redevelopment and extension of Aberdeen Art Gallery, Schoolhill, Aberdeen. The appointment followed a competitive process which started with a Prior Information Notice (PIN) advertised in a public notice (OJUE).

Aberdeen Art Gallery is a Category A listed building in the central conservation area. It is surrounded by Robert Gordon College to the north and east, with Schoolhill and Blackfriars Street forming the remaining boundaries.

Originally designed by Alexander Marshall McKenzie, it first opened in 1885, and was subsequently altered and extended in a number of phases. It is the largest public gallery in the north of Scotland with a rich and varied collection of art and design. The incremental development of the building had resulted in a range of issues. These included difficulty with public access, orientation and circulation, inadequate provision and use of facilities, insufficient space for the display of the collection and back of house areas.

The notice called for a team of professional practitioners capable of providing all disciplines of the design service to submit an offer to carry out the project. The award criteria were set as the most economically advantageous tender based on a 60 per cent quality, 40 per cent price, which was to be assessed by an internal panel. Notably, that panel was to include key staff at Aberdeen Art Gallery who would be involved in the project from inception to completion and beyond.

Following a Prior Information Notice (PIN) a notice was called for a Pre-Qualification Questionnaire (PQQ), used to shortlist a minimum of five and a maximum of eight teams.

The PQQ represented 80 per cent of the quality score. Shortlisted teams were then invited to tender and the response was split into tender (price) and tender questionnaire responses (the remaining 20 per cent of the quality score). The tender price comprised a lump sum fee for RIBA stage A-B (feasibility) and a percentage-based fee for subsequent stages, based on a construction budget of £20m. The process included interviews following tender return.

This approach of selecting a pre-assembled design team has become common, rather than simply selecting an architect and other consultants individually and directly. It allows the client to have confidence in selecting a team that has a proven track record of working together to deliver similar projects. It also simplifies the procurement process for the client with the appointment of the design team made via the architects, who appoint a number of sub-consultants.

However, this can also raise issues for the client, architect and other consultants. Whilst the client may perceive/realise a benefit in terms of simplified procurement, with a single appointment, point of payment and with management of the team transferred to the architect, the direct contractual relationship between client and other consultants is lost. The team are employed by the architect which may make it harder for the client to address issues that arise with individual consultants and maintain the same level of dialogue.

The transfer of management responsibility also engenders additional work for the architect, which may result in a reduced service if the fee for this element of work is not recognised and identified in the tender. The architect also becomes the conduit for client/consultant dialogue, and this may negatively impact on

fig. 6.1
*Aberdeen Art Gallery
View from Centre
Court balcony
© dapple photography*

all parties in ways that are not initially apparent, such as agreement to additional work, payment and performance issues.

As with all procurement, the scoring criteria is critical, and the quality/price aspect of scoring is key. Quality scores are unavoidably subjective and frequently turn out to be close, whilst price scoring is calculated via a pre-defined, logical method, often resulting in large differences in scores. A low price (in this case a fixed lump sum) can unduly distort scoring resulting in the lowest price winning the tender, regardless of the quality score. Hence, the mechanism for scoring price is critical and the comparison of tenders needs to be very carefully considered to ensure quality remains as important a factor as the client intends when selecting the team.

In this case, the inclusion of key staff from Aberdeen Art Gallery on the internal panel responsible for awarding the tender contributed significantly to the selection of the most appropriate team (quality), with whom the client was confident they could work best, with design team fees (price) given due relative consideration.

The use of a PQQ in the selection of a shortlist is common and has clear benefits for both clients and tendering teams. The result in this instance was a defined number of teams being shortlisted to go on to develop a tender (price) and response to tender questions. The response to the PQQ was also a key element in the quality score and provided the client team with key background information.

An alternative approach we have encountered more often recently is the practice of issuing open Invitations to Tender (ITTs). Instead of shortlisting via PQQ, all interested parties complete highly developed proposals, which requires significant investment on the part of design teams, without the benefit (reduced risk) of competing against a defined (smaller) number. This approach also has potential pitfalls in that the basis of fees can be unclear and that key stages of the design process are compressed or unduly accelerated.

On Aberdeen Art Gallery, following shortlisting, the Tender Questions provided an opportunity for the selected teams to focus on their understanding of issues, outline how these could be addressed and identify how to deliver the best outcome for the client.

The PQQ and tender questions were well-considered and this approach, issuing tender questions as opposed to the common practice of seeking submission of a competition scheme at tender stage, allowed flexibility for ideas to be tested with the client team during the subsequent RIBA stage A-B (feasibility). Thus, we were able to develop a proposal that suited the client's ambitions and budget, without being committed to a fixed approach from the outset.

The selection of the team was an important factor for the client and the interview allowed them to engage with the team, receive a presentation on key issues and raise questions. Although not employed on this occasion, a scored interview may also have provided a further opportunity for review and adjustment of the quality score prior to finally selecting the preferred team.

Since our appointment for Aberdeen Art Gallery, we have noticed an increase in the use of frameworks to procure architectural services. This avoids open notices and enables the client to tender on pre-agreed fee scales or fee caps. However the fees associated with these frameworks often present challenges in terms of delivering the quality and service required. Although designed to streamline the

fig. 6.2
Aberdeen Art Gallery Entrance elevation showing new rooftop extension
© dapple photography

fig. 6.3
Aberdeen Art Gallery View of new extension & rooflight; towards Gallery 19
© dapple photography

"Somewhat perversely for arts buildings procurement, this process appears to demonstrate a level of risk aversion which frequently contradicts the very nature and ethos of the client art organisations"

appointment process, it could be argued that frameworks restrict participation (and therefore competition) and that often design teams are not assigned on merits appropriate to individual projects.

An important factor in the success of this project was that the procurement model selected, one which Hoskins Architects often favours, was such that key design decisions were not made until after the original brief — and the relationship between design team and client— had been developed and ideas tested.

Aberdeen Art Gallery re-opened its doors to queues of waiting public on the 2nd of November 2019 and the response to the

redeveloped building has been exceptionally positive. Gallery staff are similarly enthusiastic and delighted with the product of this, the latest stage of development in the Gallery's long history.

Key to that success was an enlightened client who not only understood their own priorities but was able to select an appropriate procurement model, designed to ensure those priorities were upheld throughout the process of selecting their design team, thus ensuring they remained embedded throughout the entire redevelopment and are evident in the newly-opened Gallery today.

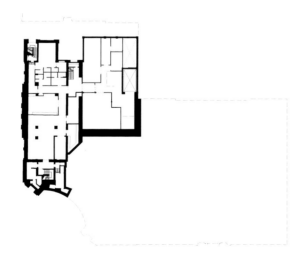
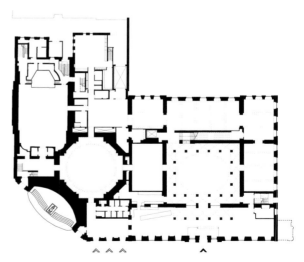

fig. 6.4
Aberdeen Art Gallery
View of carefully
refurbished Gallery 15
© dapple photography

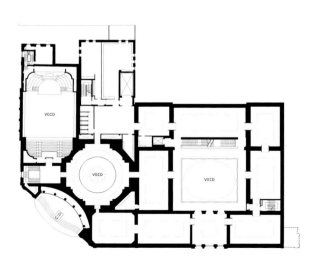

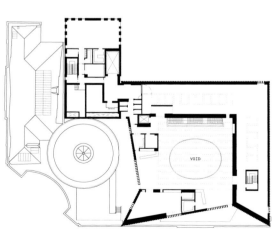

fig. 6.5
Aberdeen
Art Gallery Plans.
From left to right,
lower ground, ground,
first & second floors
© Hoskins Architects

PROJECT DATA

Name	**ABERDEEN ART GALLERY**
Location	Schoolhill, Aberdeen AB10 1FQ
Country	SCOTLAND
Year	2007

PROJECT DESCRIPTION

Type	Art Gallery complex with permanent and temporary gallery spaces, Cowdray Hall music venue, education, community and art handling facilities, a War Memorial and Remembrance Hall. The existing building has has a category A listing and lies in the central conservation area
Size	7,741 m^2
Budget Cost	£34.6m (GBP) (€38.71m)

COMPETITION DESCRIPTION

Client	**Aberdeen City Council**
	Project capital funding was provided by Aberdeen City Council, the National Heritage Lottery Fund (HLF), UK Government BP and public donations. The Scottish Government did not provide financial support
Programmer/Agent	Aberdeen City Council
Public/Private	Public
Procedure	A restricted competition procedure having a prior information notice
Procedure Reference	Directive 2004/18/EC. Art. 28 *(Directive 2014/24/EU Art.28 nearest equivalence)*
Stages	2 and an interview
Project Intention	The initial appointment was for RIBA stage A/B
Conditions Applied	Aberdeen City Council
	In the assessment quality was weighted at 70% and cost at 30%.

COMPETITION FACTS

Timescale	Competition call:	December 2007
	PQQ submission:	June 2008
	ITT submission:	October 2008
	Interview:	February 2009
	Award:	July 2009
Submission Required	**Stage 1:** PQQ (Pre-qualification questionnaire) Probity questions, statutory compliance confirmations, relevant experience	
	Stage 2: An ITT (invitation to tender) resource schedule, an inclusive lump sum fee, and a design response. No design was submitted within the tender but an approach was outlined using diagrams and text	
	Stage 3: A competitive interview	
Announcement	Stage 1: September 2008	
	Stage 2: December 2008	
	Stage 3: July 2009	
Number of Entries	19	

"Key to that success was an enlightened client who not only understood their own priorities but was able to select an appropriate procurement model, designed to ensure those priorities were upheld"

ASSESSMENT & SELECTION

Jury Numbers	5
Jury Composition	Principal Architect, Construction Consultancy
	Aberdeen City Council Art Gallery & Museum Manager
	Aberdeen City Council Service Manager, Culture
	Aberdeen City Council Elected member - Spokesperson for Culture
	Aberdeen City Council Chair of Marguerite McBey Trust
Number Shortlisted	6
Winner	Hoskins Architects with a sub-consultant team comprising: AECOM, Quantity Surveyors; Buro Happold Ltd., Structural & Civil Engineer and Mechanical & Electrical Engineers
Runners Up	Not known
Prizes & Awards	None
Conclusion of Process	The award led to a RIBA Stage A-B feasibility study, and in turn to the construction design commission with services provided up to and including RIBA stage L
Construction Contract(s)	JCT Standard Building Contract With Quantities for use in Scotland (SBC/Q/Scot 2011) was let to main contractors McLaughlin and Harvey who commenced works in 2015
Project Completion	February 2019. The fit-out followed, with the Gallery re-opening November 2019

FURTHER INFORMATION

Hoskins Architects: www.hoskinsarchitects.com
Aberdeen Art Gallery: https://www.aberdeencity.gov.uk/AAGM
Available in the following: The Scotsman (6th November 2019), The Guardian (2nd November 2019) and in the architectural press, RIBAJ (10 December 2019) and AJ (20th November 2019).
Hoskin Architects have undertaken a number of cultural projects including the redevelopment of the National Museum of Scotland; the Weltmuseum Wien (Vienna); The Bridge Arts Centre, in Glasgow's East End; designs for The Mackintosh Gallery at the Lighthouse, Glasgow, Scotland's centre for Architecture and Design and the Architecture for All Gallery at the V&A, London.

fig. 6.6
Aberdeen Art Gallery
Front range cafe
space with entrance
beyond
© dapple photography

7   Edinburgh Printmakers and associated arts spaces

Nicola Walls

Page \ Park Architects, Scotland

In April 2019 Edinburgh Printmakers' (EP) new home opened at Castlemill Works in Fountainbridge to the west of Edinburgh's city centre. This grade C listed former workshop for the North British Rubber Company (NBRC) is the last historic fragment on a major redevelopment site. Even in its dilapidated former state our client had seen the potential on this site to create 'a unique offer' allowing them to expand their production studio facilities and add a blend of gallery and retail spaces, with a dedicated education suite, café, and ancillary accommodation.

The project background

In 2012 an option appraisal study was undertaken by Oliver Chapman Architects of various buildings and sites to evaluate their suitability for EP's needs. Once the NBRC's potential suitability was identified, initial proposals were then developed by a local Edinburgh architectural practice to RIBA Stage 2 to form part of the Capital Project Feasibility Study which was submitted in November 2013. An OJEU contract notice calling for architect led design teams requiring completion of a Pre-Qualification was placed in May 2014.

The Project Vision

Edinburgh Printmakers' vision is to support artistic excellence in the medium of print by delivering a world class cultural facility that will operate as a catalyst for the development of artistic programmes of work locally, nationally and internationally

EP were seeking to create a world class cultural facility and hub supporting artistic excellence encouraging cross fertilisation of ideas and innovation across artistic platforms, with their new premises enhancing the organisation's visibility and increasing income generation.

The procurement process

The Design Team was procured through a restricted 2-stage competition. From the initial pre-qualification stage a shortlist of six architect led design teams progressed to the Invitation to Tender (ITT) stage.

In addition to the design response, a full resource schedule and an inclusive lump sum fee for the project was required, (based on RIBA Work Stage C and onwards, for a contract value of £5.7m) and design teams attended a competitive interview. The assessment was based on a quality/price split of 70/30%, and Page \ Park were advised of our success in late August 2014.

Reflections on the competitive process

Page \ Park's business development team convene weekly to review any potential 'open competition' opportunities. Given the investment required to make such submissions, and the fact that there is rarely remuneration, we carefully consider whether individual opportunities are worth pursuing. This decision is usually based on several factors including the project type, its value, and our ability to demonstrate relevant experience. A significant factor is whether there have been earlier feasibility studies and therefore an incumbent team, and if this is the case, we would try to make enquiries to determine whether this is therefore a genuine opportunity or whether it is just a procedural obligation. A competitive process affects the profitability of a project going forward; however, we also acknowledge that arts projects carry a cache and profile that bring other benefits to our practice beyond the monetary.

In the case of the Edinburgh Printmakers, whilst we had no direct relevant experience of

fig. 7.1
Edinburgh Printmakers Print Studio
© *Jim Stephenson*

"A competitive process affects the profitability of a project going forward; however, we also acknowledge that arts projects carry a cache and profile that bring other benefits to our practice beyond the monetary"

fig. 7.2

*Edinburgh
Printmakers Shop*
© Jim Stephenson

printing production studios, there were many aspects of the brief that we had covered in other projects. The fact that the project was about the creative adaptation of a historic building into cultural usage, was also a very good fit for our practice, our interests and our experience.

However, the pre-qualification questionnaire (PQQ) stage for this project presented challenges regarding eligibility, as many PQQs do, because through this process they potentially preclude less well-established practices.

A factor is the level of insurance required and another restriction on this project was the requirement to demonstrate an established working relationship across the team members, making it impossible to develop new working relationships through this type of competitive process.

Each team needed to submit three examples of buildings redeveloped for arts or other cultural facilities, and a further three examples of listed buildings converted to cultural use. Whilst not time barred, this requirement reduces the number of practices who could adequately demonstrate this experience – resulting in a situation in Scotland where we often find ourselves repeatedly competing against the same practices.

At the ITT stage, information on the earlier architectural proposal within the EP Capital Project Development Study was shared. At this stage Page \ Park proposed in our design submission a radical shift from the earlier proposals. Our designs investigated opening up the frontage onto Dundee Street to increase Edinburgh Printmakers visibility to passing pedestrians and traffic, rather than reusing the original main entrance.

Moving from the concept scheme developed within the earlier study could be perceived as risky – although it is a strategy we have adopted when we perceive other worthwhile solutions that feel more intuitive. However, when there is no dialogue with the client which might allow their aspirations and needs to be explored, this can also feel presumptive.

Inevitably the completed scheme is very different from the competition stage. It was developed in close collaboration with the client team and through thorough understanding of the organisation and the building once that creative dialogue happened after our appointment. Opening to positive reviews, the first few months of operation of Edinburgh Printmakers have seen a critically acclaimed exhibition programme, a thriving café and a growing creative community operating in Castlemill Works.

Through this competitive process Page \ Park ultimately delivered an acclaimed, successful and well used project for Edinburgh Printmakers.

However, the UK competitive process, with its focuses on early stage administrative compliance and procedures rather than ideas, makes it difficult to break into new sectors and areas of work, and for new collaborations to be forged. Somewhat perversely for arts buildings procurement, this process appears to demonstrate a level of risk aversion which frequently contradicts the very nature and ethos of the client art organisations.

fig. 7.4
Edinburgh Printmakers
Section
© Page \ Park

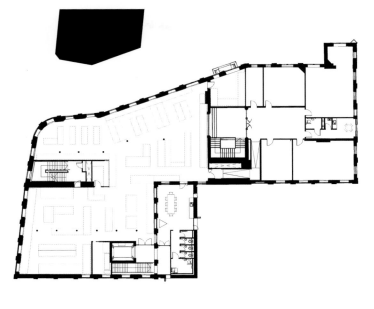

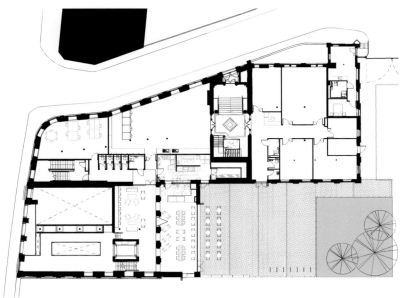

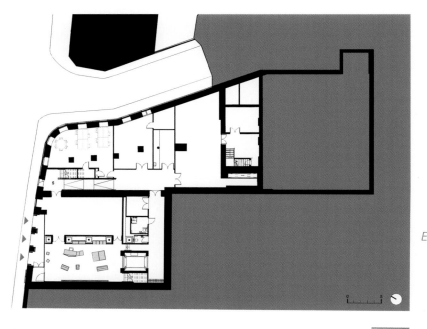

fig. 7.5
*Edinburgh Printmakers
Plans.
From bottom to top,
lower ground
ground & first floor
© Page \ Park*

PROJECT DATA

Name	EDINBURGH PRINTMAKERS: Studios, associated education & arts support spaces
Location	Castlemills, 1 Dundee Street, Edinburgh, EH3 9FP
Country	SCOTLAND
Year	2013

PROJECT DESCRIPTION

Type	Restoration and redevelopment of a grade C listed building to provide print studio, galleries, café, shop, education and creative industries units
Size	2,650 m^2
Budget Cost	£6.5m (GBP) (€7.59m)

COMPETITION DESCRIPTION

Client	**Edinburgh Printmakers Ltd. (EP)**, a charitable company limited by guarantee. Project capital funding was provided by the Heritage Lottery Fund (HLF), Creative Scotland, Scottish Government, Historic Environment Scotland and City of Edinburgh Council, supported by the Garfield Weston Foundation and Robertson Trust
Programmer/Agent	Gardiner and Theobald
Public/Private	Public
Procedure	A restricted competition procedure, with a prior information notice
Procedure Reference	Directive 2004/18/EC. Art. 28 *(Directive 2014/24/EU Art.28 nearest equivalent)*
Stages	2 and an interview (see below)
Project Intention	For a preceding feasibility design study to be developed to completion
Conditions Applied	Royal Incorporation of Architects in Scotland (RIAS). (assumed - *but unverified*). Quality was weighted 70, to cost weighted 30

COMPETITION FACTS

Timescale	Competition call: 7 May 2014 PQQ submission: 6 June 2014 ITT call: August 2014 Award: 20 August 2014
Submission Required	**Stage 1:** PQQ (Pre-qualification questionnaire) Probity questions, statutory compliance confirmations, relevant experience and a demonstration of successful working relationships with fellow team members **Stage 2:** A full resource schedule, an inclusive lump sum fee, (from RIBA Stage C for a £5.7m contract) and a design response comprising: Some hand drawn concept sketches, basic CAD plans, one section, a CAD visualisation and a model (interview only). A competitive interview, unscored
Announcement	September 2014 (with contract award notice published 25 November 2014)
Number of Entries	6

ASSESSMENT & SELECTION

Jury Numbers	5
Jury Composition	EP Chair of the Board
	EP Chief Executive Officer
	EP Financial Director
	EP Board Member (an architect)
	Gardiner and Theobald Project Manager
Number Shortlisted	6
Winner	Page \ Park Architects Ltd. (lead architects & conservation architects) working with Harley Haddow Ltd. (M&E), Will Rudd Davidson (structural engineers) and Adapt Trust (access consultants).
Runners Up	Not known
Prizes & Awards	None
Conclusion of Process	Construction design commission
Construction Contract(s)	JCT Standard Building Contract With Quantities for use in Scotland (SBC/Q/Scot)
Project Completion	3rd December 2018. Public opening April 2019

FURTHER INFORMATION

Page \ Park Architects: www.pagepark.co.uk/project/architecture/edinburgh-printmakers
Edinburgh Printmakers: www.edinburghprintmakers.co.uk
Available in the following: Wallpaper (3rd June 2019), Homes and Interiors Scotland (25th June 2019) and the architectural press (Architecture Today 20th May 2019 & AJ 28th May 2019).

RICS Social Impact Awards 2020, Scotland Winner - Project of the Year and Heritage Category. GIA Award 2019, Winner - Leisure / Arts Category.
Page/Park Architects have undertaken a number of arts projects including: The Lighthouse, Glasgow; CCA (Centre for Contemporary Arts) Glasgow; Eden Court Theatre, Inverness; Scottish National Portrait Gallery, Edinburgh; Museum of Rural Life, East Kilbride; McManus Galleries, Dundee; Leeds Playhouse; and the Birmingham Symphony Hall.

fig. 7.7
Edinburgh Printmakers
New extension &
courtyard
© Jim Stephenson

"...the new premises for the town's Oriel Gallery inside the covered market.... a hybrid place of commerce and art...the place feels right for its aspirations. It is welcoming, animated, open, unpretentious and multifarious, while also calm and dignified."
The Guardian 1 Sept. 2018

fig. 8.1

Tŷ Pawb food square
© James Morris

8   Tŷ Pawb (Everybody's House)

Sarah Featherstone

Featherstone Young Architects, England and Wales

Tŷ Pawb (Everybody's House) is an arts venue relocating the former Oriel Wrecsam (Wrexham Arts Centre) within The People's Market, one of the town's three existing markets. This was a 1980s purpose-built market hall with an integral multi-storey car park. The project was commissioned by Wrexham County Borough Council (WCBC), with capital funding and support from the Arts Council of Wales (ACW) and the Welsh Government (WG).

When reopened in April 2018 Tŷ Pawb presented a new typology which reinvents underused public infrastructure enlivening it with cultural uses, providing a diversity of functions and activities better sustaining the whole.

The Project

Externally the building's transformation is now announced by a new entrance and graphic treatment to the facades, signaling Tŷ Pawb's presence in the town.

Opportunities to attract people are offered by the market and car park, and their strategic location, which provides a pedestrian shortcut between the old town center and edge-of town attractions. This long popular route has been treated as part of the Wrexham town center by extension and by developing a new urban streetscape internally, with squares, street furniture, billboards and signposts inside.

With the Tŷ Pawb team our practice have rethought the traditional art gallery environment and the civic role of cultural programming to offer a looser more experimental space rooted in the community and everyday life. This we refer to as the 'baggy space' concept, where designers and curators create a light-touch framework which enables others to fill the gaps. This approach helps create a place that can be used habitually and opens up potential for wider and more meaningful public experiences.

The 'baggy space' concept is particularly visible at Sqwar y Bobl (The People's Square), a new flexible space at the center of the market. Experimentally this brings together the arts, market and community. It is equipped with translucent heavy plastic industrial curtains to divide the space during concurrently programmed activities, allowing for flexibility informal and spontaneous events.

The passing user experience has been transformed. Cuts introduced into the existing precast concrete building bring natural light deep into the plan, creating dramatic vertical connections between floors. There is now a varied mix of arts spaces, market trading, and food retailers with creative studios and offices on the first floor, whilst the original car park facility remains in use on the upper storey's. Bright welcoming and spacious arts and exhibition spaces are animated by cultural activities now being programmed by Tŷ Pawb, including Wal Pawb (Everyone's Wall), a large billboard with a rolling programme of locally selected artwork. More prosaically, longer trading hours for the returning market traders have also been provided alongside new food retailers providing early morning coffee to late-night drinks.

We worked closely with the furniture designer Tim Denton. He constructed much of the furniture collaboratively with community groups. These included primary school pupils who built the reception desk; local college students who built shop furniture and market hall benches, a wood-working group lathe-turned the stool hooks and table legs, and others who made the supports for the Sqwar y Bobl tables, and the stools and boxes for the Siop//Shop. The participants learnt valuable skills while visibly contributing to Tŷ Pawb.

fig. 8.2
*Tŷ Pawb Floor cut
outs let in light
and link the gallery
workshop space
with studios above*
© James Morris

fig. 8.3
*Tŷ Pawb corner with
graphics facing the
out-of-town shopping
malls*
© James Morris

*"The passing user experience has been transformed…
Bright welcoming and spacious arts and exhibition
spaces are animated by cultural activities now being
programmed by Tŷ Pawb"*

The procurement process

We find that although design competitions provide the main way to win projects which we have relevant experience in, the onerous and irrelevant questions, frequent lack of architects on the judging panel, undue complexity and multiple competitive stages are all significant obstacles.

In this case a site and building feasibility and business plan had been commissioned in 2013 prior to our engagement and our original appointment was only to planning (RIBA Stage 3).

To undertake further work and avoid another competitive process, we first had to negotiate additional fees beneath the Council's fee/cost threshold. The pressure on WCBC's programme provided a clear incentive to retain us to deliver the construction tender information. This enabled our work to continue over that summer during a two-stage contractor procurement process.

WCBC were seeking a design build contract having a design team selected and appointed by the contractor, against our recommendations and, materially, those of ACW. A negotiated hybrid model was eventually adopted. In this our appointment was transferred to the project managers who were already on the WCBC framework, and to avoid losing time from any requirement to make a further competition call. ACW's independent advisors, architect Harry James and QS Richard Pritchard, were particularly instrumental in ensuring the project design didn't go to further competition and our continuity was retained eventually through construction.

Reflections on the competitive process

The project benefited from a good passionate client team with an early and clear timeline which they adhered to, and although the assessment panel was devoid of architects it was supported ably by a good architect advisor, Niall Maxwell.

It might have helped however if the assessment panel had community representation, including a market stall holder and if better access and more responsibility in the community engagement process had been offered. A 14 week programme to planning and to allow for meaningful community engagement, we felt, was disproportionately short and the pressure diminished engagement. However, we did manage to adhere to this.

Time and resources are lost when architectural work stages are fragment by recurrent competitive procedures over the duration of a project, diminishing potential quality, values and stakeholding not to mention the insecurities generated for all.

It is also inexplicable to us that authorities investing in competitive architectural selection for culturally important projects might then prefer a design build contract, which reverses design responsibilities and leadership at the all-important construction phase, to place them with the contractor.

The terms of appointment could have been more clearly and flexibly described within the original competitive call. This could have provided flexibility and avoided the undue complexity and inefficiency of potentially multiple stage competitive procedures and without pre-emptive proscription of the contractual route.

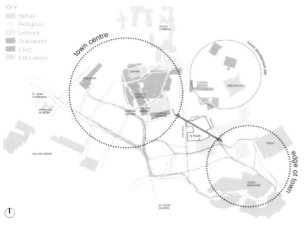

fig. 8.4
*Strategic location of
Tŷ Pawb
© Featherstone
Young Architects*

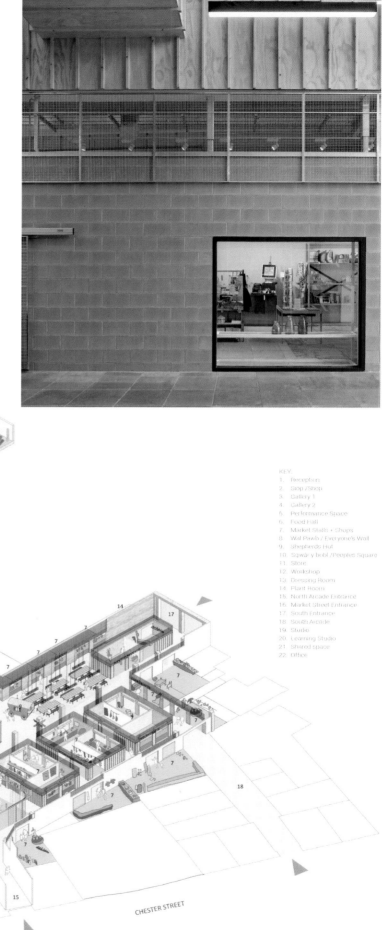

fig. 8.5
*Tŷ Pawb materials
palette of blockwork,
galvanised mesh and
plywood
© James Morris*

KEY:
1. Reception
2. Stop /Shop
3. Gallery 1
4. Gallery 2
5. Performance Space
6. Food Hall
7. Market Stalls + Shops
8. Wal Pawb / Everyone's Wall
9. Shepherds Hut
10. Sgwâr y bobl /Peoples Square
11. Store
12. Workshop
13. Dressing Room
14. Plant Room
15. North Arcade Entrance
16. Market Street Entrance
17. Sixth Entrance
18. South Arcade
19. Studio
20. Learning Studio
21. Shared space
22. Office

fig. 8.6
*Tŷ Pawb axonometric
© Featherstone
Young Architects*

"The terms of appointment could have been more clearly and flexibly described within the original competitive call. This could have provided flexibility and avoided the undue complexity and inefficiency of potentially multiple stage competitive procedures and without pre-emptive proscription of the contractual route."

fig. 8.7
Wal Pawb (People's Wall) with artwork, seating and peep windows
© James Morris

PROJECT DATA

Name	**TŶ PAWB (Everybody's House) cultural community facility**
Location	Market Street, Wrexham LL13 8DA
Country	WALES
Year	2013

PROJECT DESCRIPTION

Type	Restoration and redevelopment of a city center market hall with car park to provide two galleries, performance space, a shop, food hall, market stalls, studios and meeting rooms with 1st floor administration spaces.
Size	4,000 m²
Budget Cost	£4.3 m (GBP) (€4.7m) construction cost

COMPETITION DESCRIPTION

Client	**Wrexham County Borough Council**, with capital funding provided by Wrexham County Borough Council, the Arts Council of Wales and the Welsh Government.
Programmer/Agent	Wrexham County Borough Council,
Public/Private	Public
Procedure	Open competition procedure.
Procedure Reference	Directive 2004/18/EC. Art. 28 *(near equivalent: Directive 2014/24/EU Art.27)*
Stages	1
Project Intention	A feasibility and business appraisal with options had been prepared by Ash Sakula Architects and Bop Consulting (to RIBA Stage 0). The project intention was for a feasibility design study to be developed up to and including submission of a planning application (to RIBA Stage 3).
Conditions Applied	Arts Council Wales Quality was weighted 70, to cost weighted 30.

COMPETITION FACTS

Timescale	Competition call:	7 May 2015
	PQQ submission:	3 July 2015
	Award:	August 2015
Submission Required	Probity questions, statutory compliance confirmations, professional and team composition, and relevant experience. 4 x A4 pages describing the proposal with key issues to be addressed, milestones, the approach, and a delivery programme. An inclusive lump sum fee, day rates, a full resource schedule, and a methodology statement from the design team. An interview (at which 2No. design sketches were presented)	
Announcement	2 September 2015 (Contract Award Notice)	
Number of Entries	8	

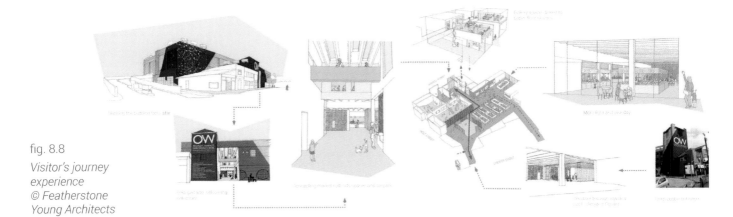

fig. 8.8
*Visitor's journey
experience
© Featherstone
Young Architects*

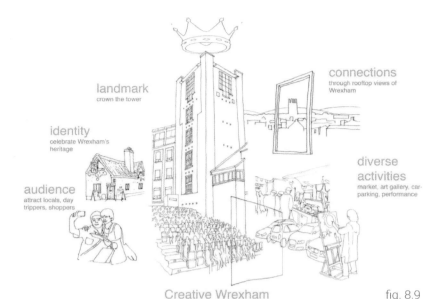

landmark
crown the tower

identity
celebrate Wrexham's
heritage

connections
through rooftop views of
Wrexham

diverse
activities
market, art gallery, car-
parking, performance

audience
attract locals, day
trippers, shoppers

Creative Wrexham
a place where ideas are developed

fig. 8.9
*Sketches undertaken
for the appointment
interview
© Featherstone
Young Architects*

ASSESSMENT & SELECTION

Jury Numbers	7
Jury Composition	**With a deliberative role:** Representatives of Wrexham Council arts team Arts Council for Wales representative, Andy Richards **With an advisory role:** Nial Maxwell (Office of Rural Architecture)
Number Shortlisted	5
Winner	Featherstone Young with design team: Civic Engineers, Ingine (M&E) and Stockdale (Q.S). Fourth Street worked with the design team as business advisors up to planning but were appointed separately
Runners Up	Curl la Tourelle with Wayne Head, Ash Sakula and two others (unknown)
Prizes & Awards	None
Conclusion of Process	Design commission to planning (RIBA Stage 3). Featherstone Young Architects commission was with agreement then extended with their appointment to complete the construction phase design works as sub-contractors to SP Projects Ltd. (the Q.S.'s and project managers stages 4-5), who were already on the client's framework. Upon assignation of the contract to Wynne Construction however new engineers (Haltec), services (ESD) and QS (SP Projects) consultancy teams were appointed.
Construction Contract(s)	JCT Standard Design & Build Contract.
Project Completion	April 2018

FURTHER INFORMATION

Featherstone Young Architects: www.featherstoneyoung.com
Ty Pawb review - an art gallery that truly is everybody's house. Moore R. The Guardian. 1 Sept 2018
www.theguardian.com/artanddesign/2018/sep/01/ty-pawb-review-art-gallery-everybodys-house-wrexham-market
Something for everybody. Astbury. J., The Architects Journal. Building Study. 13 Sept. 2018
www.architectsjournal.co.uk/buildings/something-for-everybody-ty-pawb-art-gallery-by-featherstone-young/10034988.article

fig. 8.10
*Sqwar y Bobl (The
People's Square),
Industrial curtains
transform the
space supporting a
range of activities
© James Morris*

Tŷ Pawb (Everybody's HouseH

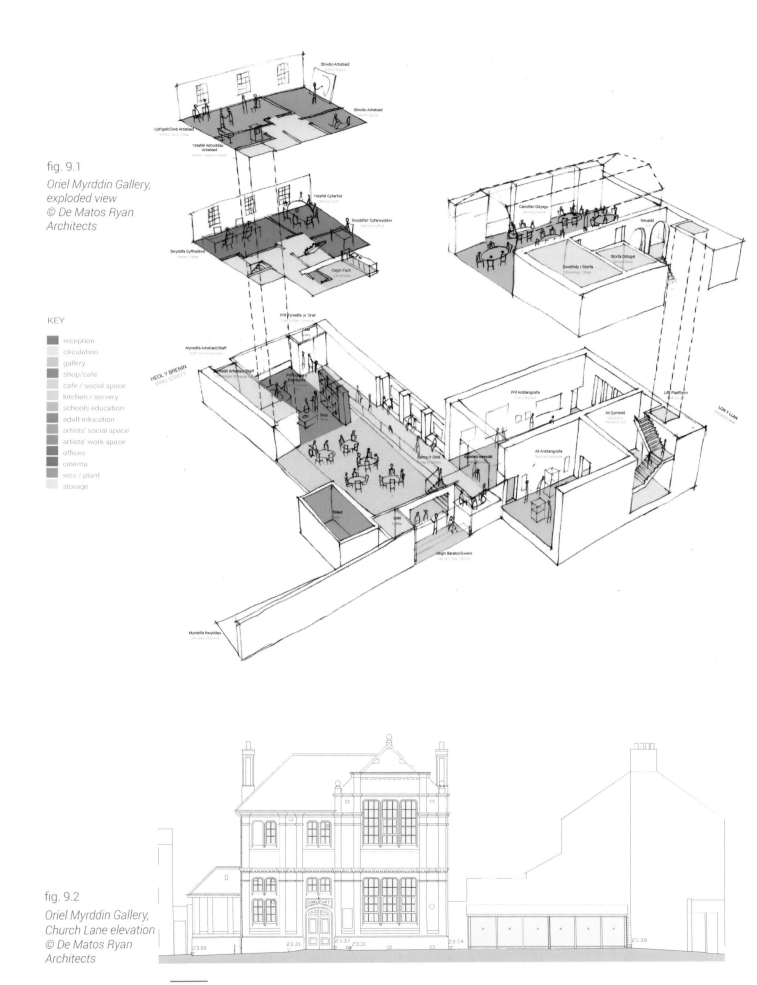

fig. 9.1

*Oriel Myrddin Gallery,
exploded view
© De Matos Ryan
Architects*

KEY

- reception
- circulation
- gallery
- shop/cafe
- cafe / social space
- kitchen / servery
- schools education
- adult education
- artists' social space
- artists' work space
- offices
- cinema
- wcs / plant
- storage

fig. 9.2

*Oriel Myrddin Gallery,
Church Lane elevation
© De Matos Ryan
Architects*

9   The Oriel Myrddin Gallery and Wyeside Arts Centre compared

Angus Morrogh-Ryan

De Matos Ryan Architects, England and Wales

Strategically, De Matos Ryan have been focused on developing an evolving portfolio within the cultural sector, building on previous experience in parallel fields, such as retail and hospitality, to ensure that the often limited capital funding of our projects is based on both meaningful community consultation and market research. This methodology has been successful in ensuring that there is always a well-reasoned mitigation to any potential capital investment. In this sense we have become well known for exploring and establishing what a community genuinely wants and then resolving the priority of these needs so that the funds available are best used to achieve optimal value and social benefit.

Oriel Myrddin Gallery

Our relationship with the cultural sector in Wales began in 2016 when responding to an OJEU notice for the redevelopment of Oriel Myrddin Gallery, Carmarthen. A well-considered RIBA Stage 0-2 Feasibility Study had already been successfully undertaken by Rural Office for Architecture. The tendered commission was to take this forward from RIBA Stage 3 through to completion.

The Oriel Myrddin Gallery project involved the renovation of an existing grade 2 listed Victorian 'art-school' which is currently used as a gallery with a small shop and community outreach and education facilities on the first floor. During the early stages of RIBA Stage 3, complexities concerning the three simultaneous land purchases required for expansion and a fresh appraisal of accessibility led to the need to develop a new strategy relative to the conclusions of the previous RIBA Stage 0-2 Feasibility Study. A shop perpendicular to the site on King Street was identified as being an opportunity to attract higher footfall and connect the high street more directly into the gallery. It also created the opportunity to add a dedicated café, shop and artists hub to the organisation's community offer.

The high street shop site allowed for a reorganisation and expansion of the brief, returning the gallery building closer to its original intention as a place of art within the community. The newly located shop was larger and more visible, allowing for a café to be added to the offer. The townhouse above rehoused staff offices and created an 'Artist's Club'; somewhere for local artists and crafts-people to consider as a genuinely shared space with a strong sense of belonging and communal facilities, such as reprographics, a library, a small commercial gallery and meeting rooms for them to use.

We focused on unlocking the potential of the buildings, the artistic and community development, the business model and making new connections so that everything the organisation needs has its space, enhancing the heritage, improving accessibility and creating greater opportunities for revenue-generating activities, which will make the gallery economically sustainable long term.

The project considered three complementary but distinct areas of engagement which together form the core of the gallery's mission — art, education and commercial activity. The existing, highly successful programme of exhibitions were to be maintained and expanded, with more secure and technical spaces to accommodate travelling shows better. Education and community outreach are key aspects of the new gallery studios, which with better spaces will provide for everything from artist's lectures, hands-on educational workshops for elderly users, families with children and school groups.

The Oriel Myrddin Gallery project is currently on hold at the conclusion of RIBA Stage 3 although it was announced in 2020 that funding has now been secured.

Following on from this commission, we continued to bid for similar scaled, community-based arts projects throughout Wales and have

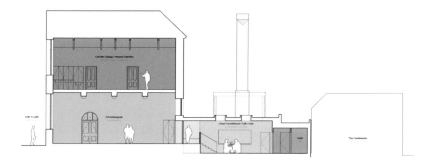

fig. 9.3
*Oriel Myrddin Gallery,
section*
© De Matos Ryan
Architects

KEY

■ reception
□ circulation
■ gallery
■ shop/cafe
□ cafe / social space
■ kitchen / servery
■ schools education
■ adult education
■ artists' social space
■ artists' work space
■ offices
■ cinema
■ wcs / plant
□ storage

always found these projects to be full of optimism in the context of local communities that genuinely value their cultural infrastructure. It has been through our particular approach to cultural sustainability that I have personally become an Associate Adviser to the Arts Council of Wales' 'Resilience Programme', assisting in scoping the potential future needs of a wide range of cultural organisations across Wales.

Wyeside Arts Centre

As was the case with the Oriel Myrddin Gallery, our involvement with Wyeside Arts Centre began with an OJEU notice advertised through the 'Sell 2 Wales' tender portal. The 'Wyeside Works' project makes for a useful comparison with Oriel Myrddin's insofar as the two commissions sit either side of RIBA Stage 2.

The brief for the 'Wyeside Works' project was for a RIBA Stage 0-2 feasibility study. It was to explore ideas for widening the scope and appeal of the art centre's offer and in doing so to put in place plans for making their future more financially resilient and sustainable. The feasibility stage has now been completed.

In an interesting reversal of the circumstances surrounding the Oriel Myrddin Gallery commission whereby we were appointed to follow on from the conclusion of another architect's feasibility study after RIBA Stage 2, if the 'Wyeside Works' project were to now proceed beyond RIBA Stage 2, we would almost certainly need to re-tender for it via a public competition. This raises interesting questions about loss of continuity and value in terms of the project and site specific knowledge acquired during the course of the initial design development, and also the relationships that are built between client and design teams. In terms of procurement regulations and funding, there may of course be many fair and reasonable reasons for the subdivision of such commissioning, but there are clear issues of value.

The 'Wyeside Works' tender requirements were not dissimilar to other OJEU processes that we have participated in previously. However, unlike some other OJEU opportunities, which often require a Pre-Qualification Questionnaire (PQQ) to be submitted in advance of then being Invited to Tender (ITT) at a later date, the selection process wrapped up the proof of suitability with the intellectual response in one submission. Thereafter, it was assessed by the steering group/jury in three stages.

1. **Initial assessment of suitability.** Failure to score more than 10% on the 'Supplier Suitability Questionnaire' (SSQ) would mean that your bid would not be considered further for the second 'Tender Assessment' stage. Typical reassurances on integrity and competence, including company policies and previous project references, were also requested.

2. **Tender Assessment.** The requirements of the ITT submission were thankfully not overly onerous in terms of time and resource required to participate insofar as they simply requested concise (300-500word max.) responses to specific topics, such as client brief, methodology, and risk assessment. Compared to some other OJEU tenders, for which we have submitted bids, we greatly appreciated the more measured approach to the ITT response requirements.

fig. 9.4
*Oriel Myrddin Gallery,
section*
© De Matos Ryan
Architects

3. **Interview:** A shortlist of four companies from seven were then invited to interview. What was interesting about this particular interview process was that all participants were set the same prescribed topic, rather like an essay, as follows: 'Balancing the immediate re-development needs of the building with the innovative, long term development aspirations in order to generate public interest, excitement and funding potential will be a challenge, how will your team meet that challenge. Discuss.' We have since learnt that this type of question is a quirk of the appointed Project Manager. Again, we appreciated this as it created a level playing field for all tendering parties. We developed a presentation called '5 Steps towards an achievable Masterplan', which thankfully did the trick.

The commission for the 'Wyeside Works' RIBA Stage 0-2 feasibility study was for a lead consultant architect with a core multidisciplinary team, including structural engineering, MEP services, costs consultancy, theatre & cinema consultants, acoustics, BREEAM, fire engineering, access consultants and CDM advisers. The extensive survey and specialist reports required included a measured survey of the buildings, condition surveys for all M&E services, building fabric surveys including damp & rot assessments, and preliminary ecological assessment, energy audit, acoustic testing and access survey reports.

Client bodies who commission increasingly prefer to request extensive multidisciplinary consultant teams and a wide range of surveys in order to reduce project risk. In the context of fixed budgets and funding grants perhaps this might be seen by them as entirely understandable. It comprehensively sets a strong foundation for any project, however asking for everything at once upfront also raise questions about the efficacy. For instance, some surveys such as transport and ecology can become out of date if not commissioned at the right time in the project's development and can run the risk of needing to be commissioned again later.

Nonetheless, a consequence of the initial surveys and reports at the 'Wyeside Works' project was that the projected lifespan of an uninsulated, asbestos roof over the Market Theatre and the overall poor condition of the existing M&E services meant that the financial threshold required for any capital investment to make a meaningful impact on the organisation was significantly higher than previously anticipated.

The objective of the original business plan was to split the existing cinema into two more commercially flexible studio cinema screens. This would unavoidably truncate the existing M&E service infrastructure, creating a tipping point for the replacement of the building's entire M&E services. Similarly, the liability of the deteriorating asbestos roof over the theatre and the risks associated with accessing its perimeter adjacent to the river meant that it was really only expedient to strip and replace the asbestos within the first phase of capital works rather than later. Furthermore, in doing so it was therefore considered sensible to prepare any new rooftop for the potential reinstatement of the Assembly Rooms as a spectacular roof extension overlooking the River Wye in the future.

A number of Option Studies were developed and assessed under a SWOT analysis before deciding on a preferred option. Whilst the project set off with the idea of reinstating the Assembly Rooms as a 'would-like-to-have' rather than 'must-have' ambition, it became clear that in order to secure sufficient future funding for all aspects of the brief, the project needed to be ambitious — and the rooftop extension would enhance the arts centre status as a landmark in the cultural landscape.

fig. 9.5
*Historic view of
the Wyeside site*

*"in both projects, there were … discoveries within
the architectural commission which significantly
impacted the previous … business plan. It raises
questions as to whether the business plan should be
further developed alongside the architectural option
studies"*

fig. 9.6
*Wyeside Arts Centre
Winter
© Pillar Visuals*

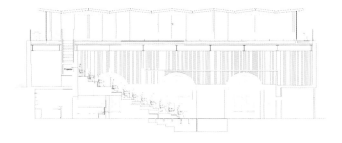

Reflections

In relation to both pieces of work for Oriel Myrddin Gallery and Wyeside Arts Centre, a business plan preceded the architectural commission. This is eminently sensible insofar as the consideration of the commercial ambitions and community needs are fundamental to the formation of a well-reasoned strategic brief. However, in both projects, there were subsequent discoveries within the architectural commission which significantly impacted the previous assumptions of the business plan. The business plan should always be further developed alongside the architectural option studies.

Similarly, it raises questions as to whether those 'due diligence' surveys and reports which have financial risk embodied within them should be commissioned in advance of any business plan or architectural commission. The opportunities and risks associated with site conditions, including legal conveyance and the building fabric & services, should perhaps be fully understood before any business case, option studies or design work is undertaken.

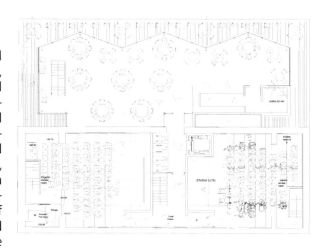

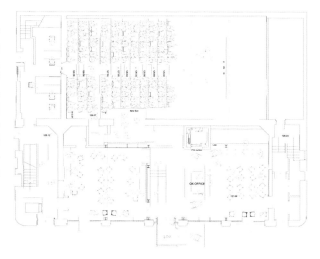

Further Information

De Matos Ryan Architects: www.dematosryan.co.uk
Oriel Myrddin Gallery: https://orielmyrddingallery.co.uk Wyeside Arts Centre: http://wyeside.co.uk
De Matos Ryan have undertaken various public arts and cultural work including York Theatre Royal, St Georges Hall, Bradford, auditorium works on Richmond's Grade 1 listed Theatre Royal, Camden People's Theatre, and the front of house refurbishment of Sadler's Wells, and is currently working on the V&A Museum of Childhood.

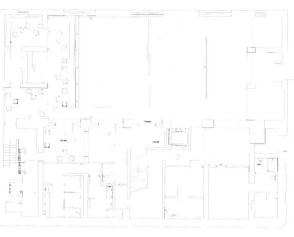

fig. 9.7
Proposed Wyeside Arts Centre.
(From top)
Section through riverside extension.
First floor plan.
Street / entry level plan.
Basement plan.
© De Matos Ryan Architects

PROJECT DATA

Name	**Oriel Myrddin Gallery**
Location	Church St, Carmarthen SA31 1LH
Country	WALES
Year	2016

PROJECT DESCRIPTION

Type	Restoration, conversion and extension of a Grade II listed Victorian structure that was formerly a School of Art, to provide more exhibition space, appropriate access, artists and administrative spaces, external spaces and a cafe.
Size	Existing 190m². Proposed 318m²
Budget Cost	£986,320 (GBP) (€1,082,220) excl. VAT

COMPETITION DESCRIPTION

Client	Oriel Myrddin Trust, co-funded by Carmarthen County Council and the Arts Council Wales
Programmer/Agent	Carmarthen County Council
Public/Private	Public
Procedure	Restricted competition procedure. *(Notice 2016/S 024 -037623)*
Procedure Reference	Directive 2004/18/EC. Art. 28 *(near equivalent: Directive 2014/24/EU Art.27)*
Stages	3
Project Intention	A feasibility and business appraisal with options had been prepared by Rural Office for Architecture (to RIBA Stage 2). The project intention was to develop the project from RIBA Stage 3 forward.
Conditions Applied	Arts Council Wales At ITT stage: Quality was weighted 60, to cost weighted 40

COMPETITION FACTS

Timescale	Competition call:	4 Febuary 2016
	PQQ submission:	25 April 2016
	Award:	17 June 2016

Submission Required	**Stage 1:** PQQ (Pre-qualification questionnaire). Probity questions, statutory compliance confirmations, professional and team approach and composition for 23 sub-consultants, with onerous evidencing of previous experience including up to 5/no less than 2 exemplary contracts successfully concluded in the past 3 years, examples of successful contemporary designs integrated into listed buildings, and the achievement of BREEAM Very good on a similar project **Stage 2:** ITT. For quality questions, a max. 18 x A4 page response required for qualitative questions. A pricing schedule with lump sum fees for future work stages to completion **Stage 3:** Interview. Forming 25% of the stage 2 quality assessment mark, with the Architects required to demonstrate at interview how their designs and approach will respond to the brief
Announcement	20 June 2016 (Contract Award Notice)
Number of Entries	4

ASSESSMENT & SELECTION

Jury Numbers	More than the 5 listed *(exact number unknown)*
Jury Composition	**With a deliberative role:** Oriel Myrddin Trust Chair and trustee Oriel Myrddin Gallery: General Manager Carmarthen County Council representative Arts Business Consultant … *and unknown others.* **Non-voting jury members:** Arts Council of Wales representative.
Number Shortlisted	4
Winner	De Matos Ryan Architects
Runners Up	Unknown
Prizes	None
Conclusion of Process	A design commission was awarded for RIBA Stage 3 to completion. Following completion of RIBA Stage 3 the project was put on hold awaiting funding approval, which was granted in summer 2020

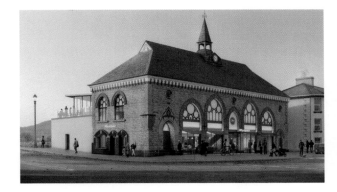

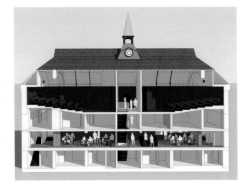

Name	**Wyeside Arts Centre** (WAC)
Location	Wyeside Arts Centre, Castle Street, Builth Wells, Powys, LD2 3BN
Country	WALES
Year	2018
PROJECT DESCRIPTION	
Type	Conversion & extension of the WAC building's 1 cinema & 1 theatre (doubling as an events space & 2nd. cinema) with an extra cinema, public, disabled & back of house facilities.
Size	Proposed 1,586m²
Budget Cost	A study to evaluate a construction cost budget: the study estimated £5.258m(GBP) (€5.79)
COMPETITION DESCRIPTION	
Client	Wyeside Arts Centre, co-funded by Arwain leader programme and the Arts Council Wales.
Programmer/Agent	Rob David, Rob David Project Management.
Public/Private	Public
Procedure	Open competition procedure
Procedure Reference	Below OJEU threshold issued via Sell2Wales
Stages	2 *(as described within the tender invite, although in the notice 1 was specified)*
Project Intention	A RIBA Stage 0-2 business case & feasibility study with a full architect lead design team comprising QS, structural & M&E engineering, H&S (CDM), BREEAM sustainability & access advisors, specialists in theatre/cinema design, lighting, acoustics, fire, green energy & tanking, with a requirement for 6 surveys
Conditions Applied	Arts Council Wales At ITT stage: Quality was weighted 60, to cost weighted 40
COMPETITION FACTS	
Timescale	Competition call: 18 March 2018 SSQ/PQQ submission: 20 June 2018 Award: 4 July 2018
Submission Required	**Stage 1:** SSQ (Supplier suitability questionnaire). Probity questions, statutory compliance confirmations, with descriptions, references and evidencing of experience of 3 previous projects offering similar service in arts /performance venues **Stage 2:** ITT. 4 questions (max. 1,600 words) plus 1 evidencing the teams CVs their skills, abilities & appropriate project empathies, a pricing schedule giving an overall cost & all consultants charge out rates. (a design team fee allocation of £55k was specified) **Interview:** The team were required to demonstrate how their designs & approach will best respond to the brief
Announcement	6 July 2018
Number of Entries	7
ASSESSMENT & SELECTION	
Jury Numbers	7
Jury Composition	**With a deliberative role:** Wyeside Arts Centre Trust. Chair and trustee Wyeside Arts Centre Trust: Deputy chair/Secretary Wyeside Arts Centre: General Manager Theatr Mwldan, co-programmer & cultural advisor Project manager Arts Business Consultant **Non-voting jury members:** Arts Council of Wales representative
Number Shortlisted	4
Winner	De Matos Ryan Architects
Runners Up / Prizes	Austin Smith Lord, Purcell, & Ferguson Mann
Conclusion of Process	The RIBA Stage 0-2 commission was awarded with works completed on 30 October 2018

fig. 9.9 (left)
Existing Oriel Myrddin Gallery
© De Matos Ryan Architects

fig. 9.10 (middle)
Proposed Wyeside Arts Centre. Town side exterior view
© Pillar Visuals

fig. 9.11 (right)
Proposed Wyeside Arts Centre section
© De Matos Ryan Architects

fig. 9.8 (bottom left)
Existing Oriel Myrddin Gallery
© De Matos Ryan Architects

"The qualification hurdle for entry into the competition was set intentionally low to encourage a wide range of interest and participation"

fig. 10.1
Winning design entry.
Exterior perspective.
© Heneghan Peng
Architects

10 The Giant's Causeway Design Competition

Jim Roberts

Fourth Street, England

The Giant's Causeway is an area of global geological importance, characterised by some 40,000 large, polygonal columns of exposed basalt rock. The scale, drama and setting of the site has attracted visitors for centuries and its imagery is symbolic of Northern Ireland.

By the turn of the century, the Giant's Causeway was already a designated UNESCO World Heritage Site and one of Northern Ireland's most popular tourist destinations. But it was suffering from a legacy of underinvestment and neglect, resulting in a confused and underwhelming visitor experience.

In April 2003 a significant programme of investment in the visitor experience was launched with much fanfare and ministerial announcement. A cornerstone of that programme was an international design competition for a new Visitor Centre. Implicit in that idea was the importance of the Giant's Causeway as a catalyst for growing Northern Ireland's tourism economy and the positive messages that a design competition might signal to an international audience.

The directive to invest in a new visitor centre came with two parallel initiatives: first, to develop an interpretation strategy for the Giant's Causeway and its coastline; and, second, a tourism strategy for the Causeway Coast and Glens. This early, strategic work helped to marshal the input, enthusiasm, and investment of important partners like the National Trust, Moyle District Council and the Environment and Heritage Service for Northern Ireland.

There was so much significantly we also had to navigate. For example an individual had been buying up neighbouring lands for years leading up to our involvement in order to develop a 'private' visitor centre and there was a critical risk that the public might be held to ransom.

Having already produced the business case that helped to define the concept and brief for a visitor centre, my colleagues and I were asked by the Department of the Economy[1] to manage the competition to procure its architectural design.

One of the first key decisions we took was to run the architectural competition according to the 'Standard Regulations for International Competitions' published by the Union of International Architects (UIA), rather than relying on RIBA guidelines, which would have been an alternative choice.[2] The UIA regulations were familiar to UNESCO, the international organisation that manages World Heritage inscription, and this decision – at a stroke – seemed to elevate the project's status to one of global importance.

A clear set of objectives was established at the outset to guide the competition, define its structure and format, and strike the best balance between two requirements that are typically in tension: the need to obtain best value for the client, on one hand; but also the desire to be fair and reasonable to the many participants – large and small – who were investing their time, energy, expense and ideas in the process.

The qualification hurdle for entry into the competition was set intentionally low to encourage a wide range of interest and participation, from individual architects to large multi-disciplinary design practices. The submission requirements were clear, concise, and limited to a maximum of three A1 sized boards and a 4-page report describing the competitor's approach to the project.

The client demonstrated real commitment to the process, putting up a prize fund that was commensurate to the project's strategic and symbolic importance. This would be

fig. 10.2

Exterior on completion
© Hufton + Crow

fig. 10.3

Interior on completion
© Hufton + Crow

fig. 10.4

Winning design entry
Interior Perspective
© Heneghan Peng
Architects

distributed to the winner, the second and third-placed entries, and three honourable mentions.

In line with the UIA regulations, an international jury was formed of six architects and a client representative – the then Permanent Secretary of the Department for the Economy. The principles of fairness, transparency and equality were baked into the competition format, including total anonymity of participants until after the jury reached unanimous agreement on a winner.

The simplicity of the competition, coupled with its international profile, helped to attract 825 expressions of interest, 479 registrations, and 201 competition entries from around the world – a level of participation that far exceeded our expectations.

The strength of the competition was reflected not only in the number and scope of entries received but also, importantly, in the overall quality of the design solutions submitted. The international panel of jurors noted the exceptional level of design quality and the innovative interpretation of the design brief demonstrated by a high proportion of entries.

The winning design, submitted by Dublin-based Heneghan Peng Architects, was developed and the building opened to the public in July 2012. The building won numerous awards and was shortlisted for the 2013 Stirling Prize.

More importantly, it has had a demonstrable impact on the volume and value of visits to the Giant's Causeway.[3] The Giant's Causeway Visitor Centre is among the best case studies of high profile, international design competitions that are held for the right reason and the right project, at the right time and in the right way. It was well-intentioned and well-conceived, properly resourced, and fairly executed – the outcome exceeding all expectations and leading to a genuinely remarkable addition to the cultural and tourist infrastructure of Northern Ireland.

References

1 Formally, the Department of Enterprise Trade and Investment Northern Ireland
2 Guidelines: Uia Competition Guide For Design Competitions In Architecture And Related Fields, Revised 2017 www.uia-architectes.org/webApi/uploads/ressource-file/32/uiacompetitionguide.pdf (accessed 18 July 2020)
3 In 2019, the visitor's centre was visited by 998,014 people. ALVA - Association of Leading Visitor Attractions. www.alva.org.uk (accessed 18 July 2020)

fig. 10.5

Winning design entry Aerial Perspective © Heneghan Peng Architects

PROJECT DATA

Name	**Giant's Causeway Visitor Centre; Architecture Competition**
Location	44 Causeway Road, Bushmills, County Antrim
Country	NORTHERN IRELAND
Year	2003
PROJECT DESCRIPTION	
Type	A visitor, exhibition and interpretation centre with landscaping, access and parking provision for visitors to the Giant's Causeway, a World Heritage Site (natural heritage)
Size	1,800m²
Budget Cost	£8.5m (GBP) (€9.43m). A 2007 based construction cost excl. land, legals, fees & contingencies for a est. £14.5m project total.
COMPETITION DESCRIPTION	
Client	The competition client and promoter was the Department of Enterprise Trade and Investment (DETI), Northern Ireland (now the Department for the Economy) in partnership with the National Trust, Moyle District Council and the Environment and Heritage Service (NI Gov)
Programmer/Agent	Fourth Street founding director Jim Roberts led, with Ray Payne the procurement advisor, and the professional and technical advisor for architecture, landscape and access
Public/Private	Public
Procedure	Open Design Contest
Procedure Reference	Directive 2004/18/EC. Art. 66 - 70 (*Equivalent to: Directive 2014/24/EU Art.78 - 82*)
Stages	1
Project Intention	An intention to build was inferred
Conditions Applied	Union Internationale des Architectes (UIA), Paris
COMPETITION FACTS	
Timescale	Prior information notice: 12 March 2004
	Competition call: 26 March 2005
	Submission: 5 August 2005
	Award: October 2005
Submission Required	3 x A1 panels (to include: a 1:1250 site plan, 1:100 floor plan, elevations & sections, a perspective & appropriate explanatory drawings with a 4 x A4 report)
Announcement	October 2005
Number of Entries	201

fig. 10.6 *(left)*

Plan of the Giants Causeway centre

@ Henegan Peng Architects

fig. 10.7 *(right)*

Exterior on completion © Hufton + Crow

"The strength of the competition was reflected not only in the number and scope of entries received but also, importantly, in the overall quality of the design solutions submitted. The international panel of jurors noted the exceptional level of design quality and the innovative interpretation of the design brief demonstrated "

ASSESSMENT & SELECTION

Jury Numbers	9
Jury Composition	**With a deliberative role:** Jochen Brandi, Architect, Germany Mario Cucinella (UIA representative), Architect, Italy Peter Hunter, Architect, England Duncan Lewis, Architect, France Aidan McGrath, Architect, N. Ireland Juhani Pallasmaa (President), Architect, Finland Bruce Robinson, Permanent Sec., Department of Enterprise, Trade & Investment, N. Ireland (nominated by the Project Promoter) **Non-voting jury members:** Claude Godefroy (UIA representative), Architect, France Frank McCloskey, Director at Royal Society of Ulster Architects
Number Shortlisted	6
Winner	Henegan Peng Architects, Dublin

Runners Up

2nd	Architectural Verstas, Helsinki
3rd	Matos Gameiro + Carlos Crespo Arquitectos Lda, Lisbon
Honorarium	Jun Aoki Associastes, Tokyo, Carlos Sousa Dias & Nuno Santos Pereira Arquitectos Lda, Sintra, and Jennifer Carré Architecte, Paris

Prizes & Awards

1st prize	£10,000	(€11,070)
2nd prize	£7,000	(€7,750)
3rd prize	£4,000	(€4,425)

Three honorariums: £1,000 each (€1,107)
Prizes - totalling £24,000 awarded (€26,560)

Conclusion of Process
Hennegan Peng Architects were awarded the construction design commission and appointed in 2006 to bring the competition winning design to completion in collaboration with Bennett Robertson, (Building Services), White Young Green (Structural Engineers), Edmond Shipway (QS & Project Managers), Dewhurst McFarlane (Facade engineering) and Turley Associates, (Planning).
The main contractor Gilbert-Ash commenced construction on site in 2010.

Construction Contract(s) NEC 3 Option A

Project Completion
Construction completed April 2012, with a public opening on the 2 July. For a total project cost of roughly £18.7m, allowing for inflation and additionally included items was regarded as a highly accurate and successful outcome.

FURTHER INFORMATION

Fourth Street www.fourth-street.com
Henegan Peng Architects www.hparc.com
RIBA Stirling Prize Shortlist: Giant's Causeway Visitors' Centre, 2013
EU Mies Award Shortlist: Giant's Causeway Visitors' Centre, 2013
Fourth Street Director Jim Roberts has been involved in many design/design team competitions including: the National Waterfront Museum Swansea, launched in 2005 following the appointment of Wilkinson Eyre Architects and Land Design Studio (exhibition design) and Farsons's Trident Park in Malta 2013 (tridentparkmalta.com), the first phase of which is due to complete in 2020.

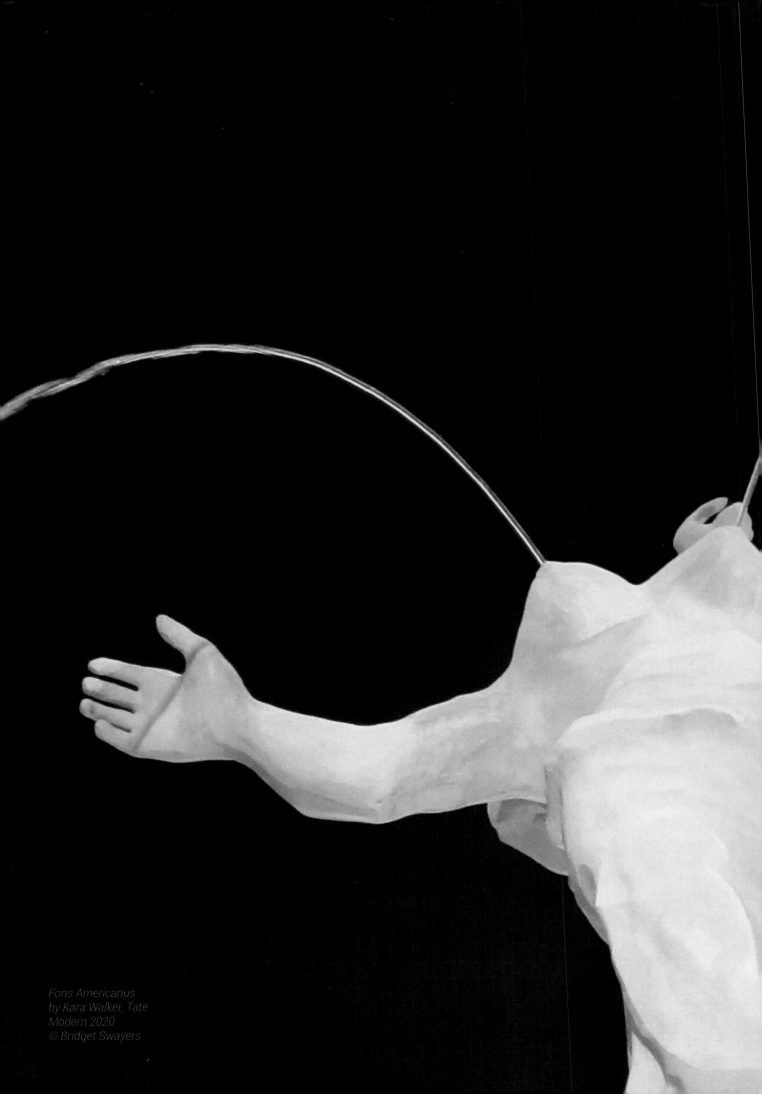

data

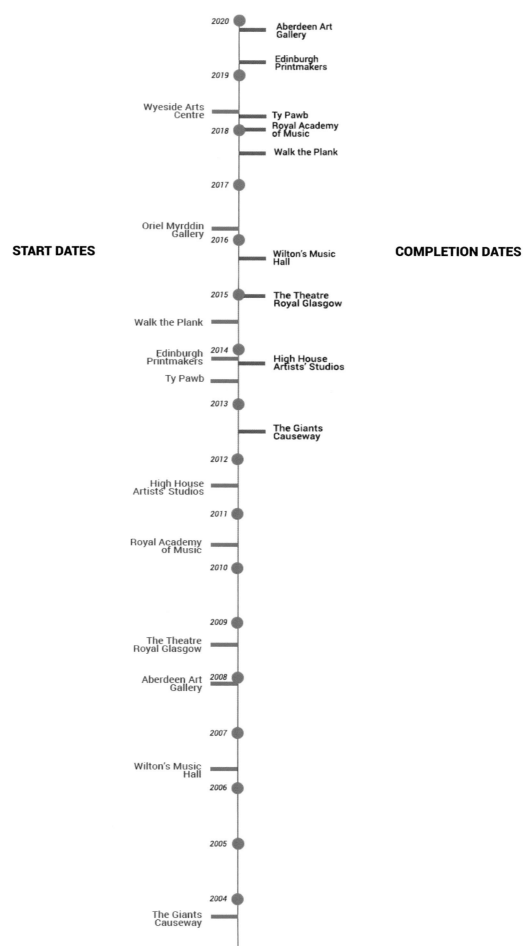

START DATES

COMPLETION DATES

2020 — Aberdeen Art Gallery

Edinburgh Printmakers

2019

Wyeside Arts Centre — Ty Pawb

2018 — Royal Academy of Music

Walk the Plank

2017

Oriel Myrddin Gallery

2016 — Wilton's Music Hall

2015 — The Theatre Royal Glasgow

Walk the Plank

Edinburgh Printmakers — 2014 — High House Artists' Studios

Ty Pawb

2013

The Giants Causeway

2012

High House Artists' Studios

2011

Royal Academy of Music

2010

2009

The Theatre Royal Glasgow

Aberdeen Art Gallery — 2008

2007

Wilton's Music Hall

2006

2005

2004

The Giants Causeway

fig. 11.1

Case Studies.
The reported timeline

2003

11 Case Study Projects — Summary Data

The conclusions from this analysis are taken forward in Chapter 15

THE CASE STUDIES ANALYSIS

This sample represents 2.61% of the Project Compass data set but allows more detailed analysis. The data here is not however statistically valid. The formatted data sheets for the case studies are standardised with those in 'Competition Culture in Europe: Voices' (2018) to allow comparative evaluation of UK processes, procedures, practices and outputs in an international context.[1]

Figures reported for time and cost, are indicative only. Costs have not been adjusted for inflation, total project costs including procurement processes, land and legal costs, or elemental analysis (where for example in the Giant's Causeway this was particularly significant), nor have costs been regionally re-based. Premiums paid for conservation and restoration works to listed building that incur high costs have also not been factored. This analysis nevertheless provides further insights.

LOCATION

The 11 case study projects compared here provide examples from each of the UK Nations 4 from England, 3 from Scotland, 3 from Wales and 1 from N. Ireland *(fig. 11.3)*.

TIME AND PROGRAMME

The Case Studies span a period commencing 2003 to January 2020 *(fig. 11.1 & 11.2)*.

Aberdeen Art Gallery took 144 months (12 years) to reach fruition. In this project the procurement process for the appointment of the architects took 20 months and at 14% of the overall programme period was the most prolonged. Although it took 10 years to complete the phases of Wilton's Music Hall, only 1.5 months (roughly 1%) of that time was spent on the architects procurement.

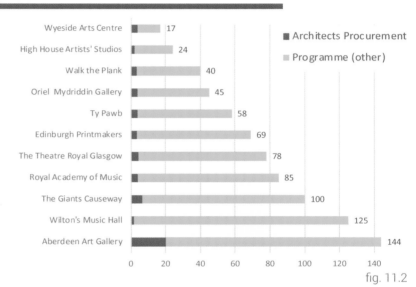

fig. 11.2
The overall programme (months) showing the proportion for design team procurement. (NB. Wyeside & Oriel remain in programme)

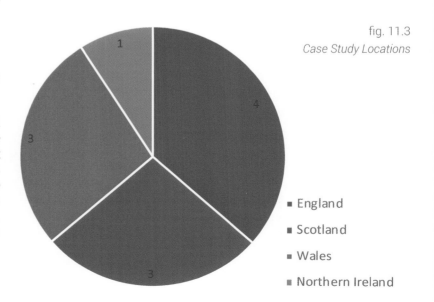

fig. 11.3
Case Study Locations

- England
- Scotland
- Wales
- Northern Ireland

fig. 11.4
The primary function provided for by the development

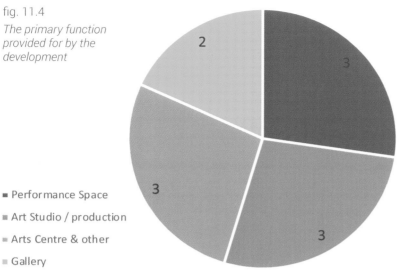

- ■ Performance Space
- ■ Art Studio / production
- ■ Arts Centre & other
- ■ Gallery

fig. 11.5
The development type

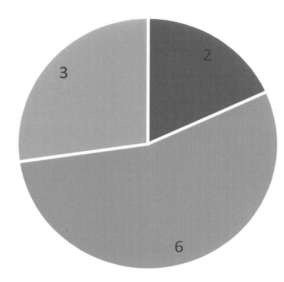

- ■ New Build

- ■ Works to a Listed Building

- ■ Existing Building

fig. 11.6
Floor areas (m²)

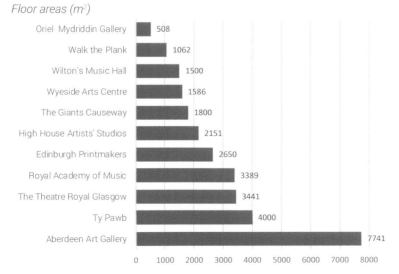

Project	Floor area (m²)
Oriel Mydriddin Gallery	508
Walk the Plank	1062
Wilton's Music Hall	1500
Wyeside Arts Centre	1586
The Giants Causeway	1800
High House Artists' Studios	2151
Edinburgh Printmakers	2650
Royal Academy of Music	3389
The Theatre Royal Glasgow	3441
Ty Pawb	4000
Aberdeen Art Gallery	7741

In the case studies the project programmes reported by the authors is based on the information known to them. The extent of unreported pre procurement preparations before the architects' appointment can however vary considerably.

In 2020 the Wyeside Arts Centre and Oriel Myrddin Gallery are still ongoing. Proportionately across all other projects the procurement averaged between 5-9% of the overall programme, and no meaningful difference could be found between the procurement time for procedures that were adopted.

High House Artists' Studios was the fastest programme to completion (24 months) and for the design team's procurement (2 months).

TYPE OF BUILDING AND FUNCTION
(fig. 11.4 & 11.5)

Of the primary functions sustained by the buildings reported in the Case Studies, artists production facilities, dedicated performance spaces and arts centres (providing mixed activities) are equally represented along with two galleries dedicated primarily to the display of works of art.

The Giant's Causeway with its extensive educational and exhibition spaces is recorded here as an arts centre.

Of these 55% (6) of the projects related to listed buildings, three were to other existing buildings (27%) and only two (18%) were free standing new buildings.

It is fitting that cultural investment in the Arts is being made sustainably, in the heritage of our building culture, and that so many of these buildings are being reused. A high level of sustainability was also targeted and delivered for the only two new reported buildings.

SIZE

The project floor areas range in size from 508 m² to 7,741m². The Aberdeen Art Gallery is by far the largest, and almost twice as large as the next biggest project Tŷ Pawb *(fig. 11.6)*.

The three largest projects and the smallest are in Scotland and Wales, not England.

COST

Project total costs range from £879k for Walk the Plank to £34.6m for the Aberdeen Art Gallery, which was £14.6m more than the next most expensive project, The Royal Academy of Music (RAM). Aberdeen £4,470 per m² cost ranked fourth against RAM at £5,901 per m² which is the most expensive but this was constructed within an educational institute that remained operational *(fig. 11.7 & 11.8)*.

The average cost per square metre across all case study projects is £3,208 per m², Walk the Plank (£828 per m²), High House Artists' Studios (£837 per m²) and Tŷ Pawb (£1,077 per m²), appear an extraordinary achievements, along with Wilton's Music Hall (£2,000 per m²), particularly given the phasing and programme timescale for this listed building.

COST AND PROGRAMME

When the two projects that remain in programme, Wyeside Arts Centre and Oriel Myrddin Gallery, are excluded from the sampling, no correlations could be found between the Project Programme and: -
- The floor area
- The m² cost factors.

The Aberdeen Art Gallery, Wilton's Music Hall and the Giant's Causeway would all appear the most uncharacteristic. The Oriel Myrddin Gallery although only at RIBA Stage 3, already falls within this same bracket.

A direct relationship between cost, quality and time which is often found within construction sector is not clearly evident. In this sector other values must be significant factors on a high proportion of these results *(fig. 11.9)*.

CLIENT TYPES
(fig. 11.10)

At their reported commencements three of this sample of projects were directly commissioned by National or Local Government, one was a private commission and seven were commissioned by independent organisations (bodies covered by public law — because they received public money).

Wilton's Music Hall is the only recorded private commission. The Royal Academy of Music was initially commissioned privately by the educational trust, but UCL required a public commission at a following stage. This project

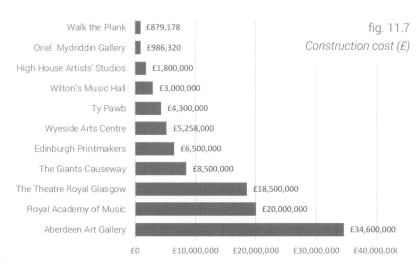

fig. 11.7
Construction cost (£)

Walk the Plank	£879,178
Oriel Myrddin Gallery	£986,320
High House Artists' Studios	£1,800,000
Wilton's Music Hall	£3,000,000
Ty Pawb	£4,300,000
Wyeside Arts Centre	£5,258,000
Edinburgh Printmakers	£6,500,000
The Giants Causeway	£8,500,000
The Theatre Royal Glasgow	£18,500,000
Royal Academy of Music	£20,000,000
Aberdeen Art Gallery	£34,600,000

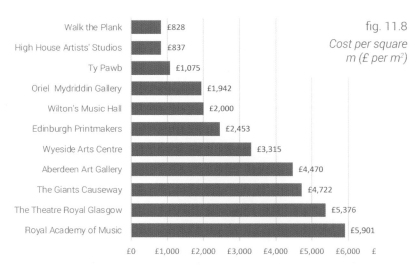

fig. 11.8
Cost per square m (£ per m²)

Walk the Plank	£828
High House Artists' Studios	£837
Ty Pawb	£1,075
Oriel Myrddin Gallery	£1,942
Wilton's Music Hall	£2,000
Edinburgh Printmakers	£2,453
Wyeside Arts Centre	£3,315
Aberdeen Art Gallery	£4,470
The Giants Causeway	£4,722
The Theatre Royal Glasgow	£5,376
Royal Academy of Music	£5,901

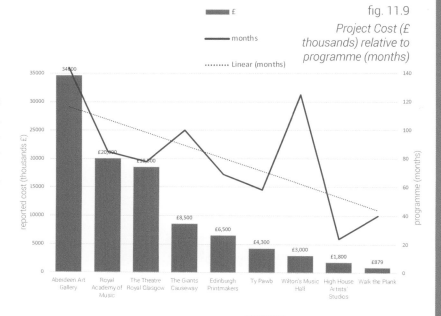

fig. 11.9
Project Cost (£ thousands) relative to programme (months)

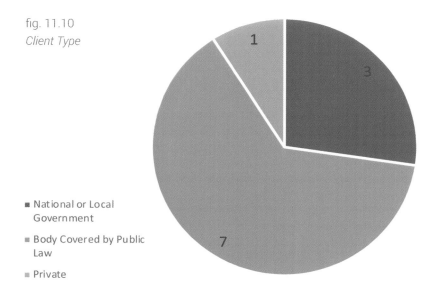

fig. 11.10
Client Type

- National or Local Government
- Body Covered by Public Law
- Private

fig. 11.11
Type of procurement procedure adopted for the architects' appointment.

- Private
- Below threshold
- Design Contest
- Open
- Restricted

fig. 11.12
MEAT assessment

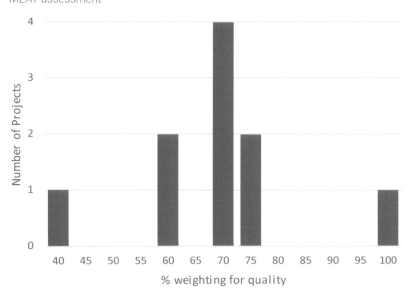

is therefore reported under a 'Body covered by Public law'. High House Studios were jointly commissioned by ACME and High House Production Park, but the latter is owned, it is understood, by Thurrock Council in the majority.

PROCUREMENT PROCEDURE
(fig. 11.11)

The Giant's Causeway was procured by a Design Contest which is a procedure specifically provided for commissioning of architectural designs. It is popular elsewhere, but is a now rarely used in the UK.[2] A Design Contest Procedure is therefore unusual as considerably less than 1% of UK public architectural commissions are procured in this way.

Although below the EU threshold values where criteria are different, Walk the Plank was modelled on a restricted procedure, and might be considered here to be very similar to an above threshold restricted procedure.[3] No negotiated procedure has been reported on within the Case Studies.

Use of Open Procedures has expanded since the transposition of EU Directive 2014/24. Use of this procedure for the two most recent Welsh projects may reflect this. There is considerable diversity of procedural types in this sample, however use of restricted procedures continues to predominate. While there an emerging trend towards more open procedures the predominance of restricted procedures remains consistent with previous findings.[4]

ASSESSMENT & SELECTION EVALUATION (MEAT)

For projects that have been assessed by the method known as 'the most economically advantageous tender' (MEAT), the weighted value for the quality (vis price) in the assessment is illustrated *(fig. 11.12)*. Wilton's Music Hall as a private commission is not included as a MEAT assessment was not used.

In making a MEAT assessment, because the financial bid is assessed mathematically and calibrated across a full range in a spreadsheet and quality is assessed subjectively, it has long been an industry recommendation that quality should be weighted at 70% or above to ensure sustainable quality.[5]

For the appointment of the architect a MEAT assessment was used on 10 of the 11 projects. Walk the Plank, which was below threshold, used a 30% weighting for quality with a 10% weighting for the interview. This has been taken as a 40% quality weighting.

The most recent two Welsh projects had a 60% quality weighting, which as noted previously appears to contradict the sustainability objectives otherwise avowed in the Arts Council for Wales and Welsh Government guidance.

Most of the projects reported here have been quality weighted at 70% or above. The Giant's Causeway used a Design Contest procedure with 100% weighting on quality, where after conclusion of the design assessment, a fee can be negotiated without prior publication. This is an accepted norm.

WORK STAGE FRAGMENTATION

This is defined as where RIBA Works Stages from Feasibility Stage to completion have been the subject of more than a single competitive procedure. This has become increasingly common, incurs additional programme time and cost for both clients and architects, because of both the competitive procedures and the need for new consultants to audit previous works. In most cases these can reasonably be avoided with sensible break clauses in the terms of an appointment (e.g. Ref: Walk the Plank).

Those projects where work stages weren't fragmented (45%) are Giants Causeway, Walk the Plank, High House Artists' Studios, Aberdeen Art Gallery, and Wilton's Music Hall (fig. 11.13).

Despite some excellent guidance provided by the Arts Council for Wales, three projects there appear to have differently staged appointment procedures, and as it appears in the case of Tŷ Pawb trying to change a professional contract at three stages with a novation to the main contractor from stage 3 doesn't typically sustain production of quality effectively. To be more sustainable Wales could aim to align its procurement process values better.

SUBMISSION STAGES

A two stage submission comprising a PQQ/SSQ stage, followed by an ITT stage and concluded with an interview is the most common methodology found in 7 Case Studies

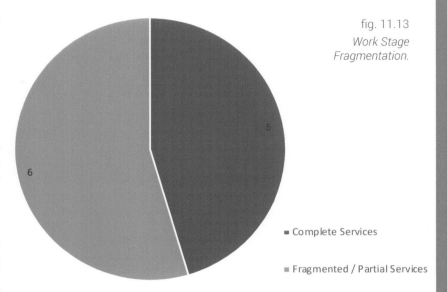

fig. 11.13
Work Stage Fragmentation.

- Complete Services

- Fragmented / Partial Services

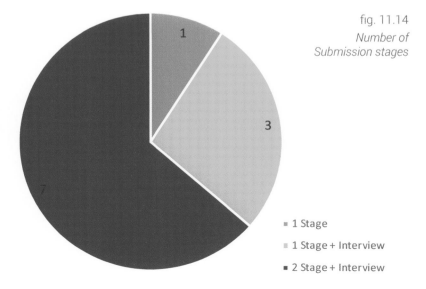

fig. 11.14
Number of Submission stages

- 1 Stage

- 1 Stage + Interview

- 2 Stage + Interview

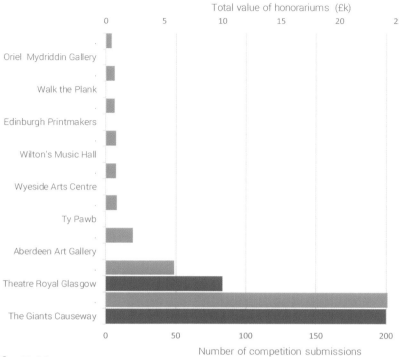

Total value of honorariums (£k)

Number of competition submissions

■ Submissions

■ Honorarium

fig. 11.15

Number of bid submissions relative to the honorarium offered.

(fig. 11.14). The three projects with the largest budgets adopted this process, and were three of the four projects having the longest overall programme. Edinburgh Printmakers is unusual in this respect as relative to the others adopting 3 procurement stages their appointment process was relatively rapid (3.5 months).

Of the completed projects three of those where an appointment was undertaken having a single submission stage followed by an interview had the fastest programme for both appointments, and for completion.

The Giant's Causeway was a Design Contest procedure which permitted a single stage submission, with a fee negotiable after conclusion of the competitive process with the competition winner (and others shortlisted if necessary if negotiations with the winner are not successful).[6]

NUMBER OF ENTRIES & HONORARIUMS
(fig. 11.15)

Any client who seeks choice on the most appropriate design solution to a well defined brief will note the direct correlation that is found between the value of honorariums awarded and the number of bid submissions received. Architects have long called for better recognition of their speculative work when submitting detailed designs. Progressive clients appear to acknowledge this and benefit accordingly. The Theatre Royal Glasgow with 49 bids and the Giant's Causeway with 201 bids, received on average 125 bids.

The total values of Honorarium offered on these two projects as a percentage of the project cost: -
* 0.312% The Giant's Causeway (£26,560)
* 0.054% Theatre Royal Glasgow (£10,000)

The size of the commission for Aberdeen Art Gallery, with 19 bids, elicited the highest number of bids where no honorarium was offered – and likely because of its significantly scale. For each other project where no honorarium was offered the average numbers of those bidding was 6.7.

The Royal Academy of Music is not included as the contract award notice does not record the numbers of bids received.

PRACTICES WINNING THEIR 1ST SECTOR COMMISSION

Of the case study projects a total of 27% were won by new architectural firms, less than 5 years old upon winning the commission and working in the sector for the first time *(fig. 11.16)*.

All the projects were won by micro and SME (MSME) practices. In this report Hoskins Architects are recorded as established, although at the time of their winning submission the practice was only ten years old.

Heneghan Peng architects success at the Giant's Causeway occurred two years after they opened their Dublin Office and heralded a highly successful international career subsequently. Two other new practices winning commissions, Architectural Emporium and HAT Projects, both achieved significant recognition for the quality and success of their case study projects.

It is very unusual in the UK construction sector to find clients that are so open and willing to employ young and emergent talent. In this sector and specific to these projects, cultural, artistic and social values appear to have informed the consultants selection with considerable success — and more so than simply the values attributed to previous experience and financial standing.

On the case study evidence this UK sector appears unusual compared to the industry more widely. The patronage remains relatively more willing to deliver good value and quality by opening up opportunities to new practices as the lead consultants.[7]

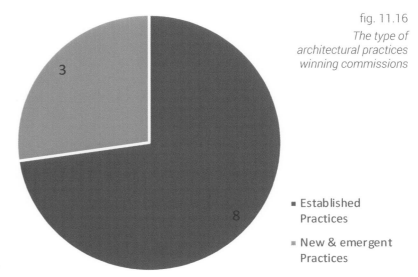

fig. 11.16
The type of architectural practices winning commissions

- Established Practices
- New & emergent Practices

References

1   Menteth W. (ed) Competition Culture in Europe: Voices. Project Compass, London 2018 ISBN 978-0-9931481-5-6. projectcompass.co.uk/index.php/compass/publications (accessed 2 July 2020)

2   Menteth W., O'Carroll O., Curtis R., Sawyers B., Public Construction Procurement Trends 2009-2014. Project Compass CIC, London 2014. ISBN 978-0-9931481-0-1 projectcompass.co.uk/index.php/compass/publications (accessed 2 July 2020)

3   The EU Treaty Principles of equal treatment, transparency, proportionality, and free movement and nondiscrimination applied above thresholds, have also been shown to apply to below-threshold contracts so were considered best practice.

4   Ibid p.24-26. Public Construction Trends

5   Ten Principles for Procuring Better Outcomes. 2016 (ed) RIBA. London p.26. www.architecture.com/-/media/GatherContent/Ten-Principles-for-Procuring-Better-Outcomes/Additional-Documents/TenPrinciplesforProcuringBetterOutcomes2016versionpdf.pdf (accessed 2 July 2020)

6   A Design Contest is a simple procedure described in Directive 2014/24/EU Art.78-82. eur-lex.europa.eu/legal-content/EN/TXT/PDF/?uri=CELEX:32014L0024&from=EN (accessed 2 July 2020)

Project Compass provide clear guidance on running a design contests in:

      Menteth W., O'Carroll O., Curtis R., Sawyers B., Design Contest Guidance: For Selecting Architects and Design Teams. Project Compass CIC 2015 ISBN 978-0-9931481-1-8 projectcompass.co.uk/index.php/compass/publications (accessed 2 July 2020)

7   Crosby P., Competition Practices in the UK and the role of the RIBA. pp. 45-50. In: The Competition Grid: Experimenting With & Within Architecture Competitions. Theodorou M., Katsakou A., (eds.) RIBA Publishing 2018 ISBN978-1-85946-710-7

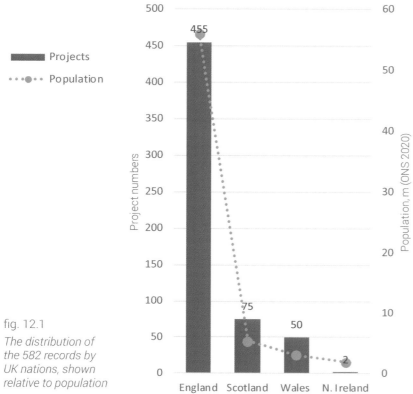

fig. 12.1

The distribution of the 582 records by UK nations, shown relative to population

Projects

Population

Project numbers

Population, m (ONS 2020)

500
450
400
350
300
250
200
150
100
50
0

60
50
40
30
20
10
0

455
75
50
2

England   Scotland   Wales   N. Ireland

■ London
■ North
■ South East
■ Midlands
■ South West

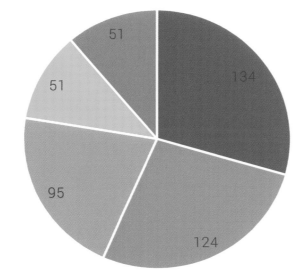

fig. 12.2

The regional breakdown for England

51
51
95
134
124

12   UK Data Research and Analysis

The conclusions from this analysis are taken forward in Chapter 15

The data set comprises 582 records of 491 arts and cultural projects from across the UK. These records were identified primarily from the funding decisions made by the National Lottery distributor bodies from January 2013-November 2018.

The available public Contract and Award Notices for the architect and design team services were located and the data analysed. (noting that some contract and award notices pre-dated staged funding decisions which followed in the 2013-2018 period). These were supplemented by further projects funded by others identified within the period of buildings. The data set covers 'capital' lottery awards, which include feasibility studies, refurbishments, building and equipment purchases and other capital funding grants. This, combined with re-procurement at different project stages has resulted in more than one procurement for a number of projects.

Because of variations in the capital funding programmes from the main national arts funding bodies, and the fact that several of these had reduced and closed capital programmes, this means that it has been difficult to evaluate data more robustly by regional locations. Notably however ACE and NLHF have made approaches to readdress some regional imbalances during the timescale.

The data set has been compiled according to the research methodology.

PROJECT RECORDS BY LOCATION

The 582 records show the project distributions by nations and regions *(fig. 12.1, 12.2, 12.3 & 12.4)*. Only Scotland records more projects than any individual English region. The total of projects in Scotland, Wales & N. Ireland, at 127 projects, is only three projects more than the 124 projects found in the north of England alone, and well below the 134 found in London.

fig. 12.3
*ACE English regions
© Arts Council
England*

England		
London	134	
North	124	
South East	95	
Midlands	51	
South West	51	
Sub total		455
Scotland	75	
Wales	50	
Northern Ireland	2	

fig. 12.4
*Distribution of project
records by location*

"There are four significant large scale London projects totaling £938m which accentuate the regional imbalance ... account for 53.3% of the total project costs in London, 24.2% of the UK total and more than the combined total for Scotland, Wales and N. Ireland"

PROJECT COSTS BY LOCATION

The estimated total project costs across the countries / regions within the data set are based on the 325 projects from the data set where an estimated total project cost could be found *(fig. 12.5 & 12.7)*. These figures exclude the projects which were subsequently discontinued, those for just equipment or building purchase / lease extension.

There are four significant large scale London projects totalling £938m which accentuate the regional imbalance *(fig. 12.6)*. These are:

Centre for Music, City of London   £288m
V&A East, Collection & Research Centre
                                          £100m
Museum of London, Smithfield   £150m
Queen Elizabeth Olympic Park - Culture & Education Quarter
                                          £400m

These four projects account for 53.3% of the total project costs in London, 24.2% of the UK total, and more than the combined total for Scotland, Wales and N. Ireland. When these projects are excluded, the average project cost in London of £11.6m is, otherwise, more similar to those found elsewhere in the UK.

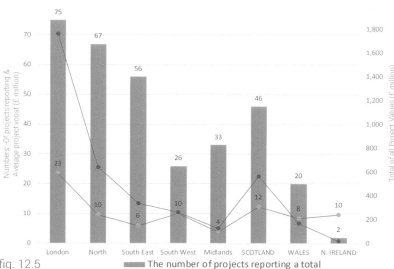

fig. 12.5

The regional distribution of 325 projects and their total costs (were the estimated total project cost could be found), shown with the average project cost.

The number of projects reporting a total
— Av. project cost (£ million)
— Total of the estimated project costs (£ million)

fig. 12.7
The estimated total project costs across the countries / regions

England
London	£1,761,110,995 on 75 projects	
	18 had no project total cost info.	
North	£638,173,000 on 67 projects	
	19 had no project total cost info.	
South-East	£335,731,466 on 56 projects	
	4 had no project total cost info	
South-West	£260,101,000 on 26 projects	
	14 had no project total cost info.	
Midlands	£128,072,815 on 33 projects	
	6 had no project total cost info.	
Sub total	£3,077,929,811 on 257projects	
	61 had no project total cost info.	
Scotland	£560,539,000 on 46 projects	
	4 had no project total cost info.	
Wales	£167,205,000 on 20 projects	
	1 had no project total cost info.	
N. Ireland.	£19,000,000 on 2 projects	
Total	£3,869,933,276 (582 records)	

fig. 12.6

The project costs of 4 London projects relative to the totals for the nations and UK whole.

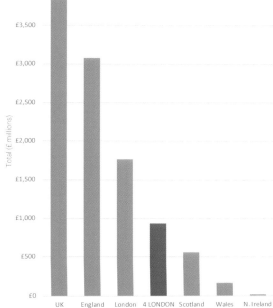

GRANTS & AWARDS SUMS

A regional comparison of the 475 grant awards and their total award sums has been made across the data set, for the different English regions *(fig. 12.8 & 12.9)*. However the regional spread of grant awards and their total award sums for the period are not possible to compare and contrast directly across the UK nations, as the staging, their periods and reporting mechanisms were so varied.

The north of England region with 138 grants received the highest by number, the highest total of grant aid at £73m and the highest average award at £532k per grant. The South West's 62 grants totalling £22m fell well behind and has the lowest average award of £357k.

London is home to a number of 'national' arts and cultural organisations such as the Science Museum, National Theatre, Royal Academy of Art, which historically has made the regional imbalance more pronounced. Due to the competition from these 'national' organisations smaller London based arts organisations also find it harder to secure sponsorship and public funding.

It is acknowledged that there is a national economic imbalance in England and that this is also reflected in a cultural infrastructure imbalance, with a strong London and South East bias. The report 'Rebalancing Our Cultural Capital' by Peter Stark, Christopher Gordon and David Powell, published in 2013 highlighted the significant regional differences.[1]

When launched in 1995 the National Lottery Arts funding was made available on a first come first served basis with no award cap, and with no national cultural infrastructure planning or strategy. Over time the application processes have been amended and all distributors are actively seeking to redress the regional imbalances.

The UK2070 Commission, an independent inquiry into city and regional inequalities in the United Kingdom was set up in 2018.[2] Chaired by Lord Kerslake, it was set up to conduct a review of the policy and spatial issues related to the UK's long-term city and regional development. Although not addressing arts and culture specifically, the final report 'Make No Little Plans: Acting At Scale For a Fairer and Stronger Future', launched in March 2020, presents a 10-Point programme of action to tackle the regional inequalities.[3]

England

London	£64,019,114	by	128 grants
North	£73,451,190	by	138 grants
South-East	£36,536,008	by	91 grants
South-West	£22,192,695	by	62 grants
Midlands	£27,333,614	by	56 grants
Total	**£223,532,621**	by	474 grants

fig. 12.8
A regional breakdown of grant awards made in England

fig. 12.9
Distribution of project grant awards in the English regions

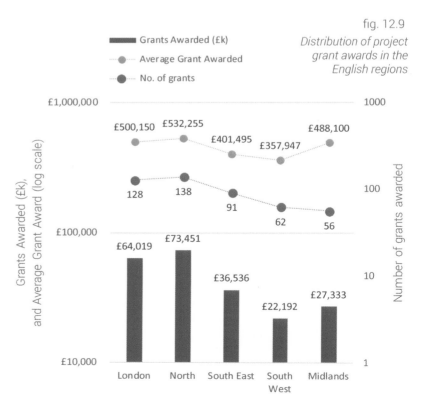

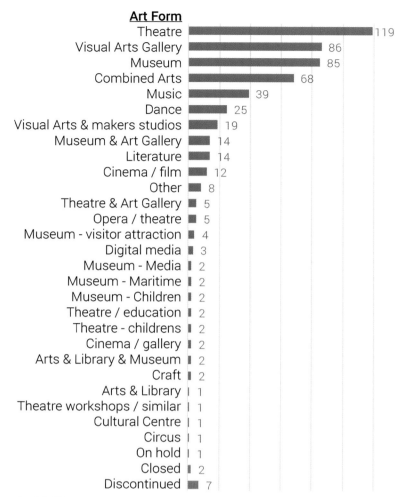

Art Form

Art Form	
Theatre	119
Visual Arts Gallery	86
Museum	85
Combined Arts	68
Music	39
Dance	25
Visual Arts & makers studios	19
Museum & Art Gallery	14
Literature	14
Cinema / film	12
Other	8
Theatre & Art Gallery	5
Opera / theatre	5
Museum - visitor attraction	4
Digital media	3
Museum - Media	2
Museum - Maritime	2
Museum - Children	2
Theatre / education	2
Theatre - childrens	2
Cinema / gallery	2
Arts & Library & Museum	2
Craft	2
Arts & Library	1
Theatre workshops / similar	1
Cultural Centre	1
Circus	1
On hold	1
Closed	2
Discontinued	7

fig. 12.10

The distribution by art forms of grant awards by numbers

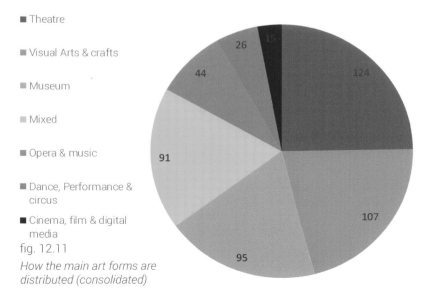

- Theatre
- Visual Arts & crafts
- Museum
- Mixed
- Opera & music
- Dance, Performance & circus
- Cinema, film & digital media

fig. 12.11

How the main art forms are distributed (consolidated)

In addition to wider consultation, including the role of arts and culture in addressing inequalities, including spatial provision, the suggested actions are now being re-considered in light of Covid-19.[4]

A detailed analysis of Art Council England's awards and regional spread can be found in the 'Capital Works! Evaluation of Arts Council England's capital investment 2012-2018 Summary Report' Alchemy, February 2018.[5]

Arts Council England has developed an interactive map where funding for 2018-2022 can now be found.[6]

ART FORMS

The distribution of art forms that have been registered by the grant award receiving organisations has been broken down.

The largest typology overall is theatre, with 22.5% by total numbers of grants awarded of those recorded *(fig. 12.10)*. This excludes those described as mixed use or specialist, for example theatre education and children's theatre. When ancillary education, children's and theatre workshop facilities are added this rises to 23.5%. The categories of individual Visual Arts Galleries and Museums follows both at roughly 16%, with music accounting for 7.4% and dance at 4.7%, of the total numbers of grants awarded.

An aggregation of the main typologies is reported, where it has been thought possible to do so indicatively. This extrapolation relates to the dominant function and those that can be clearly identified with this function *(fig. 12.11)*. The three biggest functional types being Theatre, Visual Arts and Crafts, and Museums. Mixed facilities however account for 17% of the grant awards with cinema, film and digital media showing the lowest level of awards.

BUILDING TYPE & COMMISSIONING

In the Arts sector the data indicates that the predominant building types being commissioned are works of conservation, refurbishment, upgrading, and adaptation of existing buildings *(fig. 12.12)*.

62.5% of all project commissions by numbers, of those for which descriptions could be reliably ascertained and which weren't discontinued engaged in works to existing buildings.

New buildings whether standalone or, in large part, extensions to existing facilities account for 16.9% of commissions compared to works of conservation at 26.3% and works to existing buildings otherwise at 36.3%.

This is a balance that is also well reflected in the case studies. In this sector the proportion of work being undertaken to existing buildings relative to new buildings is circumstantially thought to be far above that found in other sectors.

The detail of types has been further aggregated to provide clarity between project commissions, described as being predominantly for conservation, other works to existing buildings, and new building. The category types of project design commissions has been abstracted from the descriptions provided, with distinctions made to cover a wide range of projects. In many cases minor differences in nuance and terminology reduces clarity, while a single project may have more than one or two commissions if staged appointments are made. Where projects have discontinued, descriptions have been insufficiently clear, relate to building purchases, landscape or to unspecified call offs these are not included. A seperate residual catagory of 'Others', which are those its otherwise not possible to determine, is then included *(fig. 12.13)*.

> *"62.5% of all project commissions engaged in works to existing buildings...New buildings whether standalone or, in large part, extensions to existing facilities account for 16.9%"*

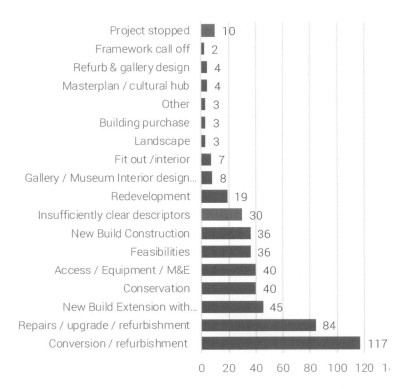

fig. 12.12
Number of project design commissions by the type of work described

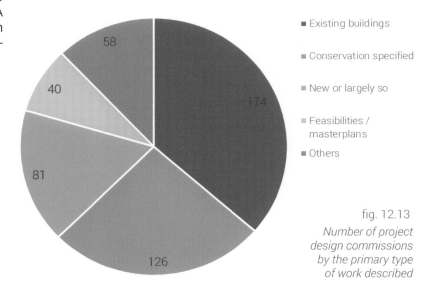

fig. 12.13
Number of project design commissions by the primary type of work described

PROCUREMENT PROCEDURES

Of the types of public competition procedures, under the UK Public Contract Regulations reported, 68.2% of these procurements used a restricted procedure *(fig. 12.14 & 12.15)*. Of the seven basic procedures available for the procurement of architectural services only two typically are being used in this UK sector. There were no recorded design contests, competitive procedures with negotiation, competitive dialogue, or innovation partnership procurement procedures.

Only 145 procedures could be adequately confirmed through the public contract notices for the 491 projects. As the information has been mapped from source funders and from the relevant Contract Notice it relies on the tendering organisation correctly and consistently assigning, for example, the project and client name, and the procurement process. In part due to mixed terminologies being used, more issues were uncovered than might be expected.

The 68.2% of restricted procedures, reported here within this sector in the period 2013-18, is less than the 81% reported nationally overall in the Public Construction Procurement Trends 2009-2014 research by Project Compass. 25% are open procedures in this data set versus 12% in the 2009-14 Trends research.[7] This indicates that the sector is using more open procedures than the country as a whole and fewer restricted procedures.

Examples of procedures that have been used follow. Along with the extracted data, these enhance insights into the main procedural types as each different approach can lead to quite different expectations, uptake, value and outcomes. Restricted, open and design contests procedures can all also be found described within the case studies *(Chapters 1-10)*.

Restricted Procedures

This is a procurement procedure typically restricted by use of a Standard Selection Questionnaire (SSQ). This was known as a pre-qualification questionnaire (PQQ) up untill 2016. This term is used here for procedures up to that date. The procedure uses set questions for shortlisting candidates in a first stage. This stage is followed by an invitation to tender (ITT) at a second stage, where the process can include an interview and/or design submissions. The optional parameters, criteria and flexibility that can be used for selecting the candidates are predetermined at the outset. When a contract is awarded onto a framework a further selection stage(s) typically applies when commissions are 'called off' that framework.

An example of an interesting high profile restricted procedure from the data set is:
Centre for Music London:
Restricted procedure
Quality/Price	70/30

Quality assessment, weighted criteria:
Response to brief:	35
Presentation & interview	21
Management & team	10.5
Project office	3.5

Price assessment, weighted criteria:
Fee	15
Resource allocation	15

Run by the City of London on behalf of the Barbican, London Symphony Orchestra and Guildhall School of Music & Drama, who are leading on the development of a detailed business case for the new Centre backed by £2.5m in funding from the City of London Corporation. The notice for the project received international applicants before shortlisting firms for each role. Companies submitted tender responses, were interviewed and marked against the published criteria. The Architect/Lead Designer, Civil and Structural Engineer, Building Services Engineer, Acoustic Consultant and Theatre Consultant were procured independently. The scope of service for the Architect/Lead Designer included Principal Designer, Fire Engineering, Façade Consultants and Access Consultancy.

The initial appointment was for concept design to support the business case with provision to instruct further RIBA design stages. All Architects invited to tender received an honorarium of £10,000 for satisfactory completion of a Response to Brief.

The contract notice stated the contract value was £12m for the architect/lead designer. The award notice gave the contract value of £350,000 as this was the maximum budget for the concept design developed sufficiently to inform the business case.

Estimated total project cost is currently £288m. To date £6.8m of funding has been provided by the City of London to develop the initial design information and associated business case. The Treasury (Central Govt.) revoked a pledge of £5.5m as the project was not considered good value for public money. It is proposed that the outstanding project costs will be met by private funding.[8]

The importance of the early SSQ/PQQ requirements in opening up or shutting down the access to smaller practices to participate in the procurement needs to be highlighted. Requirements appropriate to the scale of the project should also be balanced to allow as inclusive an approach as possible.

Accelerate restricted procedure
Public procurement rules in specified circumstances can allow contracting authorities to apply reduced timescales for the submission of tenders to projects governed by the restricted procedure. Time scales can be reduced from the traditional 80 days (where electronic means of communication are used), down to a minimum 30 days, where the reduction can be justified on the grounds of urgency. Generally the reasons for urgency should be external, i.e. not resulting from delay by the purchaser.

There were 9 accelerated restricted procedures in the dataset. Two provided justifications:
Natural History Museum, London
Justification: *due to operational constraints & need to maintain business continuity. Loss of income - existing members room has been de-commissioned & no longer offering to existing members or benefit to potential new members*
Natural History Museum, Waterhouse Link, London
Justification: *urgent requirement due to operational constraints & need to maintain business continuity*

"69.4% of these procurements used a restricted procedure. Of the seven basic procedures available ... two typically are being used in this UK sector. There were no recorded design contests, competitive procedures with negotiation, competitive dialogue, or innovation partnership procurement procedures"

Procedural type	Numbers.
Restricted Procedures:	
Restricted	90
Accelerated restricted	9
Call off frameworks	2
(awarded by restricted procedures)	
Sub total	101
Open procedures	36
Other procedures *(& types)*	8
Total	**145**

fig. 12.15
The types of public competition procedures, under the UK Public Contract Regulations

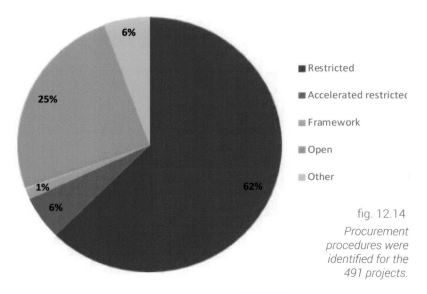

- ■ Restricted
- ■ Accelerated restricted
- ■ Framework
- ■ Open
- ■ Other

62%
6%
1%
25%
6%

fig. 12.14
Procurement procedures were identified for the 491 projects.

The following had no rational provided:
Nuffield Theatre, Southampton
Hastings Pier
Design Museum, London
HOME Manchester,
RAF Museum
Citizens Theatre.
The Factory, Manchester

The time that a competition opportunity is publicly visible naturally has an impact on the number of potential bidders who will, and can, respond. Time can be a barrier to entry unless bidders have been forewarned and this can therefore reduce access and competition. Forewarning can be provided by issue of a prior Information notice — but none are recorded for these procurements.

Frameworks

A restricted procedure can lead to the award of contract which confers only a place on a framework. This provides a pool of approved consultants or contractors who a client may call upon over a period of time (usually 4 years). A further competition stage is typically required to appoint designers. This is done by calling them off the framework, most frequently using a further mini competition stage. But these competitions are largely unrecorded.

Frameworks provide particular value where there is an anticipated and identified programme of work to be done over a period of time. Although designed to streamline the appointment process in this context, it is argued frameworks can sometimes add a further tier of procedural process, and hence restrict participation and competition.

The British Museum

Restricted Procedure with	4 Lots.
Quality/Price	60/40
Tenders received	35
Awards made	24
Firms winning those awards	11

Issued in 2015 for architectural, related design and advisory services to create a 4 year framework, having 4 Lots. 35 bids were received and 24 awards were made onto the 4 Lots, which were won by 11 individual firms.

Shakespeare North Playhouse

Restricted Procedure	
Estimated value	£243,321

The client Knowsley Council used a call off from the Merseytravel Consultancy Framework for an architectural services contract awarded in 2017.[9]

Open Procedures:

An Open procedure Is where there is no specified requirement to issue an SSQ/PQQ for shortlisting first. It is where 'the tender shall be accompanied by the information for qualitative selection required by the contracting authority'.

In open procedures however an SSQ/PQQ format may frequently be issued conjunctively, typically using more limited question sets to ensure the basic information required is provided, along with the Invitation to Tender (ITT). Interested parties therefore complete more highly developed submissions generally in a single stage. Commensurately more detailed assessment is also undertaken by the assessor for that stage. Submissions may extend over more than a single stage and comprise an interview according to how the qualitative assessment is constructed.

More time maybe invested at the outset on the part of each design team bidding, without benefit of competing against a smaller shortlist, but timescales may be shorter overall. This approach also has potential pitfalls in that key stages of the briefing and design processes can become unduly accelerated and the fee basis can be unclear.

There were 36 tenders within the sample stated as being open competitions, an example being:

Cnoc Soilleir.

Open procedure		
Quality/Price		70/30
Quality criteria:	70	
Project context & vision	10	
Challenges & risks	10	
Methodology	25	
Competence of team	20	
Community benefit	5	
Price:	30	
Tenders received		7
Estimated value:		£600,000
Lowest offer		£418,200
Highest offer		£772,200

An architect-led design team procurement for the Cnoc Soilleir project located in Daliburgh, South Uist, Outer Hebrides. Their vision is to establish there a Centre for

Gàidhlig language, music and dance. The Centre will provide learning opportunities, events and year-round performances of an international standard.

Phase 1 Detailed Design and Groundworks. The design team will lead the project design and coordination with the client
Phase 2 Superstructure, construction, fit-out and completion.
The Lead Consultant/Architect-led Design Team is to be procured for the whole project but the terms of appointment provide break clauses.[10]

TENDER PORTALS

Excluding OJEU (the Official Journal of the European Union) and where the information was available across the data set, 17 different procurement portals were identified as being used *(fig. 12.16)*. The most used being:

- DeltaeSourcing   22 projects
- Public Contracts Scotland.   19 projects
- MyTenders   10 projects
- Sell2Wales   6 projects
- Contracts finder   4 projects

The use of Contracts Finder, the national procurement portal for England, is particularly poor given the number of English notices issued relative to Scotland and Wales. Going forward after Brexit the lack of an effective single national procurement portal is a concern.

On 31 December 2020, following Brexit, 'Find a Tender' became the UK single National Portal, to replace OJEU — however the current Beta site remains woeful by comparison.

CONTRACT NOTICES (CN) AND CONTRACT AWARD NOTICES (CAN)

The data set comprises 217 public notices of which there are 135 contract notices and 82 award notices *(fig. 12.17)*.

Only 60.7% (82) of the contract notices have apparently been concluded by an award notice, while 39.3% (53) of contract notices have no award notices.

Two projects had two contract notices:
Hastings Pier
The first procurement was abandoned, the second was issued in 2010 so it has been excluded from the data set.

"The use of Contracts Finder, the national procurement portal for England, is particularly poor given the number of English notices issued relative to Scotland and Wales...a lack of Government investment and deficiencies since its establishment materially undermine its functionality, reducing accessibility, transparency and efficiency"

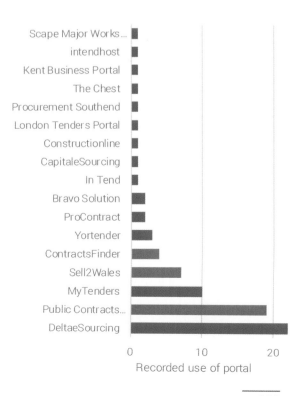

fig. 12.16

Recorded use of UK procurement portals. National Portals shown red.

Only 60.7% (82) of the contract notices have apparently been concluded by an award notice, while 39.3% (53) of contract notices have no award notices ... Any public organisation as a mandatory funding pre-requisite should stipulate that award notices must be issued, to ensure transparency is upheld and address the potential for corruption.

Kings Theatre Edinburgh
This also had two contract notices, one only 6 days before the award notice which would appear contrary to the regulations. The latter included a requirement for an access consultant on the team. The first tender notice 228739-2018, of 31 May 2018 was discontinued and no contract let. Only one has been included in the data set.

Two award notices were published in 2019 for:
Norton Priory
One award notice was issued when the contract was awarded. This was without prior publication of a contract notice, as a Voluntary Ex Ante Transparency Notice. Because a contract notice was not required for this 'negotiated procedure without prior publication' this has been excluded in the data set.

Several projects were awarded funding within the timeframe of the data captured, but the contract or award notices were issued prior to 2012. This was the case for 13 projects for contract notices and 6 projects for award notices.

The range of project scales, nature of the projects, procurement processes, sample size and difficulty in locating all of the tender information makes long term data trends difficult to accurately assess. A lack of award notices is noticeable however *(fig. 12.17)*.

The deficit in the number of award notices being issued relative to Contract Notices was identified previously in 'Public Construction Procurement Trends 2009-2014', (Project Compass 2014). It was found then that only 70% of contract notices were concluded by an award notice, in the construction sector more widely. The low proportion of award notice being issued in this new data set is below that found more generally in the UK between 2009-2014. At that stage a trend over the years towards a diminishing proportion of award notices being issued relative to contract notices was highlighted. That trend aligns with these new more recent findings.[11]

Without transparent accountability, regulatory compliance and the ability to identify aberrances (including corruption) can not be upheld. The advancing trend highlighted in this report is, therefore, a significant concern. Any public organisation as a mandatory funding pre-requisite should stipulate that award

■ Contract Notices (CN's)

■ Award Notices (CAN's)

fig. 12.17

Total number of published Contract Notices (CN) and Contract Award Notices (CAN) in this Jan. 2013-Nov. 2018 data.

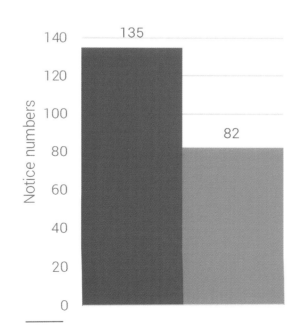

notices must be issued, to ensure transparency is upheld and address the potential for corruption.

VARIATION IN CONTRACT NOTICE, TENDER SUMS & AWARD NOTICE

Across the data set there were interesting variations noted between the estimated contract value in the Contract Notice and the final contract value stated in the Award Notice. No narrative explains these. They could be due to change of scope or other issues identified during the procurement process, or a low tender fee to secure the project. The following is an example:

Hall for Cornwall
Open procedure
Quality/Price: 70/30
Tenders received: 14
CN est. contract value   £750k - £950k
CAN contract: £1,451,275[12]

National Museum of the Royal Navy, SeaMore Project
(further details about this example can be found in this chapter under Open Procedures)
CAN contract value   £500,000
High/low offers: £928k - £363k

There is a significant variance in tenders in an instance where a multiple contract notice also arises.

Kings Theatre Edinburgh
Restricted procedure
Quality/Price   70/30
Tenders received   4
High/low offers   £1,381k - £782k

In this case there were two Contract Notices, one only 6 days before the award notice. The latter one included for an access consultant on the team. The first tender notice 228739-2018 of 31 May 2018 was discontinued and no contract let. The second procedure was also discontinued and no contract was awarded.[13]

Such degrees of variance in the bids indicate untenable expectations on the part of the commissioners and/or by those bidding.

"In assessments the most commonly used ratio between quality and price was 70/30 with 27 procedures using this proportion (39.7% of all procedures), 35.3% fell below this ratio and 25% above"

% Quality	No. of projects
100% Quality	2
85	1
80	11
75	3
70	27
65	2
60	15
50	1
40	2
0 (ie. 100% Price)	4
Total	**68**

fig. 12.18

The quality / price weightings used for assessment of tenders

ASSESSMENT & SELECTION CRITERIA

Of the 68 records in the data set that provided any criteria, a breakdown was extracted between quality and price weightings used for assessment of the tender submissions *(fig. 12.18 & 12.19)*.

In assessments the most commonly used ratio between quality and price was 70/30 with 27 procedures using this proportion (39.7% of all procedures), 35.3% fell below this ratio and 25% above. 4 projects were tendered on price alone and 2 with quality at 40%.

Examples from across the data set ranging from 100% quality to 100% price:

The Whitworth Art Gallery	
Quality	100%
V&A Museum, Members' Room	
Quality/price	80/20
Tate St Ives	
Quality/price	70/30
Dorset County Museum	
Quality/price	65/35
Bromley Museum at the Priory	
Quality/price	40/60
Kilmartin Museum	
Price	100%

Devonshire Park, Eastbourne is an example of a project having an 70/30 quality price weighting. It illustrates how the weightings are broken down further to provide more detailed criteria. Although the contract notice recorded this project as having a MEAT assessment, it did not report a quality price split. This is probably because 5% of the price bid was for a resource assessment against a capped fee. This project nevertheless has been recorded in this data set as a 70/30 split.

Devonshire Park Project

Restricted Procedure		
Evaluation criteria weightings:		
Overall Quality/price		70/30
Quality:		
Relevant experience + CVs.	20	
Outline methodology	20	
Design response.	20	
Identification of key risks.	10	
Price		
For RIBA Stage 2 & 3: -		
Lump sum fee	10	
Resourcing	5	
The average % fee: -		
across procurement routes	10	
Resources against: -		
A capped fee of £350k	5	

Tenders received:	5
CN est. contract value:	Not given
Tenders:	£1,134k - £120k
CAN contract	£1,350,835
Est. project cost	£35m

Many projects were also found where on close inspection of the actual criteria used there is a lack of distinction between price/cost factors:

National Museum of the Royal Navy, SeaMore Project

Open procedure
Quality/Price   70/30
    Quality criteria: 70
        Financial Capacity
        Health & Safety
        Technical & Professional Ability
        Added Value
    Price   30
Tenders received   20
Estimated value   £500,000
Lowest offer   £363,200
Highest offer   £928,306

An architect led integrated design team required to provide professional design services to deliver the SeaMore Project for the National Museum of the Royal Navy at Portsmouth Historic Dockyard. This project aims to consolidates various collection in the Portsmouth dockyard site including the Royal Marines collection.[14]

In the case of the SeaMore Project it is particularly difficult to understand how the quality assessment criteria used can assess the bidders architectural design quality or ability to design well in response to a brief.

The broad findings in this publication, however, tend to contrast with more general architectural procurement *(fig. 12.19)*. Across the wider construction sector, where the clients are public bodies, Project Compass has found greater emphasis on price weighting in bid selections, which appears to arise due to a narrow interpretation of accountability. But clients in the arts sector appear better educated at understanding the difference between lowest price and best value, and are placing greater emphasis on selecting designers on the basis of quality.

Although this is to be welcomed, what is evident is that 24 (35%) of 68 selections still fell short of the appropriate recommended minimum balance having a 30% price to 70% quality ratio, and more clearly still needs to be done.[15]

"none of the funders guidance notes from any of the funding bodies ... outline the need to consider the relative merits of quality and price...clear sector guidance is absent. A need to provide appropriate guidance to ensure better quality future outcomes should be a consideration"

fig. 12.19

The ranged distribution of quality weightings used for assessment of tenders, by numbers of projects

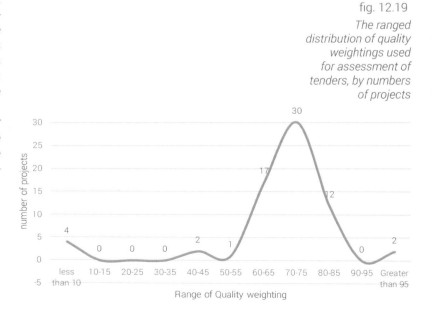

As with all procurement, the scoring criteria are critical, and the Quality/Price aspect of scoring is key. Quality scores are unavoidably subjective and frequently turn out to be close, whilst Price scoring is calculated mathematically via a pre-defined logical method, often resulting in large ranges across the scoring. A low price can unduly distort scoring resulting in the lowest price winning the tender, regardless of the Quality score. Hence, the mechanism for scoring price against value is critical and the comparison of tenders needs to be very carefully considered to ensure quality remains the important factor when selecting the team.

The only guidance notes which mention the tender price, are those provided by The National Lottery Heritage Fund which states:
> '....Your proof should be a report on the tenders you have received, together with your decision on which to accept. You must give full reasons if you do not select the lowest tender.' [16]

They do not provide guidance on reporting, however, if the best quality bid is not selected, which might confer better balanced values.

Anecdotally it was stated by one of the case study contributors that
> "the typical weighting suggested by Arts Council of Wales is 70% quality 30% pricing."

However none of the funders guidance notes from any of the funding bodies reviewed in this research outline the need to consider the relative merits of quality and price.

In the Scottish Opera case study in any future competition process the Client, in retrospect, would notably try and consider a means of assessing and balancing price versus quality to a greater extent. This was in relation to setting the criteria for the procurement of the main contractor, ensuring that the tender fee was suitably robust for the deliverability of the high quality of the intended outcome.

When establishing assessment criteria clear sector guidance to support better understanding of the distinction between quality and price, and between what might apply for a services contract, for the employment of an architect/consultant, and a works contract, for the employment of a main contractor, is absent. A need to provide appropriate guidance to ensure better quality future outcomes should be a consideration.

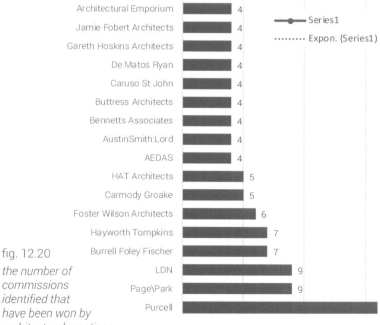

fig. 12.20

the number of commissions identified that have been won by architectural practices reportedly winning 4 or more commissions

ARCHITECTS

Of the 420 projects, the appointed architect could only be identified in 353 cases. For the remainder either the information could not be located, an architect was not appointed or the notice called for equipment, services purchasing a building, or an architect/design team was not otherwise required.

Notes:
- The data set includes one project where the design team provided their services pro bono as part of their charitable work.
- Of the projects not included 3 which were contractor design & build and 1 was engineer led with no architect appointed.
- In 26 Jan 2015 - Aedas bought UK architectural practice RHWL, and its specialist cultural and public building subsidiary Arts Team and the entries have been amalgamated.

The architects commissioned most often, for four or more projects, of the 208 Architectural firms identified over the period are reported *(fig. 12.20)*.

11.6% of commissions were won by the practices winning more than four commissions, with 16 (4.53%) being won by the most successful practice, Purcell.

A research question arising from the distributions found in the Project Compass's Public Construction Procurement Trends 2009-2014 research was to establish how much access there was to the sector for architects and by how much some architects were appointed more than others.[17] But with regards to the cohort range overall from the distribution of work that can be ascertained from this sample size and Purcell's lead in the sector, it does not suggest any natural aberration *(fig. 12.21)*. The dominance of Purcell might be a simple reflection of their reputation, national reach, longevity as a practice, reliability through delivery and their early specialism as heritage consultants in a sector where much of the work is associated with building conservation and the reworking of existing buildings.

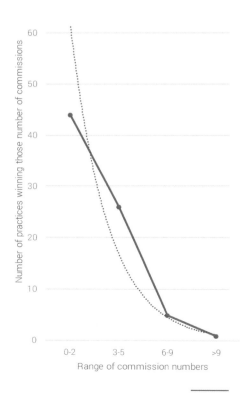

fig. 12.21

distribution of the number of practices winning a range of commissions

COMPETITION PROGRAMMERS

There were 13 competitions managed by five specialist architectural competition programmers and one other architecture organisation.

RIBA Competitions Office
  Windermere Jetty Boat Museum
  Hastings Pier
  Live Works, Newcastle
  Halle St Peter's, Manchester
  Gladstone's Library, Hawarden, North Wales
  The Whitworth Art Gallery, Manchester
  This open procedure notably had:

Submissions	139
Stage 1: shortlist	10
Stage 2: design stage shortlist	5
Honorarium:	
Stage 2 practices each received	£5k

Malcolm Reading
  Queen Elizabeth Olympic Park Culture and Education Quarter London
  Ross Pavilion, Edinburgh.
  RAF Museum, Hendon, London
  Museum of London, Smithfield
RIAS Consultancy (The Royal Incorporation of Architects in Scotland)
  Fruitmarket Gallery, Edinburgh
Collander
  Scottish Chamber Orchestra
The Architecture Foundation
  Studio Voltaire

MULTI-STAGE FUNDING PROCESSES

Complex multi-stage funding application processes are required by the various funding bodies. These are acknowledged as being necessary to ensure viable organisations, (by the review of operating budgets, art programme, outputs and impact etc.) and that the capital projects provide value for money and are on track (programme). However this can lead to more prolonged projects from gestation, inception and feasibility to construction completion and opening.

Two examples are:
Square Chapel Centre for the Arts
  In Sept 2015 construction started on Evans Vettori Architects' £6.6m building overhaul, 10 years after the firm had been appointed. Funding was from the last round of Arts Council England capital funding.
  In 2017 it re-opened, but unfortunately the West Yorkshire theatre and cultural institution, has entered into administration due to a funding shortfall.

The project extended considerably over the 12 years from architects appointment to re-opening.

Mwyafu cyfleoedd yn Pontio, Bangor University's Arts & Innovation building
  In November 2008 Grimshaw architects were appointed following a tender, to develop a new £35m building. The project was subject to various financial and construction problems and delays.
  In 2015 it was finally opened with increased costs of £49m.

The **Aberdeen Art Gallery** and **Wilton's Music Hall Case Studies** provide further more detailed examples.

Some, although not all, contract notices acknowledge the multi-stage process and need for break clauses in the contracted terms of appointment to allow for the funding assessment process, and the potential for being unsuccessful in obtaining funding. The following are examples:

The RSC Costume Workshop

Restricted procedure	
Quality/Price:	60/40
Tenders received	6
CN est. contract value	£300k - £450k
High/low offers:	£517k - £303k

The Contract Notice stated:
"the RSC is looking to appoint an architect led design team to deliver the design associated with our proposed costume workshop redevelopment project. The initial phase of the design work will take the project through to the completion of RIBA Stage D. This will support our Arts Council Stage 2 application, which if successful, will see the design team remobilised to complete the detailed design phases and prepare tender and construction"[18]

Jacksons Lane Theatre

Restricted procedure	
Quality/Price	70/30
Tenders received	22
CN est. contract value	£417k
High/low offers:	£415k - £303k

The Contract Notice stated:
'In June 2017, Jacksons Lane's application to the ACE's Large Capital Scheme was awarded a Stage One pass and development funding. This allows Jacksons Lane 18 months to develop the project to RIBA Design Stage D (RIBA Plan of work 2007) / or completed RIBA

Work Stage 3 (RIBA Plan of work 2013) & make a Stage Two application. If this is successful, then the full grant of £2,103,920, less development funding, will be awarded.

The initial application was based on a Feasibility Study produced by Citizens Design Bureau which developed an outline scheme to RIBA Stage 1. The outline construction cost for the whole project is estimated to be in the region of £2,767,000 (total budget in the region of £4,500,000).

At the point of submission of the Stage II application there will be a project break from November 2018 to February 2019, whilst ACE considers the application and makes its decision on further funding.

Jacksons Lane intends that this current procurement should result in a contract being awarded to the organisation or consortium who would also be able to continue to the next project stage (if the Stage II application to ACE is successful) without further tendering. A break clause will therefore be in effect for the required waiting period."[19]

Manchester Jewish Museum

Restricted procedure
Quality/Price: 60/40
Quality weighting:
Tender: 30
Interview: 30
Price weighting, Fee:
to RIBA stage 3:   20
RIBA stages 4 to 6:   20

The Contract Notice stated:
"The contract will be awarded for services to RIBA stage 6, but there will be a break clause to be invoked in the event that the Museum's round 2 submission to the HLF is unsuccessful (i.e. the contract will initially be awarded for services up to & including RIBA stage 3 only)."[20]

MULTI-STAGE & MULTI-FUNDER

Some contract notices clearly outline the complexity of dealing with multiple funding bodies and funding stages. This be further complicated by separate funding bodies that fund different elements of the project. An example being:

Brighton Dome & Brighton Festival Capital Redevelopment Project

Quality/Price: 70/30
Weightings:
Overall bid quality & the extent it demonstrates ability, satisfying the brief: 30
Evidence of direct experience of similar projects, including RIBA Stage D proposals & submission of planning applications for ACE or HLF funded capital projects within the arts/culture/heritage sector (to incl. experience of individual team members outlined in CV's):   40
Price (£/hrs/personnel + total)   30

The Contract Notice stated:
"Brighton Dome & Festival Ltd. is seeking an architect lead design team to...RIBA Stage D... through to a planning decision & contributing design documentation to a Stage Two Capital Bid to ACE. The design documentation will also be used sometime later in 2014 to inform the preparation of a Stage 2 HLF bid jointly with the Royal Pavilion & Museums – pending a successful pass at Stage 1...in November 2013."

A further Contract Notice (120026-2015) for an Open Procedure was issued for RIBA Stage 4 to Stage 7. Feilden Clegg Bradley Studios the same design team as previously was appointed.[21]

In 2020 following the liquidation of the main works contractor the building works are still on-going.

FUNDING

Most of the arts and cultural projects are funded from a range of sources, including the arts funding bodies, trusts and foundations, local authorities, national government funds, local donations, philanthropists, local large employers/businesses and European funding.

The full list of 82 funding sources found referenced within the procurement or funding information, excluding local authorities, the arts organisations themselves and donations, can be found in Appendix E.

An example of regional funding is:
The Northern Cultural Regeneration Fund
Launched by government in August 2017 to build a lasting regional legacy from the Great Exhibition of the North. The £15m Fund (managed by Key Fund), is a combination of support and finance via the National Lottery. Projects announced in March 2018 include:

Blackpool
to create a museum celebrating the town's history as the UK's first mass seaside holiday resort would receive £4m.

Bradford Odeon
a vacant former cinema was allocated £4m to transform it into a 4,000-capacity live music and events venue.

Lake District
cultural attractions across the Lake District were allocated nearly £3.3m to enhance the visitor experience.

Philanthropic gifts
The largest noted significant single philanthropic gift is that of £11.25 million towards Opera North's capital development.

Section 106 Funded projects
11 new arts buildings or shell and core developments which were created through S106 Agreements, 6 of which are in London.

European Funding
9 projects were found which had received EU funding directly, 8 receiving European Regional Development Funding (ERDF) and one receiving Welsh Government Rural Communities funding from the Rural Development Programme 2014-2020, funded by European Agricultural Fund for Rural Development and the Welsh Government.

European funding has supported a large number of arts and heritage capital projects over the years. Due to changes in targeted regional funding priorities and eligibility this has reduced over recent years and this source of funds will now cease.

Exceptions to the rule

There are of course a number of arts and cultural buildings commissioned by private bodies or organisations and without public funding. They have their own procurement policies.

For example the University of Cambridge is not a public body within the meaning of the Public Contracts Regulations 2015 (Directive 2014/24/EU) and is not subject to the European procurement legislation.

Where the University advertises contracts in the Official Journal of the European Union, it does so on a voluntary basis and does not undertake any obligation to comply with the procurement legislation. The University reserves its rights in full to adapt or step outside the procedures in the procurement legislation as the University considers necessary.

"Before we enter into a contract with a supplier, a competitive process will have been completed in line with University policies and strategy.[22] The Universities agreed Financial Regulations and competitive practices are transparent.[23]

Once registered, as opportunities arise organisations who meet the selection criteria defined for each tender, which may for example include listing under certain 'business classifications' and/or of a certain ownership structure, will receive further information to enable them to determine if they would like to be considered for inclusion in the tendering activity. We may, at our discretion seek quotations for low value purchases by telephone or email but a more formal tender process will be required in writing for higher value purchases exceeding £50,000 total value."[24]

CHANGE OF ARCHITECT BETWEEN STAGES

Seven of the eleven case studies highlight issues relating to continuity of works across the full RIBA plan of work stages. These include having multiple procurement processes for different stages, or the pressure on work streams and clients, and novation under a Design & Build contract.

Traditionally architects were appointed to carry a project through on behalf of a client from inception to completion, sustaining through the continuity of their engagement a relationship providing a golden thread for the responsibility, vision and quality of work. Increasingly however architects are being appointed only for particular stages of a projects production, with new appointments procured upon conclusion of those stages.

In other UK sectors it has become increasingly common, for example, to appoint a high-profile architect to achieve planning permission, and then appoint a different architect to detail the building design and see it through to completion. The diminished value and quality standards arising, considered against those publicly projected and anticipated, have become a growing concern.

The discontinuity of appointments across RIBA stages is referred to here as 'work stage fragmentation'. It has significant impacts on project costs, time, quality and value.

The extent to which this is increasingly happening has therefore been a research question. The findings from the case studies highlighting the profound fragmentation of appointments across RIBA work stages is supported by the data reported here. The grants, contract and award notices indicate that a significant number of projects are being tendered for partial work stages (fig. 12.22).

It has only been possible to evidence the fragmentation happening around RIBA work stage 2, between project preparations and feasibility stages, and stages 2-7. Data is not available for further analysis at RIBA stages 3, 4, or 5 where this fragmentation is also reputedly occurring, for example, between planning/pre commencement on site and site construction.

RIBA Stage 0-2		
Feasibilities	36	
Masterplan	3	
Masterplan / cultural hub	1	
Sub total		**40**
RIBA Stage 0-7		
Conversion / refurbishment	36	
New Build Extension/refurb	33	
Refurbishment	31	
New Build Construction	28	
Conversion	25	
Refurb /conservation /repairs	22	
Redevelopment	11	
Refurb & gallery design	3	
Sub total		**189**
RIBA Stage 2-7		
Conversion / refurbishment	25	
Refurbishment / conservation	18	
New build extension/refurb	12	
Repairs / upgrade / refurb	10	
New build construction	8	
Redevelopment	8	
Refurb & gallery design	1	
Sub total		**82**
Where terms & conditions covering RIBA Work Stages are unclear		
Refurb / Repairs / upgrade	74	
Access / Equipment / M&E	40	
Interior design & fit out:-		
To Gallery / Museum	8	
S106	7	
Other	3	
Landscape	3	
Building purchase	3	
Framework	2	
Sub total		**140**
Unknown / unclear	30	
Project stopped	10	
Sub total		**40**
Total		**491**

fig. 12.22

Table recording the number of contract notices found recording RIBA stages of appointment

The records indicate that only 38.7% of projects can be verified from the contract notices as offering service appointments at commencement, extending through Stages 0-7 *(fig. 12.23)*. 8% covered RIBA stage 0-2 only and 17% covered RIBA Stages 2-7 only. It might be thought that the number of feasibility stage investigations would be greater than the numbers of subsequent projects. However many of these may for example have been sub OJEU threshold appointments, let without equivalent transparency, or undertaken with kick-start funding privately or resourced otherwise.

Upon scrutiny of other additional source material to elicit named practices on projects, only 45 projects were found where it could actually be confirmed that the same architect undertook both the feasibility study and the main capital project (with only two for example in Wales). This amounts to 9.2% of all 491 notices. There were 12 projects where it could actually be confirmed that there was a change in architect for the different project stages where the building and site remained the same.

The 12 projects breakdown as follows:

England	7	(70%)
Scotland	2	(10%)
Wales	3	(30%)

The case studies along with these findings clearly indicate an exceptionally high preponderance of projects where the work stages are being fragmented. It can also be inferred, as is evident from the case studies, that projects when they are being retendered are then let to the same original architect - in effect these procurements might be seen as a complete waste of everybody's time and money.

Some examples of where the feasibility was undertaken by another practice are:

Cwmni Theatr Arad Goch
Commissioned George + Tomos Architects and Crafted Space to undertake design development work for the Arad Goch Centre based on a feasibility study produced by Featherstone Young Architects.

Ty Pawb, Wrexham (Case Study)
Featherstone Young completed the design development and delivery following a feasibility study by Ash Sakula. Issues as reported in the Case Study then arose with their subsequent appointment by novation through to completion.

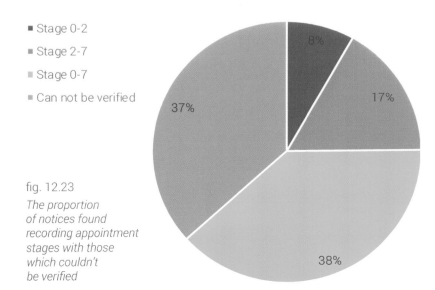

- Stage 0-2
- Stage 2-7
- Stage 0-7
- Can not be verified

fig. 12.23
The proportion of notices found recording appointment stages with those which couldn't be verified

Cwmni'r Fran Wen

Ellis Williams Architects were appointed to undertake the feasibility study for a new building following a tender process in 2016. The project was then re-tendered in 2019 for the conversion of a Grade II listed church for the £3.2m new creative arts centre centre, this was won by Manalo & White.

The data set included one project where the design team were required to adopt an existing design.

Rothesay Pavilion

Restricted Procedure	
Quality / Price	80/20
Tenders received	1
CN project cost est.	£6m
CAN project estimate	£10.6m

In 2014 following its competition process, Argyll and Bute Council appointed a Design Team (excluding QS), led by a Conservation Accredited Architect with expertise in the repair of listed modernist concrete structures, for the Delivery Stage of the Rothesay Pavilion Project.

"The Design Team will be required to adopt the existing design (which has been developed to RIBA Stage D/3), to specify and implement a phase of urgent works to tackle severe areas of cast stone deterioration, to undertake a value engineering exercise on the Stage D design, and then on approval to develop the project through RIBA Stage 4 Technical Design, Stage 5 Construction, and Stage 6, Handover and Close Out".

The construction cost is estimated to have risen to £14m in 2019.
As of April 2020 the refurbishment of the building has yet to be completed.[25]

New architects were also appointed following changes, for example, of the site, funding, and lease, and where on occasion an architect went into liquidation.

The Fruitmarket Gallery, Edinburgh

This is a complex project which was originally a 1990s SAC funded conversion by Richard Murphy architects. In 2011 the Gallery was awarded £100k Stage One Capital Funding from Creative Scotland to develop improvement plans. A further £1.4m was ring-fenced subject to the submission of a Stage Two Application and fully developed design and business plans.

In 2013, the Gallery appointed Hoskins Architects following a competition process that also included SHS Burridge, Oliver Chapman Architects, Reiach and Hall Architects, Richard Murphy Architects and Malcolm Fraser Architects. Unfortunately, the Gallery was unable to secure the support from the HLF on which the proposal's fundraising depended, resulting in the project being abandoned and Hoskins Architects stepping down.

A smaller revised project, which received backing from Creative Scotland with other public and private funders, is now expected to cost around £3.7m. The Fruitmarket Gallery engaged RIAS Consultancy to manage the process of procuring an architect led multi-disciplinary design team, to take the project forward. A total of 18 practices submitted with relevant examples of their work. In Nov 2018 the panel announced unanimously awarding Reiach & Hall the appointment and the project is believed to be ongoing.[26]

Blackpool Museum

This is another project that was reconsidered and reduced in scale. The initial project was to create a new museum for the town located within the Grade II* listed Pavilion Theatre and Horseshoe within the Winter Garden. £1.24m HLF funding was awarded in 2014 to undertake a feasibility study for a full scale museum. However, the costs of the renovation and development were £26m, resulting in an £8m funding gap that could not be met. The Council decided not to proceed with that project.[27]

In August 2017 alternative sites and options were considered and the potential for inclusion of the museum within a new development was proposed. The Palatine Building is being redeveloped into a 5* hotel and leisure complex and the museum will be located on the first floor. The revised scheme has a budget of £13m.

Northern Cultural Regeneration Funding (NCRF) was received, in addition to £4m from HLF and Blackpool City Council. Buttress Architects and Casson Mann were retained as the architects and exhibition designers. It is unclear if any S106 funding was involved.[28] It is currently under constructed and anticipated to open in 2021.

Mountview Academy of Theatre Arts

This was originally to be accommodated in Hornsey Town hall, London with development proposals to RIBA stage 3 put together by Purcell. It was identified that the existing listed building was too constraining and that a larger building was required. LB Southwark identified a site in Peckham with the intention that a new build academy could be created on a brown field site to enhance the cultural offer in Peckham. The £30m 200-seat theatre space has been designed by Carl Turner Architects in partnership with Southwark Council. The development includes a number of rentable/commercial units. For the architect's specific procurement on this project no contract notice or award notice have been located. It is understood the services were acquired by a call off from the London Borough of Southwark framework. The building opened in 2018.[29]

There are however anomalies:

Tate St Ives:

The original tender for the St Ives expansion was in 2010 (or earlier) which Jamie Fobert Architects won, but in 2011 the scheme was scrapped. In 2012 it was re-tendered and Jamie Fobert won again. The gallery re-opened again in October 2017 with the new extension following shortly after.

For one project there was a need to retender the architectural services for two different phases:

The Garden Museum, London:

In 2008 phase I was built to address the pressing needs for dedicated spaces with a 'museum for a nation of gardeners': five new galleries, space for a hundred public events a year, and the first archive of garden design. In 2013 Dow Jones won a competitive tender to design the second phase of the Garden Museum.

The Museum, located in a Grade II* listed church adjacent to Lambeth Palace, received a grant in September 2014 of £3,510,600, 53% of eligible delivery costs towards the redevelopment of the site to establish a museum of gardens through the construction of new collections galleries inside the old church, building an extension for schools, a community space, and a new café, creating a new centre of learning about gardening inspired by Tradescant's vision of an Ark (collection) and an Eden (botanical garden).

The Museum now sought a grant increase of £247,800. Total project costs had increased due to two archaeological discoveries, one included the discovery of an unknown vault in which five Archbishops of Canterbury were buried. Other increases included the extra costs of the two-stage tender process. An unexpected fee which Thames Water had requested, was to undertake a 'sewer walk' and some adaptations to the sewerage connections and there were extra costs for installing heating ducts in the nave and drains. A National Heritage Memorial Fund Grant increase of £247,800 was awarded.

Following planning consent the research also found several instances of the commissioned architect being replaced by another. An example being:

Oldham Coliseum,

Mecanoo were originally the architect having first secured planning permission in 2015, but were replaced in 2018 by Ellis Williams as delivery architect. The procurement process for that is not clear. Mecanoo had delivered the HOME project and Birmingham Library, but for two other Manchester projects Mecanoo had also not been retained as delivery architect.

The reason given was that the Council did not want the project run from Mecanoo's Delft office, after they had closed their Manchester office. However, a statement from Cllr Jean Stretton, Oldham Council leader, said: "Mecanoo informed us that they're unable to resource the architectural services side of this project beyond the end of our initial contract with them"

But due to cost increase and reduced value for money the project was later abandoned in November 2018. Alternative plans for a new performance space in the town centre have been developed with the organisation, council and ACE.[30]

In Wales it has been noted that there are smaller practices only undertaking feasibility studies. They are not getting appointed for later project stages or even being novated forward. This appears to be contrary to the Welsh Governments reputed policy on economic sustainability. It is not clear if this is by choice, a reflection on practice size and experience, or if this is due to the requirement from many clients to include within SSQ's/PQQ's/ITT's unduly onerous criteria. Calling for evidence of multiple similar completed projects and specific levels of turnover are factors which for example prevent smaller and emerging practices being appointed. Quality or reduction of risk is not guaranteed by those who have designed a similar building previously. But thresholds, criteria, quotas and work stage fragmentation could be restricting innovation and opportunities across the sector.

The Case Study on Wilton's Music Hall highlights how important it is however for the client to ensure the continuity of an architect for the duration of a project. When so many projects are reported as being prolonged, requiring all parties share a common vision as stakeholders, share those empathies and can retain the integrity of the design intent for the duration, they appears more better capable of robustly producing quality.

As highlighted in several other Case Studies there is a contradiction between the process and the end purpose where multiple staged procurements can prevent practices participating in the process due to the costs, compliances and/or commercial risk. This also arises when post feasibility a new competitive process is required by funding bodies, where there might otherwise be an assumption that the original architect would be appointed.

A well-considered and robust feasibility is important, but then re-selecting another design team to take this forward is not ideal. Inevitably as work flows become fragmented into more individual work stages throughout projects there is a need for the newly appointed design to review, audit and potentially repeat work from previous stages. This also places additional cost and management burdens upon a client who must also re-tender, re-engage the processes and briefing. The knowledge lost can be significant.

This is not the most effective, efficient or best value call. The current predilection for slicing and dicing projects into separate work stages referenced within this report as 'work stage fragmentation' may sometimes result in an excellent outcome – as evidenced by Edinburgh Printmakers but equally this can be a loss of opportunity and other potential benefits.

All of the funding bodies operate strict rules on procurement which is appropriate as public funding is being used, however there are more effective ways in which the procurement can be structured that address the requirement for a competitive process but which can make for a more streamlined approach.

Arts and cultural projects are quite particular as they generally need to work within the processes required by the funding bodies. In order to apply for funding a feasibility study or options appraisal needs to be completed and a detailed brief developed, along with the associated business plan and the artistic programme requirements established. As the process is so lengthy the funding criteria can change during the life of a project.

These tend to be very individual projects, to meet the specific project requirements, needing a close collaboration between all of the design and client team, other consultants, funding bodies and other stakeholders and funders. This does not fit well with certain forms of contract or project management.

Providing break clauses in the terms of consultancy appointments, is a well tried and tested means of better addressing these issue, as is evidenced in this analysis, but the popularity of this approach is declining. Funding organisations guidance would do well in future to incorporate more and better guidance on how best this maybe addressed, by use of break clauses.

DESIGN & BUILD (D&B)

For the majority of the projects the researchers were unable to find sufficient information regarding the contractor procurement process used. But 9 projects were identified as being constructed under a D&B contractor procurement. ACE was the main funder for all these projects with the exception of Tŷ Pawb, Mountview Theatre and the Science museum:

Tara Theatre
National Skill Academy
Bridport Arts Centre
Ferens Gallery
Tŷ Pawb
Milton Keynes Gallery
The project was previously advertised and tendered based upon a Traditional Two Stage procurement route. This did not result in a satisfactory outcome and it was decided to complete the design sufficient for a Design and Build procurement route, by which time planning issues had progressed to an appropriate stage and funding secured.
Mountview Theatre Academy
Main funders London Borough of Southwark, Garfield Weston, Lloyd Webber Foundation
1 Collection Project, Science Museum
Main funder Science Museum Group

Self-build In-house design and build
Beamish the Living Museum of the North,
Unusually this 'Remaking Beamish' project, undertook most of the design and build elements in-house, appointing an Architectural Assistant to provide the capacity to achieve an ambitious programme. Doonan Architects completed the initial design stages, prepared measured drawings, secured planning permission and prepared constructional details for the museum's staff to complete the projects on site.

This example provides an interesting counterpoint as it might appear the construction forms an integral part of the project, where in other instances the use of D&B is not.

QUESTIONABLE PROCUREMENTS

Several projects were found where there were some examples of bad practice. In terms of fees, levels of risk and intellectual property specifically the following Llandudno project is an example. Here the design team were required to undertake initial design work for no fee / at risk and with assignment of all copyright. The Terms and Condition's required handover of all copyright of documents and images to the client for this work. The also shows significant variation in tender fees.

Llandudno Museum Development Project

Tenders received	6
High/low offer:	£120,000 - £5,750
Estimated total project	£1.5m

The Contract Notice states:
*"It is anticipated that the contract for the project up to RIBA Stage B will be undertaken on **an 'at risk/no fee' basis** and tenders are therefore invited on that basis and the assumption that the project will proceed to completion, subject to funding. At this stage it is estimated that the total project budget (incl. capital and revenue costs) will be in the region of £1 to £1.5million. In line with its vision, an Initial Design Brief has been prepared and the Museum now wishes to appoint an Architect to develop architectural design proposals in response to the brief up to RIBA Stage B (now RIBA Stage 1). The Architect's report will inform and be integrated into the development of a First Round application and request for a Development Grant from the Heritage Lottery Fund to enable the design proposals to be further developed to RIBA Stage E (now Stage 4) and which, if approved, will form the basis of a Second Round application: it will also be used for applications to other potential grant funding sources and sponsors.*

For Stage C onwards, it is anticipated that the architect will be responsible for the appointment and management of the architectural design team, including any specialist contractors such as structural or mechanical engineers, Quantity Surveyors" etc."

PROJECTS DISCONTINUED

Of the 491 projects in the data set 10 projects were stopped for a variety of reasons, with the following providing reasons.

Museum for Birmingham

A planned £318m redevelopment of the grade II* listed Council House site, which the museum co-occupies with Birmingham City Council. The brief set a provisional date for submitting a stage 1 bid to the Heritage Lottery Fund in October 2017, and for completion in 2022.

Birmingham Museums Trust stated that the tender had been cancelled, but said there were still plans for the redevelopment to go ahead. Birmingham Museum and Art Gallery have stated that the project will resume after the 2022 Commonwealth Games. The procurement has clearly been put on hold, although no further details have been provided and nothing notified by any public contract notice processes.

St Peter's Seminary Cardross

The seminary, designed by Gillespie, Kidd & Coia, opened in 1966 as a training college for Roman Catholic priests. Since 1987 the building has lain empty and become derelict. It is the most significant post war modern building in Scotland and is statutory listed Category A, entered on the Buildings at Risk Register and the World Monuments Watch List of 100 Most Endangered Sites.

Avanti Architects were engaged by the Archdiocese of Glasgow to produce a definitive Conservation Assessment for the buildings. This led to Avanti being commissioned by NVA a not-for-profit arts charity to develop plans in collaboration with ERZ Landscape Architects and McGinlay Bell to partially restore, consolidate and adapt the buildings to create an education, performance, exhibition and public arts centre within the 57 hectare site. The project was part funded by Heritage Lottery Fund and Creative Scotland. However due to the escalating costs and risks this project was stopped.

A report considering options for St Peter's Seminary prepared for Scottish Ministers by Historic Environment Scotland at the request of the Scottish Government, was published in June 2019 . This recommended that the building should not become a Property in Care, which would then receive government support, due to the significant costs required and inability for income generation on the scale required.[31]

Thames Estuary Museum

An initial scheme for the Southend-on-Sea Museum was developed by AEW but at £55m (budget £40m) and with spiralling costs this was unaffordable and the project halted.[32]

Swindon Museum and Art Gallery

This HLF Funding bid failed. There has been no official public competition, but MAKE won an earlier competition to draw up designs for a scheme to provide a vision for the fundraising. The project was then proposed to be a refurbishment of the existing Wyvern Theatre to provide gallery space. However funding from the LEP is being used to look at the potential for a smaller new build project or relocation into the Mechanics' Institution.

Oriel Davies Gallery, Newtown Powys.

A feasibility study was completed but the Contract Notice for the next stage was cancelled in July 2017. The reason provided is 'discontinuation of procedure'.[33]

Bromley Museum at the Priory

In June 2011 a £2.3m 1st round application was made to the LLF's Heritage Grants programme with match funding of £447k from London Borough of Bromley. The application was given a Stage 1 HLF Approval, including a project Development Grant of £186,300. Further investigations and design development determined significantly more conservation work was needed. Project costs increased from £2.46m to £3.61m in the Stage 2 application, requiring £1.06m of Council match funding and a commitment to 25 years' revenue funding of some £275k per annum, representing a full 70% of the museum's projected operating budget. Members elected to withdraw the application prior to a final HLF decision and the project was suspended. The museum is closed and due to be sold.[34]

References:

1   Peter Stark P., Gordon C. & Powell D., *Rebalancing Our Cultural Capital: A contribution to the debate on national policy for the arts and culture in England 31 Oct 2013* http://www.gpsculture.co.uk/downloads/rocc/Rebalancing_FINAL_3mb.pdf (accessed 28 May 2020)

2   UK2070 Commission website: uk2070.org.uk/ (accessed 28 May 2020)

3   *Make No Little Plans: Acting at Scale for a Fairer and Stronger Future. UK 2070 – An Inquiry into Regional Inequalities Towards a Framework for Action.* UK2070 Commission. Feb. 2020 www.gpsculture.co.uk/downloads/rocc/Rebalancing_FINAL_3mb.pdf (accessed 28 May 2020)

4   *UK2070 Commission: An Inquiry into Regional Inequalities Towards a Framework For Action* uk2070.org.uk/ (accessed 3 June 2020)

5   Langley D., Royce S., Dinnen A, *Capital Works! Evaluation of Arts Council England's capital investment 2012-2018 Summary Report'.* Alchemy research & consultancy, February 2018. www.artscouncil.org.uk/sites/default/files/download-file/ARC_summary_report_June%202018_0.pdf (accessed 3 June 2020)

6   *Interactive map: our funded organisations, 2018-2022* Arts Council England www.artscouncil.org.uk/funding-map-2018-2022 (accessed 3 June 2020)

7   Menteth, W., O'Carroll, O., Curtis, R., Sawyer, B. *Public Construction Procurement Trends 2009-2014.* Project Compass CIC. Dec 2014. ISBN (Print): 9780993148101. projectcompass.co.uk/wp-content/uploads/2019/10/Project_Compass_CIC_Procurement_Trends_2009-2014.pdf (accessed 28 May 2020)

8   Centre for Music London. *Contract Notice 2017/S 090-177398* ted.europa.eu/udl?uri=TED:NOTICE:177398-2017:TEXT:EN:HTML
         Contract Award Notice 2018/S 079-177073. ted.europa.eu/udl?uri=TED:NOTICE:177073-2018:TEXT:EN:HTML&tabId=1 (accessed 3 June 2020)

9   Shakespeare North Playhouse. *Contracts Finder Award Notice.* www.contractsfinder.service.gov.uk/Notice/94528c02-f6c3-4216-8269-f80d1c2b6011?p=@QxUlRRPT0=NjJNT08=UF (accessed 28 May 2020)

10   *Contract Notice 2017/S 027-047833* ted.europa.eu/udl?uri=TED:NOTICE:47833-2017:TEXT:EN:HTML&src=0
         Contract Award Notice 2017/S 130-266295 ted.europa.eu/udl?uri=TED:NOTICE:266295-2017:TEXT:EN:HTML&src=0 (accessed 3 June 2020)

11   *Ibid Public Construction Procurement Trends 2009-2014 pp.10-11*

12   Hall For Cornwall. *Contract Notice - Open Procedure. Notice No. 2015/S 076-134351.* ted.europa.eu/udl?uri=TED:NOTICE:134351-2015:TEXT:EN:HTML&src=0 (accessed 28 May 2020)

13   Kings Theatre. *Contract Notice - Restricted procedure. Notice No. 2018/S 100-228739.* ted.europa.eu/udl?uri=TED:NOTICE:228739-2018:TEXT:EN:HTML&src=0 (accessed 28 May 2020)
         Contract Award Notice - Restricted procedure, Notice No. 2018/S 103-235981 ted.europa.eu/udl?uri=TED:NOTICE:235981-2018:TEXT:EN:HTML&src=0 (accessed 28 May 2020)

14   *Contract Notice 2016/S 232_422810* ted.europa.eu/udl?uri=TED:NOTICE:422810-2016:TEXT:EN:HTML&src=0
         Contract Award Notice 2017/S 089-174982 ted.europa.eu/udl?uri=TED:NOTICE:174982-2017:TEXT:EN:HTML&src=0 (accessed 3 June 2020)

15   *Ten Principles for Procuring Better Outcomes.* RIBA 2015 p.27 www.architecture.com/-/media/GatherContent/Ten-Principles-for-Procuring-Better-Outcomes/Additional-Documents/TenPrinciplesforProcuringBetterOutcomes2016versionpdf.pdf

16   *Writing a brief for the procurement of goods or services* HLF www.heritagefund.org.uk/publications/writing-brief-procurement-goods-or-services (accessed 3 June 2020)

17   Ibid. Public construction Procurement Trends 2009-2014 pp. 52-59

18   Royal Shakespeare Co. Costume Warehouse Contract Award Notice. ted.europa.eu/udl?uri=TED:NOTICE:84010-2014:TEXT:EN:HTML&src=0 (accessed 3 June 2020)

19   Jackson Lane Community Theatre. Contract Notice - Restricted procedure. Notice No. 2017/S 194-398534 ted.europa.eu/udl?uri=TED:NOTICE:398534-2017:TEXT:EN:HTML&src=0
      Contract Award Notice ted.europa.eu/udl?uri=TED:NOTICE:42046-2018:TEXT:EN:HTML (accessed 28 May 2020)

20   Manchester Jewish Museum Contract Notice ted.europa.eu/udl?uri=TED:NOTICE:386384-2015:TEXT:EN:HTML&src=0
      Contract Award Notice ted.europa.eu/udl?uri=TED:NOTICE:137783-2016:TEXT:EN:HTML&src=0 (accessed 3 June 2020)

21   Brighton Dome & Brighton Festival Project. Contract Notice - Open Procedure. Notice No. 2015/S 067-120026 ted.europa.eu/TED/notice/udl;JSESSIONID=09C33AB09E0DBEF29A073D6976ABDED8.backend-a1?uri=TED:NOTICE:120026-2015:TEXT:EN:HTML&src=0 (accessed 3 June 2020)

22   Becoming a supplier. University of Cambridge. April 2019. www.admin.cam.ac.uk/offices/purchasing/suppliers/new/becoming.html (accessed 3 June 2020)

23   Financial Regulations. Cambridge University Jan. 2020. www.finance.admin.cam.ac.uk/policy-and-procedures/financial-regulations (accessed 3 June 2020)

24   How we buy goods, works and services. University of Cambridge. April 2019. www.procurement.admin.cam.ac.uk/supplier-portal/how-we-buy-goods-works-and-services (accessed 4 Sept. 2020)

25   As described in the Rothesay Pavilion Redevelopment Works Contract. Notices - Notice Nos. 2014/S 138-248090 2015/S 179-324451 & 2015/S 067-117345 www.publiccontractsscotland.gov.uk/search/show/search_view.aspx?ID=SEP220318 ted.europa.eu/udl?uri=TED:NOTICE:489236-2017:TEXT:EN:HTML and: 'Rothesay Pavilion prepares to open its doors after £14m restoration.' The Herald, 26 Jan 2019 www.herald-scotland.com/news/17386782.rothesay-pavilion-prepares-to-open-its-doors-after-14m-restoration/ (accessed 3 June 2020)

26   Fruitmarket Gallery Contract Notice & Contract Award Notice. www.publiccontractsscotland.gov.uk/search/show/search_view.aspx?ID=NOV337172 (accessed 3 June 2020)

27   Changes to plans for a Blackpool Museum , 15 Aug. 2019. Blackpool Council. www.blackpool.gov.uk/News/2017/July/Changes-to-plans-for-a-Blackpool-Museum.aspx (accessed 3 June 2020)

28   Launch of Blackpool Museum. Visit Fylde Coast. 10 Jan. 2020. www.liveblackpool.info/about/history/blackpool-museum/(accessed 3 June 2020)

29   https://turner.works/works/view/mount-view-academy/ (accessed 3 June 2020)

30   Oldham Colieum Place North West website 5 Jan 2018 www.placenorthwest.co.uk/news/council-preps-for-architect-switch-at-oldham-coliseum/
      Architects Journal 17 April 2018 www.architectsjournal.co.uk/news/ellis-williams-replaces-mecanoo-on-oldham-coliseum-job/10025394.article
      Place North West website 26 Nov 2018 www.placenorthwest.co.uk/news/oldham-scraps-27m-coliseum-plan/ (accessed 3 June 2020)

31   Report on St Peter's Seminary, Cardross Historic Environment Scotland. 27 June 2019. www.historicenvironment.scot/archives-and-research/publications/publication/?publicationId=e33d06cf-91dd-45b4-a7e9-aa7800fe1749 (accessed 3 June 2020)

32   Cliffs Museum, Southend, plan SCRAPPED www.southendstandard.co.uk/news/16989977.cliffs-museum-southend-plan-scrapped-after-news-it-will-cost-55million/ (accessed 3 June 2020)

33   Oriel Davies Gallery, Powys. Contract Notice No. 2017/S 128-261167. ted.europa.eu/udl?uri=TED:NOTICE:261167-2017:TEXT:EN:HTML&tabId=1
      Contract Award Notice No. 2017/S 214-445063 ted.europa.eu/udl?uri=TED:NOTICE:445063-2017:TEXT:EN:HTML (accessed 3 June 2020)

34   Bromley Museum at the Priory cds. bromley.gov.uk/documents/s50030161/Exec%20100615%20Bromley%20Museum%20and%20the%20Priory%20Orpington%20-%20Appendix%20B.pdf
      www.museumsassociation.org/museums-journal/news/02022015-council-proposes-to-close-bromley-museum (accessed 3 June 2020)

context

13　Capital Programme Funding

How national capital programmes are distributed and proportions allocated nationally. Urban, regional and rural breakdowns are unavailable.

NATIONAL ARTS FUNDING OVERVIEW

This report is concerned with the procurement of arts and heritage buildings across the UK. As this is primarily undertaken by the National Lottery distributors, these national funding bodies are central to our research. We have outlined the structure and funding programmes for the five main national distributors who lead on arts and heritage funding.

Capital programmes have been historically funded since 1994 via receipts from the National Lottery. This is due to the additionality principle, the definition of which is shared by all National Lottery distributors: "National Lottery funding is distinct from government funding and adds value. Although it does not substitute for Exchequer expenditure, where appropriate it complements government and other programmes, policies and funding."

This enabled the Lottery distributors to use this funding for new projects which would not otherwise happen, and – when first introduced – enabled differentiation of capital from revenue and therefore the specific support of capital projects. These include purchase of buildings, equipment, vehicles, musical instruments and conversions, refurbishments and new buildings. There has been some shift from just capital to part funding new programmes of activities, so including revenue funding, creating a key part of the mixed funding model which many arts and cultural organisations depend on.

The advent of the National Lottery in 1994 has enabled a huge increase in capital projects and expansion of the arts and cultural infrastructure of the UK. From 1994 to 2019 over £40 billion has been raised for good causes.[1]

The money raised by National Lottery players is donated to good causes through the twelve National Lottery distributors:
- Arts Council England
- National Lottery Heritage Fund
- UK Sport
- Sport Scotland
- Creative Scotland (previously Scottish Arts Council)
- Sport England
- Arts Council Northern Ireland
- Sport Northern Ireland
- British Film Institute
- Arts Council Wales
- Sport Wales
- The National Lottery Community Fund

Funding for the arts through the National Lottery has continued its gradual recovery after years of turmoil, increasing by just under £30m in the first half of 2018/19 on the equivalent period in the previous year.

Total sales were up 5.4% to £3.5bn, according to the latest figures released by National Lottery operator Camelot, translating into £793.2m for good causes. A fifth of this is allocated to the UK's four Arts Councils, meaning they will collectively receive just under £159m – a 23% increase on the £129m lottery funding they received this time last year.

National Lottery sales have been under consistent pressure, which reached a peak in the summer of 2016 when it was announced that a slump had reduced the contribution to the arts by £55m in one year.[2]

The National Lottery distributors are entitled to receive a share of receipts from the sale of land on Queen Elizabeth Olympic Park in return for their contribution of an additional £675m to the funding of the London 2012 Olympic and Paralympic Games.

This was announced in 2007. The arrangements, in a legal agreement between the Secretary of State and the Greater London Authority (GLA) dated 29 March 2012, sets out the distribution of funds between the GLA and the Lottery distributors (via DCMS). Land sales are likely to take place over a lengthy period, estimated to be from 2016/17 to 2036/37. DCMS estimates the first payments to the Lottery distributors to come through around 2020/21.[3]

However in January 2021 it was being reported that costs were spiralling at East Bank, the waterside development of buildings including V&A East and Sadler Wells East, and for the new BBC and London College of Fashion buildings and that the London Legacy Development Corporation (LLDC) had gone from having a net £210m of assets in 2014/5 to a net £171m in liabilities in 2019/20, potentially jeopardising projected receipts.[4] As there is already a disproportionately high UK cultural funding commitment to the V&A East and Olympic Park Cultural quarter, these projects are under increasing pressure (fig. 12.6).

UK PUBLIC INVESTMENT IN CULTURE

This has been steadily falling overall and was anticipated to reduce significantly in the foreseeable future prior to Covid-19, the impact of which has yet to be fully realised.
- UK public investment in culture has fallen by over £0.5bn over the 4 years, from £4.4bn in 2012/13 to £3.9bn in 2016/17, a reduction of 11%.
- Local authorities are still the biggest funders of culture across the UK, but this income stream has seen the largest contraction – 80% of the net loss in funding. This is the context of a fall in Government funding to local authorities by almost 50% since 2010.[5]
- There has been a downward trend in Lottery funding distributed by Arts Councils and Heritage Lottery funds, but an increase in funding from the Big Lottery Fund.[6]

Investment from and income to the National Lottery varies from year to year and has decreased in a number of recent years. This is a further reason why the current economy underpinning our cultural sector, based as it is on grant funding for revenue and capital purposes, will need to be revisited to make it fit for the future.
- Tax relief has partially offset the reduction in other funding streams for some of the larger cultural organisations, with the introduction of theatre tax credits in 2014, orchestra tax credits in 2016 and museum and galleries tax credits in 2017.
- Data for Arts Council England shows that EU funding to the cultural sector in England

has averaged £22.3m annually in recent years.[7]

Cultural organisations have increased private (i.e. from trusts foundations, and philanthropists) funding, but this has been more challenging for smaller organisations and those outside major towns and cities.
- Cultural organisations have responded to reductions in public funds by increasing income from private sources. Private investment in culture grew by 20% across the UK over the period 2012 – 15.
- Private investment accounted for 18% of cultural organisations' total income in 2014/15. The smallest organisations are almost twice as reliant on private investment as major organisations. Private investment accounts for 29% of total income for those with a total income under £100,000.
- But size matters when growing private income: the increase in private investment has been primarily driven by high value donations to the largest recipients. Overall, private investment grew by 21% from 2012 to 2015, but just 50 organisations received 60% of total private funding across the UK.
- Smaller organisations found it harder to catalyse private investment, and grew their private funding portfolio by just 8% a year.
- Funding models also vary substantially by region, reflecting proximity to sources of private income. Cultural organisations in London, the East and the South East have greater proportions of private investment than those in the North. London-based organisations account for 66% of total private investment.[8]

Earned income, through building hire, ticket sales, café and bar sales, has also grown strongly, and represents a greater share of income in larger organisations, and those in London particularly. The current closure of arts and cultural buildings will have a significant impact on these organisations, whose reserves are usually restricted to three months of full running costs.
- Cultural organisations have also increased their earned income. Data from UK Arts Councils' National Portfolio Organisations (excluding Creative Scotland) suggests that earned income has grown by 21% between 2012/13 and 2016/17, representing 95% of income growth for these organisations.
- Earned income represents 54% of income for large organisations, but only 30% of income for small organisations.[9]

ENGLAND

There are some English national museums and galleries sponsored by the Department for Culture Media and Sport (DCMS):
- British Museum, London
- Museum of the Home, London (*formerly the Geffrye Museum*)
- Horniman Museum & Gardens, London
- Imperial War Museums, London & Salford
- National Coal Mining Museum for England, Wakefield, West Yorkshire
- The National Gallery, London
- Royal Museums Greenwich, London
- National Museums, Liverpool
- National Portrait Gallery, London
- Natural History Museum, London
- Tate Group, London; Liverpool; St Ives
- Royal Armouries Museum, Leeds
- Victoria & Albert Museum, London (*V&A Museum of Childhood, V&A Dundee*)
- Science Museums Group (*Science Museum London, Science & Industry Museum Manchester, Science & Media Museum Bradford, National Railway Museum York, Locomotion near Darlington*)
- Sir John Soane's Museum, London
- Wallace Collection, London.[10]

These are primarily the 'national' organisations. The list is intermittently reviewed and amended. Previously it also included The Design Museum and at one time the Architecture Foundation.

The Northern Cultural Regeneration Social Investment Fund is a £3m Department for Culture, Media and Sport (DCMS)-supported fund launched in 2019, and run by Key Fund, offering grants and repayable finance of £25,000 to £150,000 to charities, social enterprises and creative businesses in the North, for capital and revenue funding.

Arts Council England (ACE) Activity

'ACE champions, develops and invests in artistic and cultural experiences that enrich people's lives. We support a range of activities across the arts, museums and libraries - from theatre to digital art, reading to dance, music to literature, and crafts to collections. Great art and culture inspires us, brings us together and teaches us about ourselves and the world around us. In short, it makes life better.'

Between 2018 and 2022, they will invest £1.45 billion of public money from government and an estimated £860 million from the National Lottery to *'help create art and culture experiences for everyone, everywhere.'* [11]

The Arts Council England launched *Let's Create, Strategy 2020-2030* their new 10-year strategy on 28 January 2020. This outlines their aims and priorities for the next ten years, although does not set out their policy for capital funding.

Arts Council England Structure

ACE is a registered charity, and was established by Royal Charter on 1 April 1994, taking over those responsibilities in England previously discharged by the Arts Council of Great Britain.

The objectives as stated in their Royal Charter, its governing document, are to develop and improve knowledge, understanding and practice of the arts and to increase accessibility of the arts to the public. To this end, it makes grants to arts organisations and engages in other activities on behalf of the sector.

ACE is an arm's length Government non-departmental public body, and is regulated in accordance with a Management Agreement issued by the Secretary of State.

ACE receives grant-in-aid from DCMS and is one of the bodies designated to distribute funds from the National Lottery by the National Lottery etc. Act 1993 (as amended by the National Lottery Act 1998). The level of this funding is determined as part of a 4 year cycle of spending reviews. The next review is due in 2022.

Capital Investment

Capital investment is part of their core business and typically supports organisations that are in receipt of revenue funding through their national portfolio funding. The national portfolio of arts organisations is reviewed every 4 years. The National Portfolio Organisations (NPOs) are regularly funded organisations across England. There are 840 (including 183 Museums) organisations within the current 2018-22 portfolio.

Arts Council England's total annual income for 2018/19 (the most recent year available) was £712 million (a combination of Lottery and DCMS direct funding). Their remit is to use these funds to support arts and culture for the benefit of the English public.

They currently disburse these funds via three streams:

1. **The National Portfolio:** a core group of arts organisations, museums and libraries, ranging in size and location, in which we invest over multi-year periods
2. **National Lottery Project Grants:** a rolling programme that provides support for one-off projects
3. **Development funds:** which support specific strategic initiatives identified by the Arts Council

In 2018/19 two thirds (68%) of ACE's income came from grant-in-aid and with much of the remaining from National Lottery receipts (31%).

ACE has a funding agreement with its collection of National Portfolio Organisations (NPOs), which receive annual funding allocations. In 2018/19 two thirds (£327m) of ACE's grant-in-aid was spent on NPO funding.

ACE's income from the National Lottery Distribution Fund in 2018/19 was £240m (2017/18 was £245m; although the figure of £224m was stated for 2017/18 in the *Let's Create, Strategy 2020-2030*). £820k additional income came from other sundry orgnisations, central government bodies and public corporations. There were also grants, sponsorships and donations received from joint activities with other lottery distributors, of £632k.[12]

Their capital investment is funded from both central government and the National Lottery. The Arts Council's share of proceeds from the National Lottery Distribution Fund is:

2018/19	allocation	£223,296,000
2017/18	allocation	£228,192,000

There is a Lottery reserves policy in place to ensure that the minimum balance is not less than £50m. The capital investment in individual projects varies in scale depending on the available budget set in each funding period, but it is typically in the region of £100,000 to £5 million.

Over the period 2015-18, they committed over £120 million to c122 capital projects. Many of these remain in the various stages of the design and construction process.

In 2020, they have budgeted £11.3 million for capital grants between £100,000 and £499,999 and £30 million for grants from £500k and above.

In the annual reporting the awards made are not broken down into rural, urban or regional.

Capital Funding

Arts Council England typically supports capital investment through two funding channels to support the delivery of their strategy:

National Lottery Project Grants: Typically, capital investment may form part of an application for project activity and investment is typically less than £100,000. The programme is managed as a rolling programme with no deadlines for applications.

Capital Investment Programme: Typically split into two application processes:
  Small capital grants – grants from £100,000 to £499,999. The programme is typically managed as one round per year which includes an Expressions of Interest phase followed by a full application.
  Large Capital grants – grants from £500,000 and above which is managed as a two-stage process. The programme is typically managed as a single round over a 2-3-year period.

The Arts Council England grant decision-making process is outlined below:
  Stage 1: Organisations tell us about their capital project and how they plan to contribute to our goals and priorities. We use this information to decide whether to invite organisations to make a Stage Two application. We may award development funding to support the development of their Stage Two application. Projects are expected to be developed to at least Stage 1 (RIBA Plan of Work 2013) to submit a Stage One application.
  Stage 2: Organisations complete a detailed application to secure a grant within eighteen months of our Stage One decision. Projects are expected to be developed to at least Stage 3 (RIBA Plan of Work 2013).

Arts Council England also receives funding directly from the Department for Digital, Culture, Media and Sport to deliver specific programmes or projects on their behalf. For example the £20m Cultural Development Fund which aims to allow cities and towns to invest in creative, cultural and heritage initiatives that lead to culture-led economic growth and productivity.[13]

In 2017/18 ACE received funding from DCMS specifically for the following capital projects:

The Factory, Manchester	£34m
(£20.7m also awarded in 2018/19)	
Colston Hall, Buckinghamshire	£5.18m
Shakespeare, Knowsley	£5m
Drapers Hall, Coventry	£1m
Hall for Cornwall, Truro	£2m
Dance Hub, Birmingham	£0.5m
S1 Artspace, Sheffield	£0.5m [14]

Status as of December 2019

The Arts Council of England Large Capital Grants programme is closed to new applications.

The National Lottery Project Grants is their new open access programme for arts, museums and libraries projects. The fund is aimed at supporting individual artists, community and cultural organisations. The grants available range from £1,000 to £100,000 and prioritise the consolidation and improvement of existing arts buildings and equipment, as opposed to significant redevelopment or new buildings.

To apply for the following, applicants are required to obtain written agreement to apply to Project Grants for more than £15,000 towards:
- building works for existing arts facilities (including fit-out and refurbishment)
- improving access for existing arts facilities
- buildings works for new arts facilities (including fit-out)

- buying property or leasing a building
- the purchase of new premises for arts use (freehold or leasehold interests)

'We can consider supporting:
- refurbishing, modernising or improving existing arts buildings
- buying assets such as equipment, instruments and vehicles, including installing new technologies
- professional fees associated with capital spending on your project
- VAT that you cannot recover from HM Revenue and Customs
- costs resulting from temporarily having stopped activities during the project
- environmental sustainability costs including installing or retrofitting sustainable technologies
- commissioning artists or craftspeople to contribute to the capital project
- additional staffing for specific work during the capital project.'[15]

However in early 2020 is was announced that:

- There will be one round of large capital funding opening with a budget of £30 million in 2020/21 and an annual small capital funding programme of £11 million per year from 2018/19.[16]

The Arts Council England currently holds a framework for the provision of construction expertise that may be called upon by them during their decision-making on capital investments (assessment and monitoring) and this framework expired on 31 March 2020, after an initial 3 year term for the framework. The construction advisors, primarily quantity surveyors, work closely with the Capital team of Arts Council England as well as with relationship managers and senior managers in each area.

(See Appendix A for further information)

SCOTLAND
Creative Scotland (Alba Chruthachail)

Creative Scotland is the development body for the arts and creative industries in Scotland. Based in Edinburgh, it is an executive non-departmental public body of the Scottish Government.

Creative Scotland is a national lottery distributor under the National Lottery etc. Act 1993 and maintains a National Lottery Distribution Fund (NLDF) which is entitled to receive 1.78% of the proceeds allocated to good causes from National Lottery ticket sales. The purpose of the NLDF is the support of artistic and creative activities in Scotland.

Creative Scotland has three current funding programmes, Regular Funding for up to three years for organisations, Open Project Funding for individuals and organisations for programmes of work for up to two years, and Targeted Funding to support specific sectors, projects and initiatives.

In 2018/19 they supported the network of 121 Regularly Funded Organisations comprising arts, screen and creative industries in Scotland. This included £101.6 million grant-in-aid funding across three years from the 2018-21 round of Regular Funding.

They support creative activity by individuals and organisations through the Open Project Funding (supported by The National Lottery). This includes creative work across crafts, dance, design, digital, film and screen, literature and publishing, multi-art form, music, theatre and the visual arts. In 2018/19 awards totalling £10.5 million were made to 487 applicants. Of these, 201 awards (41%) were made to individual artists and practitioners and 286 (59%) to organisations.

In 2018/19, Creative Scotland committed £79.2 million of grant funding to the arts, screen and creative industries in Scotland arising from £57 million of Scottish Government grant-in-aid funding and £22.2 million of National Lottery funds.[17]

Creative Scotland Structure

Creative Scotland is the public body that supports the arts, screen and creative industries across all parts of Scotland on behalf of everyone who lives, works or visits here.

We enable people and organisations to work in and experience the arts, screen and creative industries in Scotland by helping others to develop great ideas and bring them to life. We distribute funding provided by the Scottish Government and the National Lottery.[18]

The recently published *A Cultural Strategy for Scotland*, by the Scottish Government (February 2020), sets out their overarching vision for culture in parallel with the existing strategies for Scotland's historic environment, museums, galleries and libraries. There are no specific actions related to capital programmes as such.

Capital Investment

Creative Scotland and its predecessor organisation, the Scottish Arts Council (SAC) have run several Capital funding programmes for the development of Scotland's arts and cultural infrastructure since the inception of Lottery funding in 1994. The large-scale capital programme was set up to support organisations to improve, refurbish and/or develop cultural facilities which offered enhanced access to, or the presentation and enjoyment of, the arts and film.

Scottish Arts Council funding programmes included 857 capital awards which constituted almost half of all Lottery awards made from 1995-2010, with an overall value of £151,584,998.

Through Creative Scotland capital funding programmes, 32 large projects each received over £100,000 of Creative Scotland funding. These arts and cultural infrastructure projects received a total of £25,012,956 of Creative Scotland funding.[19]

The last Large Capital Project was awarded funding in January 2018. The programme ended during 2018/19, with 1 application contracted during the year: the redevelopment of the Fruitmarket Gallery in Edinburgh. (£1.3 million).

Over the course of the programme, £28.5 million has been invested in large scale capital projects throughout Scotland.[20]

Status as of December 2019

The Large Capital Fund is now closed to applications.

Previously the Large Capital funding supported organisations to improve, refurbish and/or develop cultural facilities which offered enhanced access to, or the presentation and enjoyment of, the arts and film. The programme also provided funding for the renewal and refreshment of equipment. The National Performing Companies and Collections were only able to apply by invitation.

The 2013/14 budget available for Large Capital projects was £15 million and a maximum total award to a single project of £2 million. An application submission deadline was given for all Stage 1 applications.

Capital funding was allocated in two stages:

Stage 1: applications are required to outline their proposal against the purpose of the fund. This includes the design proposal developed to at least RIBA Plan of Work (Stage B) covering the outline capital costs, evidence of approach to environmental sustainability and a risk assessment.

If successful, initial development funding is awarded to enable applicants to develop their proposals. At this point funding for the project delivery and start-up costs are earmarked. The applicant is supported to develop their proposals, including attending a two -day induction. The maximum award is £100,000 and will not be more than 50% of the total costs. The rest will need to be met by match funding.

Stage 2: applications include a fully developed and costs design proposal, comprehensive Business Plan and Artist Plan. In addition to information on accessibility and environmental sustainability. The award is towards the capital costs of delivery of the project and for up to £100,000 of start-up operational and programming costs for up to three years, but again for not more than 50% of the total costs.

The stated purpose of the Large Capital Fund was:

'To provide and improve cultural facilities, refurbishment, and equipment which deliver access to, and presentation and enjoyment of, the arts and film across the country for the population of Scotland. The programme aims to achieve high standards of design.
It is not the purpose of the Capital Programme to enable uses for unused or problem buildings. We will always support a vision of a project that seeks to fulfil an evidenced need, rather than focus on a building's development for its own sake.'[21]

The Large Capital – application Guidelines 2013-14 document does not include any information on the Stage 2 application requirements.

Creative Scotland in 2019 had £30m budgeted in the Large Capital Programme for projects which are at various stages of development. These projects, which will improve and develop the infrastructure for the arts across the country from Dumfries to Aberdeen, are set to come to fruition over the next 3 to 4 years.

They are currently reviewing previous capital investments and looking to what the future needs for the arts in Scotland are likely to be.

Creative Scotland commissioned a historical review of capital infrastructure for arts and culture created with the help of Lottery funding in Scotland in July 2019. The findings of this research have yet to be published.

Creative Scotland are continuing to support smaller capital projects through the Open Project Fund. Applicants can apply for up to £100k (in exceptional circumstances and with prior permission, up to £150k), for projects for which the total costs are estimated not to exceed £200k.

(See Appendix B for further information)

WALES
Arts Council of Wales (ACW) Activity

The Arts Council of Wales - Cyngor Celfyddydau Cymru - is an independent charity, established by Royal Charter in 1994. They are also a Welsh Public Sector Organisation. Their Council members, independent trustees, are appointed by the Welsh Government. They are Wales' only national funding and development organisation for the arts.

Their principle sponsor is the Welsh Government. They are also responsible for the administration and distribution of funds raised by the National Lottery and raise additional money from a variety of public and private sector sources.

The National Assembly for Wales/Welsh Government is regarded as a related party and details of transactions with the National Assembly for Wales/Welsh Government are given in the separate accounts covering the Council's general activities.

The National Lottery Distribution Fund is administered by the Department for Culture, Media and Sport which is regarded as a related party. During the year the Council had no material transactions with the Department for Culture, Media and Sport.

For 2015/16 they received around £19million from the National Lottery. The Arts Council of Wales receives 1% of the funds earmarked for the Good Causes across the UK. Their share is fixed, although actual income received varies according to Lottery ticket sales.

Grant funding is allocated in three ways:
1. **Revenue funding:** This is the funding to key strategically important organisations across Wales who present a year-round programme of work and depend on Arts Council funding to secure their core costs. This Portfolio of revenue funded organisations are reviewed every five years. There were 67 organisations in the portfolio in 2017/18
2. **Project funding:** There are a number of open application funding programmes ranging from events to major capital awards.
3. **Tendering:** Where the Arts Council is trying to achieve a specific outcome and seeking the best organisations to deliver this, they will undertake a procurement exercise.

In 2018 ACW published *For the benefit of all...* Arts Council of Wales Corporate Plan 2018-2023. The plan is based on two priorities. The first is developing the capability and potential of those working in the arts, helping artists and arts organisations to do their best work. The second is about diversity, equality and inclusion.[22]

Cyngor Celfyddydau Cymru
Arts Council of Wales

This, along with all other funding bodies corporate plans and strategies, will need to be reviewed to address the impact of Covid-19.

Capital Investment

From March 1995 to 2019 the Arts Council of Wales has funded 13,813 projects throughout Wales and distributed £294m of Lottery funding.

> 'New landmark buildings have opened to the public including the Wales Millennium Centre, Galeri Caernarfon, Riverfront, Newport, Pontio, Bangor and most recently Ty Pawb in Wrexham *(Chapter 9 Case Study)*. There have also been a number of important refurbishment projects which have brought new life to old buildings - the Glynn Vivian Art Gallery in Swansea, Theatr Mwldan in Cardigan, Valleys Kids in Tonypandy, Arad Goch in Aberystwyth and Mostyn in Llandudno. National Lottery funding has reached across all corners many parts of Wales and helped us create spaces for people to enjoy and take part in the arts where previously there were few opportunities.'[23]

The principal activity during 2017-18 was monitoring delivery against the Council's five year Capital Development strategy (2012-17). A reported milestone was the opening of Ty Pawb in Wrexham, the

> 'culmination of a decade or more of careful advocacy and development.'[24]

Capital Funding

The investment from the National Lottery in capital building projects has helped organisations to enhance and extend their activities by creating appropriate buildings and physical environments within which to deliver their work.

Capital grants are only available to organisations and can

'support the purchase, improvement, resto-ration, building or creation of an asset that will be used for the benefit of the public to develop the organisation's work.'[25]

The reduction in Lottery funding is expected to continue:

Arts Council Wales share of proceeds from the National Lottery

2017-18	£16,351,000
2016-17	£16,300,000[26]
2015-16	£19,233,000[27]

The above figures represent the total of Lottery funding, much of which is distributed via dele-gation agreements in place with the following bodies:
- Ffilm Cymru Wales for film
- Nesta for Digital Red projects
- BBC Cymru Wales for the Horizons scheme
- Literature Wales for writers' bursaries
- Ty Cerdd for amateur music

For all of the Lottery distributors there is a contingent asset – the sale of the Olympic Park. The National Lottery Distributors are entitled to receive a share of receipts from the sale of land on Queen Elizabeth Olympic Park in return for their contribution of an additional £675m to the funding of the London 2012 Olympic and Paralympic Games. This was announced in 2007. The arrangements are set out in a legal agreement between the Secretary of State for DCMS and the Greater London Authority (GLA), dated 29 March 2012 which sets out the distribution of funds between the GLA and the Lottery Distributors via the DCMS. Land sales are likely to take place over a lengthy period, estimated to be from 2018-19 to 2036-37. DCMS estimates the first payments to the Lottery Distributors to come through around 2020-21.[28]

Capital scheme value of grants

2017-18	£1,607,000
2016-17	£2,192,000[29]
2015-16	£2,640,000[30]

Arts Council Wales ring-fenced £22m for the capital grants programme from 2012-13 to 2016-17. They then extended this into 2017-18 due to the long lead in time from the applica-tion submission to the issue of a formal offer. This has an impact on the total value of grants made each year. For 2017-18 they expected to make capital grants of around £4m but offered £1.6m, which is reflected in the reduction in net grants made compared with the previous year.

'With support from our expert Capital Committee, we work with officers to ensure that the projects we support are fit for purpose and financially viable. Capital projects can often be complex, and develop over a period of many years. Our compre-hensive processes for feasibility, design, procurement and build ensures that projects are well-conceived and planned.'[31]

All capital projects are expected to meet Building Research Establishment Environmental Assessment Method (BREEAM) sustainability standards.

The Arts Council of Wales holds a framework of advisers for the provision of construc-tion expertise that may be required by Arts Council during their decision-making on capi-tal investments (assessment and monitoring). Generally the advisors have been an architect paired with a quantity surveyor, who then work closely with the officers. An Arts Council officer participates in all selection procedures.

The large-scale capital application process was a 3-stage application, assessment and award process:

Stage 1:	RIBA Stages 0-3 feasibility
Stage 2:	RIBA Stages 3-4 design development
Stage 3:	RIBA Stages 4-7 construction.

Status as of December 2019

The capital programme for major projects is currently closed.

'We don't have the resources to fund all of them, so we have decided to prioritise members of Arts Portfolio Wales. By focus-ing our Capital Lottery funding on support-ing members of Arts Portfolio Wales we're making sure that there's a joined-up approach to arts development and growth for the key arts organisations in Wales. In exceptional circumstances we may consider funding an organisation outside of Arts Portfolio Wales that has a strategic role to play in addressing our priorities, or that we consider to be of major local, stra-tegic importance. If you think your organ-isation meets this description you must discuss this with us before planning a Capital Lottery application.

The majority of our capital budget has now been allocated and we are no longer able to accept applications for funding towards new major capital projects. Our capital programme for major projects (including public art initiatives) is therefore now closed. We will not be registering any new projects for the foreseeable future.'[32]

In the face of the underlying trend of reducing levels of Lottery income for the good causes, Arts Council Wales undertook a detailed strategic review which has led to a focusing of their spending plans for the future. They have undertaken a major consultation of the Lottery programme (Nov 2018 – Feb 2019). This coincided with the publication of their new corporate plan *"For the Benefit of All..."*

They are also undertaking an Investment Review in 2020 to look at the Lottery and Revenue funding streams and how these might work better for the Portfolio Organisations.[33] Their stated actions include:

'We will...
Ensure that we communicate our decision-making process in a more effective way.
Our new programme Guidelines will include a step-by-step guide to the assessment process, and all criteria will be clearly explained. We're also looking at how we will involve external stakeholders in our decision-making. Demonstrating that all applications are subject to a fair and open process is fundamental to good governance and accountability.'[34]

'Although our Capital Programme is closed to any major new projects, we recognise that we need to consider the maintenance of a very focussed programme which can offer support to some of the areas noted above. As Lottery funding has declined in real terms, the budget will be relatively modest and any projects supported will clearly need to be aligned with the three priority areas.'[35]

'We will...
• Establish a modest Capital investment programme with a clear focus on environmental sustainability and efficiency, improving physical access in all areas, improving financial and operational resilience.
• Work with other partners to explore how we can help increase access to workspaces for artists and smaller organisations
• Undertake a feasibility study to explore an equipment loan scheme.'[36]

A common theme which emerged both in the public consultation meetings and through the written responses is the need for more support from the Arts Council throughout the application process. There is clearly a desire for Officers to be more visible and to offer clear, practical and consistent advice and support through face to face dialogue.[37]

'We will...
• Undertake a root and branch review of the current process which aims to simplify and streamline
• Replace the current 'strands' with are more open format guided by the 3 key principles of our Corporate plan
• Devise a new entry-level programme for first time applicants
• Amend the current small grant banding 'cap' from £5,000 to £10,000, and explore the financial implications of raising the upper cap on larger applications above £30,000
• Introduce structured professional support for disabled applicants
• Ensure that our Officers are available to provide advice and support throughout the application process.'[38]

There is no further detail on the proposed changes at this time.

(See Appendix C for further information)

NORTHERN IRELAND
Arts Council of Northern Ireland (ACNI) Activity

The Arts Council of Northern Ireland (Arts Council) is the statutory body through which public funding for the arts in Northern Ireland is channelled. It was established by the Arts Council (Northern Ireland) Order 1995 and came into existence on 1 September 1995. The Arts Council took over the assets and liabilities of the Arts Council of Northern Ireland Limited which was a company limited by guarantee established in 1994 as an interim body between the previous Arts Council (established in 1943) and the new statutory body.

The origins of the 1943 Arts Council date from when the Council for the Encouragement of Music and the Arts in Northern Ireland was set up. Initially funds were provided by the Pilgrim Trust and matched by the Ministry of Education for Northern Ireland. At the present time the Arts Council is funded via grant-in-aid by the Department for Communities (DfC).

Statutory Background

The National Lottery was established by the National Lottery etc. Act 1993, as amended by the 1998 Act, to raise money for 'good causes' through the sale of lottery tickets.

The National Lottery Distribution Fund (NLDF) was established in 1994 to receive and hold monies generated by the National Lottery for good causes. Section 21 of the National Lottery etc. Act 1993 places the NLDF under the control and management of the Secretary of State for Digital, Culture, Media and Sport (DCMS).

The Arts Council of Northern Ireland is charged under the Act with responsibility for distributing Lottery proceeds allocated to the arts in Northern Ireland. Lottery proceeds are also distributed through other distributing bodies to Sport, National Heritage, Charities, and to the Arts in England, Scotland and Wales.

DCMS manage the flow of funds between Camelot (the operator of the National Lottery) and the distributing bodies. DCMS seek annual assurances from the Accounting Officer of each lottery distributing body that they have in place adequate systems of internal control and have complied with the current Financial Directions.

The Arts Council is responsible for the administration and distribution of funds raised by the National Lottery. The Board made its first awards to applicants for Lottery funding in 1995-96. The principal function is to fund applications for a broad range of capital and revenue projects in the Arts which will make an important and lasting difference to the quality of life of the people in Northern Ireland.

The Arts Council also provides funding for a number of key arts organisations through its Annual Funding Programme (AFP). This is the most significant funding for the arts in Northern Ireland each year. In 2020 £12.9m was awarded to 97 key organisations from its exchequer and National Lottery resources. The non-lottery funding is allocated by the DfC in Northern Ireland.[39]

Capital Investment

The Arts Council Northern Ireland (ACNI) Capital Build Programme began in 1994. Since then, ACNI has distributed over £70m of capital funding to establish a wide range of dedicated cultural venues in towns and cities across Northern Ireland. As a result, Northern Ireland has enjoyed a period of sustained investment in the physical infrastructure of the Arts on a scale never seen before.

In total, 39 projects (from 1994 to 2008) received funding for new-build capital works or refurbishment and renovation.

Status as of December 2019

'In light of capital resources from the National Lottery having diminished and the total fund available now standing at approximately £1m per annum, the Arts Council of Northern Ireland has taken the decision to prioritise minor works, refurbishment and equipment applications under its capital programme from now until further notice.'[40]

(See Appendix D for further information)

NATIONAL LOTTERY HERITAGE FUND
The National Lottery Heritage Fund (NLHF) Activity

The parent body is the National Heritage Memorial Fund (NHMF).[41] The NHMF allocates Lottery funds to heritage: The National Lottery Heritage Fund is the distributor.

In recent years the organisation has changed names from the Heritage Lottery Fund (HLF) to the National Heritage Memorial Fund (NHMF) and is now called the National Lottery Heritage Fund, abbreviated to Heritage Fund. The Heritage Fund covers the whole of the UK.

The NHMF
> '...champions, develops and invests in artistic and cultural experiences that enrich people's lives. We support a range of activities across the arts, museums and libraries - from theatre to digital art, reading to dance, music to literature, and crafts to collections. Great art and culture inspires us, brings us together and teaches us about ourselves and the world around us. In short, it makes life better."

Between 2015 and 2018, they will invest £1.1 billion of public money from government and an estimated £700 million from the National Lottery to
> 'help create art and culture experiences for everyone, everywhere.'[42]

The National Lottery Heritage Fund Strategic Funding Framework 2019-2024 sets out their vision and the principles that will guide National Lottery investment for the next five years.[43]

The National Heritage Memorial Fund Structure

The National Heritage Memorial Fund (NHMF or 'the Fund') is vested in, and administered by, a corporate body known as the Trustees of the National Heritage Memorial Fund. This consists of a Chair and not more than 14 other members appointed by the Prime Minister.

The Fund was set up on 1 April 1980 by the National Heritage Act 1980 (the 1980 Act) in succession to the National Land Fund as a memorial to those who have given their lives for the United Kingdom (UK). It receives an annual grant-in-aid from the government to allow it to make grants.

The powers of the trustees and their responsibilities were extended by the provisions of the National Lottery etc. Act 1993 (the 1993 Act), the National Heritage Act 1997 (the 1997 Act) and the National Lottery Act 1998 (the 1998 Act).

Under the 1993 Act NHMF became responsible for the distribution of the proportion of National Lottery proceeds allocated to heritage. NHMF has to prepare separate accounts for the receipt and allocation of grant-in-aid and for its operation as a distributor of National Lottery money. Trustees have chosen to refer to the funds as NHMF for sums allocated under the provisions of the 1980 Act and HLF for receipts under the provisions of the 1993 Act.

Under section 21(1) of the 1993 Act a fund known as the National Lottery Distribution Fund (NLDF) is maintained under the control and management of the Secretary of State for the Department of Digital, Culture, Media and Sport. All sums received from the licensee of the National Lottery under section 5(6) are paid to the Secretary of State for Digital, Culture, Media and Sport and placed into the NLDF. NHMF applies to the NLDF for funds to meet its liabilities for Lottery grant payments and administration expenses.

Under section 22 of the 1993 Act, the Secretary of State for Digital, Culture, Media and Sport shall allocate 20% of the sum paid into the NLDF for expenditure on, or connected with, the national heritage.

Section 23(3) establishes the trustees of NHMF as distributors of that portion. The percentage allocation was reduced to 16% in October 1997 following the government's creation of the New Opportunities Fund. It reverted to 20% from 1 April 2012, having been 18% for the whole of 2011-12.

The National Lottery Heritage Fund has 6 area offices where their officers lead the day-to-day relationship with heritage organisations including the delivery of National Lottery Project Grants.

For applications of up to £100,000 the decisions are made on a monthly basis at Area/County-delegated decision meetings. For applications between £100,000 and £5million the decisions are made by committees in Northern Ireland, Wales and across England. These meet every three months. For awards

HERITAGE FUND

over £5million the decisions are made by the Board of Trustees who meet nine times a year.[44]

Capital Investment

The National Lottery Heritage Fund is the largest dedicated grant funder of the UK's heritage. Since 1994, they have awarded over £8bn to more than 44,000 projects across the UK.

National Lottery funding by heritage sector since 1994 to 2019 is:

Heritage Area Historic buildings & monuments	37%
Museums, libraries, archives & collections	29%
Nature and landscapes	22%
Industrial, maritime and transport	7%
Intangible heritage	4%
Community heritage	1%

(introduced as a category in 2012)

NLHF operates two funds: its original grant-in-aid fund (NHMF) and its National Lottery distribution activities (HLF). It is required, by the accounts' direction of the Secretary of State for Digital, Culture, Media and Sport, to report these activities separately and so no consolidated accounts are prepared. This review discusses solely the activities of NHMF's National Lottery distribution work.

'NLHF receives National Lottery applications from thousands of organisations across all communities of the UK and awards grants on the basis of its aims. Since the National Lottery started in 1994 we have received over 80,000 applications requesting £22.8billion. During that time we have made over 50,000 awards with a value just over £8bn resulting in over 123,000 grant payments to a value of £6.1bn.'[45]

'Lottery income fell from £388m to £327m in 2016-17, but remained steady at £328m in 2017-18.'[46]

Their capital investment is funded from both central government and the National Lottery. The capital investment in individual projects varies in scale depending on the available budget set in each funding period, but it is typically in the region of £100,000 to £5m.

Over the period 2015-2018, they committed over £120m to roughly 122 capital projects. Many of these remain in the various stages of the design and construction process.

In 2020, they have budgeted £11.3m for capital grants between £100,000 and £499,999 and £30m for grants from £500k and above.

NHMF also act as a fund holder administering grants for the Department for Digital, Culture, Media and Sport.

Funding beyond 2020 is subject to the spending review settlement from Government and confirmation of National Lottery income.

Capital Funding

The National Lottery Heritage Fund supports capital investment through several funding programmes to support the delivery of their strategy. In March 2020 these comprise heritage grants of varying scales:

£3000	to	£10,000
£10,000	to	£100,000
£100,000	to	£250,000
£250,000	to	£5m

Grants of £5m and over – Heritage Horizon Awards
Heritage Enterprise awards.

All of these contain elements of capital funding. Prior to 2020 the capital programme was made up of:
National Lottery Project Grants: capital investment may form part of an application for project activity and investment is typically less than £100,000. The programme is managed as a rolling programme with no deadlines for applications.
Capital Investment Programme: usually split into two application processes:

Small capital grants: from £100,000 and £499,999. The programme is typically managed as one round per year which includes an Expressions of Interest phase followed by a full application.

Large Capital grants: from £500,000 and above which is managed as a two-stage process. The programme is typically managed as a single round over a two to three year period.

The National Heritage Memorial Fund grant decision-making process is outlined below:

'Stage One: Organisations tell us about their capital project and how they plan to contribute to our goals and priorities. We use this information to decide whether to invite organisations to make a Stage Two application. We may award development funding to support the development of their Stage Two application. Projects are expected to be developed to at least Stage 1 (RIBA Plan of Work 2013) to submit a Stage One application.

Stage Two: Organisations complete a detailed application to secure a grant within eighteen months of our Stage One decision. Projects are expected to be developed to at least Stage 3 (RIBA Plan of Work 2013).'

NLHF also receives funding specifically from DCMS to deliver specific programmes or projects on their behalf.

Status as of December 2019

£100m of National Lottery funding will be given to 'transformational' heritage projects over the next three years (2020-22). The National Lottery Heritage Fund has unveiled plans to make awards of £5m and over, with £50m to be allocated in 2020 and a further £50m in 2022. The organisation says applications from a wide range of heritage projects are welcome, but all projects will need to have substantial proposals for recognising the funding contribution made by The National Lottery – which for the first time could include naming rights.[47]

To assist the officers, the NLHF appoint a team of Construction Advisors, primarily project managers. An open procurement process was undertaken: National Heritage Memorial Fund – Register of Support Services 2018-22 – Construction Project Management Services.

(See Appendix E for further information)

EU FUNDING

Historic England commissioned Euclid to find out how much money from EU sources has been invested in England's heritage between 2007-16. The report concluded that heritage focussed or related projects received a minimum of £450m in EU funding during 2007-2016.[48]

The publication aligns with similar reports for Creative Scotland and Museums Galleries Scotland.[49]

Creative Scotland commissioned Euclid to identify EU funded projects focused on or linked to the arts, media and creative industries across the last ten years. The report estimates at least £23m has been awarded to over 380 arts, media and creative industries projects during 2007-17.[50]

However the majority of that funding was for activities and revenue as opposed to capital funding.

The DCMS has confirmed that the UK will not try to stay in the Creative Europe scheme which had awarded 20.9m Euros (£19.2m) to projects involving British organisations in 2019 alone.

References:

1   National Lottery website www.lotterygood-causes.org.uk *(accessed 22 May 2020)*

2   *Lottery arts funding up £30m. Arts Professional 16 Nov. 2018. www.artsprofessional.co.uk/news/lottery-arts-funding-ps30m (accessed 22 May 2020)*

3   *Arts Council Annual Report & Accounts 2018/19, Arts Council England, Grant-in-Aid and National Lottery Distribution 2017/18. p.171. Contingent assets, point 22. www.artscouncil.org.uk/sites/default/files/download-file/ Arts%20Council%20annual%20report%2017-18%20-%20 Web%20version.pdf (accessed 22 May 2020)*

4   *The London Assembly's budget and performance committee findings reported in: ''Olympic Park could become 'costly disaster', mayor of London warned' Z. Garner-Purkis, W. Ing AJ. 21 January 2021. www.architectsjournal.co.uk/news/ olympic-park-could-become-costly-disaster-mayor-of-london-warned#comment-10230 (accessed 21 January 2021*

5   *Private Investment in Culture Survey. Arts Council England and MTM. 1 Dec. 2016 ISBN 978-0-7287-1569-1. www.artscouncil.org.uk/publication/private-investment-culture-survey (accessed 22 May 2020)*

6   *Financial sustainability of local authorities 2018. NAO 8 March 2018 HC 834 session 2017-2019. www.nao.org. uk/wp-content/uploads/2018/03/Financial-sustainabilty-of-local-authorites-2018.pdf (accessed 22 May 2020)*

7   *Arts Council England EU Exit Guide, updated 1 Oct 2019 www.artscouncil.org.uk/sites/default/files/download-file/Arts%20Council%20England%20Brexit%20Guide%20 -%20October%202019.pdf (accessed 22 May 2020)*

8   *Cultural Cities Enquiry, Core Cities, Feb. 2019. p.30 sponsored by Core Cities, Key Cities, Arts Council England, Arts Council of Wales, Creative Scotland and Belfast City Council, and supported by London Councils and Arts Council Northern Ireland. Research partners were BOP Consulting and Oxford Economics. www.corecities.com/sites/default/ files/field/attachment/Cultural%20Cities%20Enquiry%20 %5Bweb%5D.pdf (accessed 22 May 2020)*

9   *ibid. Cultural Cities Enquiry p.30*

10   *DCMS/Wolfson Museums and Galleries Improvement Fund 2018-20. Department for Culture Media & Sport and The Wolfson Foundation March 2018. assets. publishing.service.gov.uk/government/uploads/system/ uploads/attachment_data/file/698973/DCMS_Wolfson_ Guidance_for_Bidders_2018-20__1_.pdf (accessed 28 November 2019)*

11   *ACE website, www.artscouncil.org.uk/about-us-0 (accessed 22 May 2020)*

12   *Let's Create Strategy 2020_2030 Arts Council England, 2021 (sic) p. 77 www.artscouncil.org.uk/sites/ default/files/download-file/Strategy%202020_2030%20 Arts%20Council%20England_SP.pdf (accessed 22 May 2020 Arts Council England, Grant-in-Aid and National Lottery Distribution 2018/19 Annual Report & Accounts. © Arts Council England, 2018 ISBN 978-1-5286-1379-8 p.103. www.artscouncil.org.uk/publication/arts-council-england-grant-aid-and-lottery-distribution-annual-report-and-accounts-2 (accessed 28 May 2020)*

13   *Cultural Development Fund www.artscouncil.org. uk/funding-finder/cultural-development-fund (accessed 22 May 2020)*

14   *ibid. ACE, 2017/18 Annual Report & Accounts*

15   *Arts Council National Lottery Project Grants, Capital (buildings) projects. August 2019. pp 3-6 www. artscouncil.org.uk/sites/default/files/download-file/ACPG_ Capital_buildings_projects09082019_0.pdf (accessed 22 May 2020)*

16   *Arts Council Development Funds www.artscouncil.org.uk/our-investment/arts-council-development-funds (accessed 27 June 2020)*

17   *Creative Scotland National Lottery Distribution Fund, Annual Report and Accounts for the year ended 31 March 2019, ISBN 978-1-5286-1675-1, Creative Scotland 2019. www.creativescotland.com/__data/assets/pdf_ file/0009/77670/CCS001_CCS1019353416-001_Scot-National-Lottery-Distribution-Fund-ARA-2018-19_PRINT.pdf (accessed 22 May 2020)*

18   *Creative Scotland website www.creativescotland. com/ (accessed 22 May 2020)*

19   *Public contracts scotland. Tender document for a historical: 'Review of Capital Infrastructure for Arts & Culture created with Lottery funding in Scotland.' for Creative Scotland. Notice Ref. MAY355031, 23 May 2019 www.public-contractsscotland.gov.uk/search/show/search_view.aspx-?ID=MAY355031 (accessed 28 May 2020)*

20   *Creative Scotland National Lottery Distribution Fund, Annual Report and Accounts for the year ended 31 March 2019. Creative Scotland November 2019. ISBN 978-1-5286-1675-1. www.creativescotland.com/__data/assets/ pdf_file/0009/77670/CCS001_CCS1019353416-001_Scot-National-Lottery-Distribution-Fund-ARA-2018-19_PRINT.pdf (accessed 22 May 2020)*

21   *Large Capital − Application Guidelines 2013-14 v1-5, p.1 Creative Scotland. www.creativescotland.com/funding/archive/large-capital (accessed 22 May 2020)*

22   *For the benefit of all... Arts Council of Wales. Corporate Plan 2018 - 2023. Arts Council of Wales 2018. https://arts.wales/sites/default/files/2019-02/Corporate_ Plan_2018-23.pdf (accessed 28 May 2020)*

23   *Transformation and change: A new National Lottery strategy for the Arts Council of Wales. Arts Council of Wales June 2019. Foreword. arts.wales/sites/default/ files/2019-06/Transformation%20and%20change_0.pdf (accessed 22 May 2020)*

24   *Arts Council of Wales Lottery Distribution Account 2017-18. July 2018. ISBN: 978-1-5286-0655-4. p.40. senedd. cymru/laid%20documents/agr-ld11698/agr-ld11698-w.pdf (accessed 22 May 2020)*

25   *ibid. ACW Accounts 2017-18. p.20*

26   *ibid. ACW Accounts 2017-18. p.67*

27   *Arts Council of Wales Lottery Distribution Account 2016-17. July 2017 ISBN: 978-1-910305-73-7. p.62. senedd. wales/laid%20documents/agr-ld11138/agr-ld11138-w.pdf (accessed 22 May 2020)*

28   *ibid. ACW Accounts 2017-18 p.66, item 10*

29   *ibid. ACW Accounts 2017-18. p.21*

30   *ibid. ACW Accounts 2016-17. p.18*

31   *ibid. ACW Accounts 2016-17. p.14*

32   *Arts Council of Wales website, arts.wales/capital-funding (accessed 22 May 2020)*

33   Transformation and change: A new National Lottery strategy for the Arts Council of Wales. Arts Council of Wales June 2019. arts.wales/resources/transformation-and-change-new-national-lottery-strategy-for-arts-council-wales (accessed 22 May 2020)

34   ibid. ACW Strategy. p.19

35   ibid. ACW Strategy. p.23

36   ibid. ACW Strategy. p.23

37   ibid. ACW Strategy. p.24

38   ibid. ACW Strategy. p.25

39   Arts Council of Northern Ireland website. artscouncil-ni.org/news/acni-awards-12.9million-in-grants-to-sustain-key-arts-organisations?utm_source=NewZapp&utm_medium=email&utm_campaign=06_April_2020 (accessed 22 May 2020)

40   ACNI Press release, 14 July 2004. http://artscouncil-ni.org/news/announcement-on-arts-council-of-northern-ireland-capital-programme (accessed 22 May 2020)

41   National Heritage Memorial Fund www.nhmf.org.uk/ (accessed 27 June 2020)

42   Heritage Fund website www.heritagefund.org.uk/ (accessed 22 May 2020)

43   Inspiring, leading and resourcing the UK's heritage. The National Lottery Heritage Fund Strategic Funding Framework 2019–2024 www.heritagefund.org.uk/sites/default/files/media/attachments/Heritage%20Fund%20-%20Strategic%20Funding%20Framework%202019-2024.pdf (accessed 28 May 2020)

44   National Lottery Fund, National Heritage Memorial Fund Distribution, Annual Report and Accounts for the year ended 31 March 2018. ISBN: 978-1-5286-0600-4. assets.publishing.service.gov.uk/government/uploads/system/uploads/attachment_data/file/731175/Heritage_Lottery_Fund_ARA_2017-18.pdf (accessed 22 May 2020)

45   ibid NLF, NHMF Accounts. p.6

46   ibid NLF, NHMF Accounts. p.8

47   Heritage Horizon Awards: grants of £5million and over www.heritagefund.org.uk/funding/heritage-horizon-awards (accessed 28 May 2020)

48   Assessing the European Union's contribution to England's historic environment. Euclid Report, Feb 2017. p.2. historicengland.org.uk/content/docs/research/assessing-eu-contribution-to-englands-historic-environment-pdf/ (accessed 22 May 2020)

49   Assessing the European Union's contribution to the arts, media and creative industries in Scotland. Euclid, May 2017. www.creativescotland.com/__data/assets/pdf_file/0020/41753/EUFundstoScotlandCS-FINAL.pdf and Assessing the European Union's Contribution to the museums and galleries sector in Scotland. Euclid.for Museums Galleries Scotland. June 2017. www.museumsgalleriesscotland.org.uk/media/1317/eu-funding-research-report.pdf (accessed 22 May 2020)

50   ibid. EU arts, media and creative industries in Scotland. Euclid Report. p.2

fig. 13.1
The MAC (Metropolitan Arts Centre) Belfast
© Bridget Sawyers

14 Funding Bodies'
Current Procurement Guidance

Referencing current UK and nationally identified commissioning guidance, documents and advisory publications, providing options for clients and national characteristics.

REVIEW OF AUTHORITIES STRATEGIES

UK's Arts Councils, Creative Scotland and National Lottery Heritage Fund most recent guidance documents on the capital funding of projects were reviewed, along with those relating to recently completed projects which were still available. The review revealed many common themes across all funding bodies. Guidance to assist applicants is however offered in different formats, providing different levels of information and support, and with varying degrees of detail.

The complexity of funding applications are typically proportionate, with increasing requirements and stagings relating to funds being sought, with variable degrees of guidance, support and its accessibility.

In late 2019 the guidance available to the applicants was also clearly impacted by the level of funding available from each body, but in some instances, the documents were written a few years ago for previous funding rounds specifically when funding for capital projects was greater.

The source documents and guidance notes were accurate as of December. 2019 except where otherwise noted.

In April 2020 the situation changed dramatically with the Covid-19 virus and the resulting impact on arts organisations, Lottery ticket sales and the development and delivery of projects. All of the funding bodies responded with restructuring of their available funding to provide emergency resources and opportunities for digital and online project funding, and measures in response are anticipated to be ongoing.

ARTS COUNCIL ENGLAND

Overview of Guidance

Since 1994, ACE has supported capital developments with £1.5 billion of Lottery funding. This investment has supported an unprecedented number of building projects, refurbishment and extensions to existing arts buildings, as well as new buildings across the country.

ACE will publish their new strategy in Spring 2020 which will set out their plans for future capital investment. The large capital grants programme is currently closed.

Between 2015-18 the ACE's capital investment has prioritised the consolidation and improvement of the existing arts infrastructure, rather than investing in significant expansion or new buildings. They supported organisations to develop resilience by having the right buildings and equipment to deliver their work and become more sustainable and innovative businesses. This included increasing the environmental performance of buildings and equipment to support a reduction in carbon emissions.[1]

Capital funding was allocated on the value of the project and the amount of funding required:
• Small Capital Grants
• Large capital Grants – no longer available

For both funding options, Arts Council England require the projects to support the delivery of their five goals (see below) by ensuring arts and cultural organisations have the right capital assets to support the delivery of their work.

In particular, capital investment is an important way of helping to deliver resilience (Goal 3).

Goals:

Goal 1: Excellence is thriving and celebrated in the arts, museums and libraries

Goal 2: Everyone has the opportunity to experience and be inspired by the arts, museums and libraries

Goal 3: The arts, museums and libraries are resilient and environmentally sustainable

Goal 4: The leadership and workforce in the arts, museums and libraries are diverse and appropriately skilled

Goal 5: Every child and young person has the opportunity to experience the richness of the arts, museums and libraries.

There are two stages to the funding awards: firstly Stage One; for which the applicant must have achieved RIBA workstage 3 for their project before applying for funding, and then Stage Two; to deliver the project..

Procurement

'You must comply with all applicable current UK public regulation procurement laws when buying any goods or services that will be used directly or indirectly in relation to the capital project. In relation to contracts for good or services, you must:
• *demonstrate that procedures to recruit consultants and contractors are fair and open and keep to the relevant legislation*
• *have quotations and tenders for contracts for goods or services available for inspection by us*
• *have contract appointment procedures available for inspection by us if requested before the terms and conditions of each appointment are agreed.'*

'In addition to our requirements set out above, your project may be covered by European Union (EU) procurement rules. You will need to follow the Public Procurement Regulations if your goods, works or services are above certain financial thresholds and if:
• *you are subject to the Public Procurement Regulations in your own right*
• *the amount of money given solely by Arts Council England, or in conjunction with other public funding or other lottery distributor, exceeds 50 per cent of your project costs.'[2]*

This means that all applicable services and construction works notices above EU Thresholds are tendered through the Official Journal of the European Union (OJEU).

Notices are not published consistently, either on the English national procurement portal 'Contracts Finder' or through the plethora of other private competing procurement website services, which diminishes access and transparency. Unlike in Wales, in England there is no requirement stated within the guidance to use the national procurement portal.

Guidance

Arts Council National Lottery Project Grants Capital investment: Large capital grants, Round 5 Guidance for stage two applicants.[3]

Arts Council National Lottery Project Grants Capital (buildings) projects, Arts Council National Lottery Project Grants is the open-access programme for arts, museums and libraries projects. Arts Council England, 12 Feb 2018.[4]

Arts Council England, Grant-in-Aid and National Lottery Distribution 2018/19 Annual Report & Accounts. Arts Council England, 2018.[5]

(Relevant sections of the ACE guidance notes and details can be found in Appendix A)

CREATIVE SCOTLAND

Overview of Guidance

The Large Capital Fund was closed to applications in 2019. Previously, Creative Scotland had a £30m budget in the Large Capital Programme for projects at various stages of development. These projects, which will improve and develop the infrastructure for the arts across the country, are set to come to fruition over the next two to three years.

Creative Scotland invites organisations who are planning a Large Capital project to contact them about their plans, however they also state that the position remains that they are not inviting any new proposals for support for Large Capital funding.

> 'We are currently reviewing previous capital investments and looking to what the future needs for the arts in Scotland are likely to be. If you are planning a Large Capital project we would be interested in hearing about your plans, so please contact us. Our position remains that we are not inviting any new proposals for support for Large Capital funding.'

In 2013/14 the lottery budget available for Large Capital projects was £15m. The Creative Scotland Large Capital Guidelines 2013/14 are the most recent guidelines available.[6]

The purpose of the fund was:
> 'To provide and improve cultural facilities, refurbishment, and equipment which deliver access to, and presentation and enjoyment of, the arts and film across the country for the population of Scotland. The programme aims to achieve high standards of design.

> 'It is not the purpose of the Capital Programme to enable uses for unused or problem buildings. We will always support a vision of a project that seeks to fulfil an evidenced need, rather than focus on a building's development for its own sake.'

> 'Our funds can be used for the following, if these meet the purpose of the fund:
> * The renewal and refreshment of equipment, or the enhancement of existing buildings, but not routine or cyclical repair and maintenance
> * The construction of new buildings'

ALBA | CHRUTHACHAIL

> 'We will consider the inclusion of the cost of the acquisition of buildings and sites, but only as part of a wider development proposal. Funds cannot be used for:
> * Cyclical repairs, maintenance or replacement where we consider this should have been dealt with as part of an ongoing replacement/ maintenance programme.'[7]

> 'We will offer funding as follows:
> * Towards the construction of new, and the enhancement of existing, buildings, and for equipment: with awards ranging from £100,000 to £2,000,000.
> * Costs associated with the development of proposals between Stage 1 and Stage 2. This can include, for example, design development, business planning, fundraising, etc. We will expect to contribute no more than 50% of these costs up to £100,000.
> * Time limited start-up operational and programme costs on opening/re-opening following the completion of a capital project to a maximum of three years post completion, tapering off over a period of months/years. We will expect to contribute no more than 50% of these costs. Our maximum contribution will be £100,000.'

The total award for all 3 elements above, could not come to more than £2m. They did not offer financial support before Stage 1 application, or retrospectively for pre-application costs.[8]

A specific deadline of 19 August 2013 was established for all Stage 1 applications.

The application requirements included:
* 'A detailed options appraisal that clearly demonstrates that you have explored alternative options and that proves there is a need for the proposed facility.
* A design proposal developed to at least RIBA, Stage B, Plan of Work.
* Appropriate drawn information, showing the scope of the works to be funded.
* Outline costs covering all aspects of the development and delivery of the capital project including a contingency for unforeseen costs.
* A comprehensive Risk Analysis covering the delivery of the project and the operation/management of the project after completion.

- *Evidence of a clear understanding of the need for a plan for your capital project within your organisation. We will need to see what actions/ provision you will take to manage the change process and the implications of such a plan on your resources both physical and financial.*
- *Evidence of good governance and management of your organisation, and your ability to deliver and manage the capital project, as well as managing your organisation after completion. You will need to provide us with details of the constitution and nature of your organisation, with names , skills and experience of your board members.*
- *Evidence of how you are adopting an approach to environmental sustainability in the construction of your project, its operation as well as throughout all your activities.*[9]

This potentially required a degree of input from specialist consultants at this stage, whose fees would need to be met by the applicant client.

To March 2020 Small capital projects were still available through the Open Project Fund for small capital funding up to £150,000 and 'Capital Programme – Large Capital' for a funding to a maximum of £2m. The current guidance for the Open Project Funding is relatively recent and was revised in August 2019.

The Open project fund does not support large scale capital development projects, such as costs for major renovations or building projects – and this includes any pre-application development costs (such as feasibility studies). They will accept applications for up to £100k towards a smaller capital or building project, provided the total costs (for the whole capital project) do not exceed £200k.[10]

Procurement

Notices for services are frequently published in Scotland through the Scottish Government's 'public contracts scotland' portal, a platform developed to improve procurement access and transparency. However this is not apparently a requirement stated in the guidance, and is not consistently undertaken.[11]

Creative Scotland's Large Capital Guidelines 2013/14 are the most recent capital guidelines available.

For applicants whose proposal is approved at Stage 1, Creative Scotland work with the application to develop their proposals towards a Stage 2 application, including a two-day induction to the programme.

There is no specific reference to procurement within the document, although there is a reference to environmental sustainability.

The guidance states that they expect applicants to take all reasonable steps for ensuring value for money when buying any assets, goods and services whereby the arts organisation have to demonstrate this by obtaining like-for-like quotations or applying competitive tendering.

Guidance

The Creative Scotland Large Capital Guidelines 2013/14 (now closed to applicants) are the most recent capital guidelines available.[12]

Creative Scotland Open Fund for Organisations: Sustaining Creative Development 2020/21. Application Guidance. Updated July 2020.[13]

In response to Covid 19, Creative Scotland provided an update to their Open Fund on 21 July 2020 to enable individuals and organisations to explore ways of working that will help them to adapt and respond to the current changing circumstances.[14]

ARTS COUNCIL OF WALES

Cyngor Celfyddydau Cymru
Arts Council of Wales

Overview of Guidance

The Arts Council of Wales' Capital Programme is currently closed to any major new projects.
'The majority of our capital budget has now been allocated and we are no longer able to accept applications for funding towards new major capital projects. Our capital programme for major projects (including public art initiatives) is therefore now closed. We will not be registering any new projects for the foreseeable future.'[15]

The Arts Council of Wales has a well structured series of guidance documents for applicants which remain current for projects still in development.[16]

This suite of guidance notes helps the applicant for an Arts Council of Wales funding and assisting the organisation to complete the forms properly and accurately with all the relevant information and attachments required for assessing the project.

These 'Help Notes' can be read as a "standalone" document or the applicant can follow the hyperlinks to look at specific sections of the notes as they fill in the form online. They should be read alongside the *General Guide to the Arts Council of Wales' Capital Programme and Capital Strategy 2012-17*.[17]

The guidance notes state that they refer to capital project funding in 2012-17 in their text, however, the date of publication for each is 2017. There do not appear to be any updates or new guidance publications/notes so it has been assumed that these remain the most current and relevant for giving advice to any prospective arts organisation looking for funding (as at December 2019).

The guidance notes are fundamentally divided into project types based on value i.e. Major Capital Projects over £100,000, and Minor Capital Projects below £100,000 and the different project stages. The stages relate to release of capital funds by Arts Council Wales, essentially in three parts: feasibility (Stage 1), design development (Stage 2) and construction (Stage 3).

Procurement

All procurement notices are required to be advertised in Wales through the Welsh Government's 'Sell2Wales' portal, a platform developed to help SMEs work successfully with the public sector.[18]

The *General Guide to the Arts Council of Wales' Capital Programme March 2017* provides an overview of the funding body, funding options, what is funded, and how to apply, and finally directs the applicant to the suite of guidance notes specific for the Capital project, size and stage. There is no direct mention of procurement in this document, instead the applicant is directed to the additional guidance.[19]

The definition of a major project is any project over £100,000.[20] Much of the required application submission information will be developing as the RIBA Work Stages 1-3 are undertaken and the project team should include professional consultants familiar with the project (building) requirements. Arts Council of Wales ask to be informed if there have been any changes to the project team since the completion of the design development phase (RIBA Stage 3 Developed Design), and why these changes were made.

The statutory obligations of the organisation and UK and EU procurement legislation are highlighted.[21] *Additional Guidance Notes Major Capital Projects 2017* contains more detailed information on each specific project stage. Reference is made to appointing the relevant consultants and the fact that the Arts Council of Wales will 'want to be involved in the appointment process'.[22] This is left open and could suggest it is more about compliance rather than assistance in the procurement. Again, when mentioning the appointment of professional consultants it is stated that the Arts Council of Wales would want to be 'involved in the appointment process.'[23]

The Arts Council of Wales want to see an options appraisal 'to evaluate the benefits and constraints of each option against your stated project aims', although it does not state how this is to be done. The opportunities will depend on the type of project and whether this is something done in-house or with an extended team of consultants. If appointment of a team of consultants is required there is a note on their procurement.[24]

There is also a broader section on procurement. *'Procurement means the way that you buy the goods and services needed to deliver your project. It covers all of the appointments you will make, including your design team and your building contractor, and also the way that you buy any new equipment for your project. When buying goods and services you must comply with all current UK and EU legislation on procurement that apply to your organisation and your project.'[25]*

This also provides a useful link for the uninitiated taking the applicant to the EU (OJEU) thresholds to determine current financial threshold values.[26]

The document comments on the appointment of the design team as individual appointments or as a whole team under one appointment, such as the architect, and that the organisation making the application should make it clear which route they are taking. It is also incumbent of the organisation to identify the duration of the contract.
'Regardless of the procurement process the guidance notes highlight the need to demonstrate that at all stages of the project's development the organisation has followed procedures that are fair, competitive and auditable and that they meet the relevant legislation.'[27]

There is no specific advice provided on procedures, contracts or how to manage the appointment of the design team for the project duration via break clauses in the contract or similar.

The Arts Council Wales employs independent specialist external advisers to assist the Arts Council Wales with independent advice on particular specialist areas:
'They include architects, quantity advisors, business advisers and public art specialists.'

'An external adviser will be involved in reviewing your completed feasibility study. When you submit your application for the implementation of your major capital project, a team of external advisers will be appointed to evaluate your application on our behalf. Each member of this team will complete a report, and this will be sent to you so that you can respond to its findings and identify any factual inaccuracies.'

The Additional Guidance Notes require that at least 1% of the construction cost be used for commissioning public art.[28] That applicants can consult with the Design Commission, including the Design Review Service, and the role of the Design Commission for Wales are highlighted.[29]

Applicants are furthermore required to appoint an appropriately qualified independent project manager to manage the construction project.
'We know that appointing an independent project manager will increase the cost of your project, but our experience of major capital projects shows that they are vital to their success.'[30]

The definition of a minor project is any project up to £100,000. The guidance for this references the appointment of professional consultants, directing the applicant to comply with all UK and EU legal requirements of commissioning goods and services especially for high value projects. It notes the OJEU procedures and requests that evidence is provided on the selection process to ensure the correct procurement procedures have been adhered to.[31]

In addition, the applicant must state how they 'will meet [their] statutory obligations during the construction phase with regards to:
- Building Regulations
- Health and Safety at Work
- Construction (Design and Management) Regulations (CDM) 2015
- The Control of Asbestos Regulations'

However, there is no advice in this document about how applicants should go about the appointment of consultants, but the guidance does invite contact with the Arts Council of Wales 'If you are unsure what information you need to submit with your application, please check with us'.[32]

Guidance

General Guide to the Arts Council of Wales' Capital Programme March 2017

Lottery Capital Programme, Additional Guidance Notes, Major Capital Projects. Arts Council of Wales, March 2017

Lottery Capital Programme Help Notes, Minor Capital Projects, Arts Council of Wales, 2017[33]

ARTS COUNCIL OF NORTHERN IRELAND

Overview of Guidance

The Arts Council of Northern Ireland has closed their Lottery Project Funding programme for 2019-20, which did not include funding for building design. Under the heading of project funding eligibility the Application Guidance Notes, published April 2019 state that you cannot apply for 'building design (architecture)'.[34]

The Small Grants Programme is ongoing, although it is for grants of up to £10k. It does not appear that capital funding includes any buildings or their designs.

The aim of this programme is to assist organisations to deliver arts projects which contribute to the growth of arts in the community for new and existing audiences, and which reflect the diversity of Northern Ireland's society and culture. Organisations currently in receipt of an Arts Council Annual Funding Programme award can apply for equipment and projects of 'an exceptional nature which were not anticipated at the time of their AFP (annual funding programme) application'.[35]

The Rural Needs Small Grants programme, also ongoing, excludes capital projects.

Guidance

Arts Council of Northern Ireland.[36]

Public Procurement Policy in Northern Ireland[37]

NATIONAL LOTTERY HERITAGE FUND

The National Lottery Heritage Fund's National Lottery Grants for Heritage is an open programme for all types of heritage projects in the UK. There are a range of funding programmes:

> Grants of £3,000 - £10,000
> Grants of £10,000 - £100,000
> Grants of £100,000 - £250,000
> Grants of £250,000 - £5 million
> Grants of £5m and over (Heritage Horizon Awards)
> Heritage Enterprise

All of the above include funding for repairs and conservation, purchase of heritage buildings, repair and adaptation of empty and derelict buildings, fit-out to a basic level (Category A), urgent repairs and new temporary structure to support meanwhile uses during the project development phase.

National Lottery Heritage Funding for less than £250,000 is generally split into a two-stage application process and includes a project enquiry form, to be completed first.

- **Stage 1** is about explaining the project and its suitability for funding. The project must have been developed to at least Stage 1 of the RIBA Plan of Work 2013 before submission.
- **Stage 2** is a detailed application about how the proposed project will be developed to completion. A project consultant will be allocated to each applicant awarded a grant to support the applicant in developing and delivering the project.

For the larger grants of over £250,000 there is a third stage. After development there is a requirement for a delivery phase application to be submitted.

The process requires the submission of an Expression of Interest Form, development phase application, and finally a delivery phase application. NLHF review the project at suitable stages coinciding with the payment schedule, including during the development phase at RIBA works stage 2. This is a point where if there are serious concerns which the applicant does not address, they may fail the review and NLHF will recommend that they do not apply for a delivery phase.

There is a suite of best practice guidance notes online: including on inclusion, environmental sustainability, project management tasks and writing a brief for the procurement of goods or services.[38]

Overview of Guidance

Grants for Heritage of £3,000 to £10,000:
- An initial online project enquiry form needs to be completed, and if the project meets the NLHF requirements then applicants are offered advice to help develop their project further.
- Applicants then submit the full online application. There is no further application stage and the grant is awarded in one tranche.[39]

Grants for Heritage £10,000 to £250,000: There is one guidance document setting out the requirements and application information for both scales of grants, although the processes are different with the grants for funding of over £100,000 being a longer and more detailed process.

Applicants are directed to the website, where more detailed information is available, including environmental sustainability, conservation plan guidance, management and maintenance plan guidance.

For both scales of grants an initial online project enquiry form needs to be completed, and if the project meets the NLHF requirements then applicants are offered advice to help develop their project further. Applicants then submit the full online application, to meet the relevant deadline if over £100,000, or if the value is less, at any time. There is no further application stage and the grant is awarded in one tranche.[40]

Grants for Heritage £250,000-£5 million: The Application Guidance, National Lottery Grants for Heritage £250,000-£5 million clearly sets out the application and assessment process.
- An initial online Expression of Interest form needs to be completed, and if the project meets the NLHF requirements then applicants are offered advice to help develop their project further.
- Applicants then submit the Development phase online application to meet one of the six annual deadlines.
- A final Delivery phase application is required to be submitted prior to commencement of any capital works.[41]

Heritage Horizon Awards: There is a total of £50m available in the first year (2020-21). The process is now closed to new applicants until the next round in 2022.

The concept behind Heritage Horizon Awards is:
> *"Backing big ideas, unlocking possibilities*
> *This means, we expect all projects to be:*
> - *transformative*
> - *innovative*
> - *collaborative*
> *We want you to show clear and ambitious plans for how the project will bring about positive changes and benefits to people, places and wider heritage. We expect you to have plans to share your learning from the project widely across the sector.'*

NLHF strategic priorities are:
- landscapes and nature
- heritage at risk

Again this is a three-stage process and the Application Guidance for National Lottery Grants for Heritage £250,000-£5m is also applicable for this fund.[42]

Heritage Enterprise Awards: The Heritage Enterprise process is for projects that
> *'...seek to achieve economic growth by investing in heritage'. It is aimed at enterprising community organisations and commercial organisations working in partnership with community organisations to help them rescue neglected historic buildings and sites and return them to a viable productive use.'*

> *'Heritage Enterprise is designed to bridge the funding gap that prevents a historic asset in need of repair from being returned to a beneficial and commercial use. The case for grant funding will depend on there being a conservation deficit. This is where the existing value of a heritage asset plus the cost of bringing it back into use is greater than the value of the asset after development has been completed'.[43]*

Applicants are required to submit an initial Expression of Interest (EOI) form and successful applicants are then invited to submit a development phase application, following which a delivery phase application and a delivery award for the project.

Procurement

The Heritage Enterprise, Grants from £250,000 to £5million, Application Guidance, sets out the guidance on buying goods, works and services and the need for at least three competitive quotes.[44] It also outlines:

'For all goods, works and services worth more than £50,000 (excluding VAT), you must provide proof of competitive tendering procedures. Your proof should be a report on the tenders you have received, together with your decision on which to accept. You must give full reasons if you do not select the lowest tender.'

'Your project may be covered by European Union (EU) procurement rules if it exceeds the thresholds noted below. This will require that all services for both fees and construction will need to be tendered through Tenders Direct, previously known as Official Journal of the European Union (OJEU).'

'If you are a non-public body, and your grant exceeds 50% of the estimated cost of a contract, or the grant together with other public funding exceeds 50% (e.g. ERDF, local authority, or other lottery distributors), and exceeds the thresholds noted below, you must adhere to EU Procurement Regulations.'

'The applicable thresholds can be found on the Cabinet Office website. Thresholds are reviewed annually in January. If you are a public body, different thresholds apply, and you will have to comply with those that are already relevant to you. The thresholds apply to all individual consultant appointments (or to the aggregate fee as a single appointment) and to construction works.'

'If you are looking to recruit a consultant or member of staff for your development phase and your delivery phase, you should make sure their contract clearly states that this is the case, and allow for break clauses (in case your delivery phase application is unsuccessful). If you do not, we may ask you to re-recruit after the delivery phase decision has been made.'

The HLF suite of best practice guidance notes, including for a template brief for the procurement of goods and services.[45]

For all other scales of grant the basic advice/requirements are the same:

'You must follow our procurement guidelines. As an overview, projects with any goods, works or services worth more than £10,000 (excluding VAT), must get at least three competitive tenders/quotes. For all goods, works and services worth more than £50,000 (excluding VAT), you must provide proof of competitive tendering procedures.'

'Your proof should be a report on the tenders you have received, together with your decision on which to accept. You must give full reasons if you do not select the lowest tender. Depending on the nature of your project you may be required to comply with European Procurement Rules and UK Public Procurement Regulations 2015.'

'If a project partner is providing goods or services paid for through the grant, then you need to tell us why they have been chosen and why an open tender process is not appropriate. We will consider whether this is the best way to carry out your project and expect you to show value for money and meet any relevant legal requirements.'[46]

'If you are unsure about your obligations, we advise you to take professional or legal advice. If you have already procured goods, works or services for the project that are worth more than £10,000 (excluding VAT), you will need to tell us how you did it. We cannot pay your grant if you have not followed the correct procedure.'[47]

TRENDS

Each funding body has developed a bespoke funding application process and approach over a number of evolutions of their capital funding programmes, so trends in their development can not be readily assessed.

All the guidance notes for each funding body highlight the responsibility of the applicant to conform with 'all applicable current UK public regulation procurement laws' and, if applicable, current European Union (EU) procurement rules in relation to all capital projects.

None of the guidance documents outline the different procurement routes which might be possible, such as design contests, open competitions or the negotiated route, all of which can deliver different outcomes. There is also no mention of the use of frameworks. There is no information provided for applicants on the different forms of contract and the appropriateness of these, i.e. between traditional vs design and build. It is assumed that all guidance and advice is sought by the applicants from consultants.

The Arts Council of Wales and National Lottery Heritage Fund directly referenced the advisers appointed by the funding bodies to assist the applicants. Of these the National Lottery Heritage Fund is the most proactive with their Construction Advisers, who are more directly engaged than ACE's Project Monitors. No detailed information is available for the ACW's Architect Advisers beyond outlining their role in assessing applications. (More information can be found on these in the Appendices).

None of the guidance notes from any of the funding bodies reviewed as part of this research outline the need to consider the relative merits of quality and price. Anecdotally it was stated by one of the case study contributors that
> "the typical weighting suggested by Arts Council of Wales is 70% quality 30% pricing"
...but this is not stated in their guidance.

National Lottery Heritage Fund clearly set out the need for contracting through to completion of the delivery phase, and to include break clauses within contracts to allow for unsuccessful applications but avoiding the need to re-procure the design team.

Arts Council of Wales and the National Lottery Heritage Fund have the most comprehensive guidance notes, with detailed information and links to other useful organisations and resources.

Both funders also outline the importance of design quality and sustainable development and provide relevant supporting information on these, ACW within their specific capital projects guidance notes and online resources and toolkits, and NLHF via their online supporting information. The digital portals are also clear and accessible, and of the organisations reviewed these provide the most exemplary models of guidance and practices.

With no remitted work being programmed Arts Council of N. Ireland is the most aberrant.

For publishing contract notices Wales in particular mandates use of its national procurement portal. Although Scotland doesn't appear to mandate its use, the majority of its notices are issued on its national procurement portal. In England this is not the case. Reliance is placed on notices being issued through private portal providers, with the issue of notices on the national portal being noticeably low. Because there are a multitude of such portals, each with different interfaces, this appears to offer significantly reduced access and transparency.

References:

1   Arts Council National Lottery Project Grants Capital investment: Large capital grants, Round 5 Guidance for stage two applicants. Introduction p.2 www.artscouncil.org.uk/sites/default/files/download-file/Round_5_Stage_2_Capital_Guidance_june2018_0.pdf (accessed 28 June 2020)

2   Ibid p.12 Large Grants AC

3   Ibid Large Grants AC

4   Arts Council National Lottery Project Grants Capital (buildings) projects, Arts Council National Lottery Project Grants is the open-access programme for arts, museums and libraries projects. Arts Council England, 12 Feb 2018. www.artscouncil.org.uk/projectgrants (accessed 28 June 2020)

5   Arts Council England, Grant-in-Aid and National Lottery Distribution 2018/19 Annual Report & Accounts. © Arts Council England, 2018 ISBN 978-1-5286-1379-8 www.artscouncil.org.uk/publication/arts-council-england-grant-aid-and-lottery-distribution-annual-report-and-accounts-2 (accessed 28 June 2020)

6   The Creative Scotland Large Capital Guidelines 2013-14 v1-5. Creative Scotland. www.creativescotland.com/funding/archive/large-capital (accessed 28 June 2020)

7   Ibid. p.1 Large Capital Guidelines Scotland.

    Capital Programme – Large Capital Application Guidelines 2013-2014 p.1. www.creativescotland.com/__data/assets/word_doc/0005/37562/Large-Capital-Guidelines-2013-14-v1-5.doc (accessed 28 June 2020)

8   Ibid p.3 Large Capital Application Guidelines

9   Ibid p.6-7 Large Capital Application Guidelines

10   Creative Scotland Open Fund for Organisations: Sustaining Creative Development 2020/21. Application Guidance. Updated July 2020 p.18. www.creativescotland.com/__data/assets/pdf_file/0018/83223/CS_Open_Fund_for_Organisations_July.pdf (accessed 28 June 2020)

11   public contracts scotland website www.publiccontractsscotland.gov.uk/ (accessed 28 June 2020)

12   Ibid The Creative Scotland Large Capital Guidelines 2013/14 www.creativescotland.com/__data/assets/word_doc/0005/37562/Large-Capital-Guidelines-2013-14-v1-5.doc

13   Creative Scotland Open Fund: Sustaining Creative Development. Project Funding, Application Guidance 2019/2020. www.creativescotland.com/__data/assets/pdf_file/0003/28695/Open-Project-Fund-Guidance-Aug-2019-FINAL.pdf

14   Update to Open Fund: 21 July 2020 Open Fund: Sustaining Creative Development www.creativescotland.com/funding/funding-programmes/open-fund-sustaining-creative-development (accessed 8 August 2020)

15   Arts Council of Wales website, arts.wales/capital-funding (accessed 28 June 2020)

16   General Guide to the Arts Council of Wales' Capital Programme March 2017, arts.wales/sites/default/files/2019-04/General-Guide-to-the-Arts-Council-of-Wales-Capital-Programme.pdf

    Major Capital Projects and Additional Guidance Notes Major Capital Projects, 2017 arts.wales/sites/default/files/2019-02/Major-Capital-Projects-Help-Notes.pdf

    Lottery Capital Programme Help Notes for: Minor Capital Projects, 2017. arts.wales/sites/default/files/2019-02/Minor-Capital-Projects-Help-Notes.pdf (all accessed 28 June 2020)

17   Ibid. The General Guide to Capital Programmes

18   Sell2Wales' website www.sell2wales.gov.wales/ (accessed 28 June 2020)

19   Ibid. General Guide to ACW's Capital Programme

20   Ibid. Capital Programme Help Notes, Major Capital Projects ACW

21   Ibid. p.13 Capital Programme Help Notes, Major Projects ACW

22   Ibid. p.4 Capital Programme Help Notes, Major Projects ACW

23   Ibid. p.4 & 6 Capital Programme Help Notes, Major Projects ACW

24   Ibid. p.5 & 6 Capital Programme Help Notes, Major Projects ACW

25   Ibid p 12 & 13 Capital Programme Help Notes, Major Projects ACW

26   www.ojec.com/thresholds.aspx/

27   Ibid p 13 Capital Programme Help Notes, Major Projects ACW

28   Ibid p. 14 & 15 Capital Programme Help Notes, Major Projects ACW

29   Ibid p. 4 Capital Programme Help Notes, Major Projects ACW

30   Ibid p. 18, Capital Programme Help Notes, Major Projects ACW

31   Ibid. Capital Programme Help Notes, Minor Projects ACW

32   Ibid. p.28. Capital Programme, Help Notes, Minor Projects ACW

33   Ibid The General Guide to Capital Programmes; Capital Programme Help Notes, Major Projects ACW, Capital Programme, Help Notes, Minor Projects ACW

34   Lottery Project Funding Programme Application Guidance Notes. arts council of Northern Ireland p. 6 www.artscouncil-ni.org/images/uploads/funding-documents/ACNI-LPF-Guidance-Notes-19-20.pdf (accessed 28 June 2020)

35   Arts Council of Northern Ireland, Small Grants Programme Guidance Notes, dated November 2015. p1 www.artscouncil-ni.org/images/uploads/funding-documents/ACNI-Small-Grants-Guidance-Notes-Dec2019.pdf (accessed 28 June 2020)

36   Arts Council of Northern Ireland www.artscouncil-ni.org/ (accessed 28 June 2020)

37   Department of Finance. Public procurement policy in Northern Ireland www.finance-ni.gov.uk/topics/procurement/public-procurement-policy-northern-ireland

38   Heritage Lottery Fund. Good practice guidance www.heritagefund.org.uk/hub/good-practice-guidance (accessed 28 June 2020)

39   Application Guidance National Lottery Grants for Heritage £3,000–£10,000. Heritage Fund www.heritagefund.org.uk/sites/default/files/media/attachments/HF%20Application%20Guidance_A_SMALL_v2.pdf (accessed 28 June 2020)

40   Application Guidance National Lottery Grants for Heritage £10,000–£250,000. Heritage Fund www.heritagefund.org.uk/sites/default/files/media/attachments/HF%20Application%20Guidance_B_MEDIUM_v2.pdf (accessed 28 June 2020)

41   Application Guidance National Lottery Grants for Heritage £250,000–£5 million. Heritage Fund www.heritagefund.org.uk/sites/default/files/media/attachments/HF%20Application%20Guidance_C_LARGE_v2.pdf (accessed 28 June 2020)

42   Heritage Horizon Awards: grants of £5million and over. www.heritagefund.org.uk/funding/heritage-horizon-awards (accessed 28 June 2020)

43   Heritage Enterprise, Grants from £250,000 to £5million, Application Guidance, January 2019. www.heritagefund.org.uk/sites/default/files/media/attachments/WEB_DC_1.PDF (accessed 28 June 2020)

44   Ibid. p.18 Heritage Enterprise Grants £250k - £5m Application

45   Ibid HLHF Good practice guidance

46   Ibid. p.20 HLHF Guidance Grants£10,k- £250,k

47   Writing a brief for the procurement of goods or services www.heritagefund.org.uk/publications/writing-brief-procurement-goods-or-services (accessed 28 June 2020)

conclusions

15   Conclusions

NATIONAL FUNDING

The key findings from reviewing the funding are that:

- Northern Ireland does not have an Arts capital programme. Nationally over the surveyed period 2013-18 Northern Ireland received a disproportionately small amount of arts investment (£19m), overall and by proportion to its population, and only two projects are recorded (fig. 12.1).

- The other main UK Arts Councils in England, Scotland, Wales and the Heritage Lottery Fund adopt similar capital funding strategies requiring staged bid submissions for all but their smaller programmes.

- Advice and guidance available from funders to those procuring and commissioning buildings on considerations for achieving best value in architectural design and construction commissioning is extremely thin.

- Only Arts Council Wales and Heritage Lottery Fund reputedly sustain those they fund to commission buildings with independent expertise to support the procurement and commissioning processes and procedures, by secondment, appointments or placement.

- No public Arts organisation could be identified as having Social Value policies or toolkits that informed funded organisations commissioning of capital programmes.

- The Arts Council of England and Heritage Lottery Fund do not advise that procurements for buildings and services be advertised on the English National Procurement Portal, Contracts Finder.

- Within the data set since 2013 over 90 organisations were found contributing towards arts capital programmes.

Since 2015-2016 Arts Council Wales has faced a 14.98% reduction in Lottery receipts, reflecting on planned expenditure commitments, and a decline is expected to continue.

By January 2021 it was being reported that costs were spiralling at the Olympic Park's cultural quarter and that the London Legacy Development Corporation (LLDC) had gone from having a net £210m of assets in 2014/5 to a net £171m in liabilities in 2019/20, potentially jeopardising projected Lottery receipts which underpin future income for funding *(Chapter 13 National Arts Funding Overview)*.[1] As there is also already a disproportionately high UK cultural funding commitment to the Olympic Park Cultural quarter, something may need to give *(fig. 12.6)*.

Since the UK Brexit European Funding programmes are no longer accessible. Brexit and the pandemic may also impact the significant arts funding provided from trusts, foundations and private sources.

EARNED INCOME

The earned income of arts organisations, which up until 2020 had grown strongly, represents a greater share of income in larger organisations, and those in London particularly. Closure and restricted use of arts and cultural buildings in consequence of the pandemic will continue to have a significant impact on all these organisations, who have restricted reserves to three months of full running costs *(Chapter 13 UK Public Investment in Culture)*. Few however have the reserves to address the current crisis to secure cultural assets forward and emergency provisions will continue to be needed.

PROJECT COSTS BY LOCATION

Four large scale London projects totalling £938m account for a significant 53.3% of the total project costs awarded for arts buildings in London. These accentuate the London regional imbalance as they represent 24.2% of the UK total and more than the combined total for Scotland, Wales and N. Ireland *(fig. 12.6 & 12.7)*.

However, when these projects are excluded, the average project cost otherwise awarded in London, of £11.6m, is more similar to those found elsewhere in the UK. Due to the competition from 'national' organisations based in London, smaller London based arts organisations find it harder to secure funding.

GRANTS & AWARDS SUMS

The regional distribution within England, of grant awards by total numbers and total sums awarded, is revealing *(fig. 12.8 & 12.9)*.

The north of England region with 138 grants received the highest by number, the highest total of grant aid at £73m and the highest average award at £532k per grant. On all counts London then comes in second. The South West's 62 grants totalling £22m fell well behind and has the lowest average award of £357k.

REGENERATION STRATEGIES

A recurrent theme in the case studies is the provision of creative arts as a key catalyst within cultural led regeneration plans, whether through providing facilities in converted buildings or in new buildings. The evidence points to creative arts-based production being highly valued as a contribution towards wider redevelopment strategies *(Chapters 4, 6, 7 & 8)*.

This development model gained particularly currency after construction of the Bilbao Guggeheim, and led to a number of high profile UK projects such as the V&A Dundee by Kengo Kuma Associates *(fig. II.2)* and the Turner Contemporary in Margate by David Chipperfield Architects *(fig. II.3)*.

New arts facilities forming an integral part of a wider master-planned regeneration strategy, such as Edinburgh Printmakers, Aberdeen Art Gallery and High House, can be considered models of this master-planning approach, although they are of different scales. As a crucial component of an integrated redevelopment strategy the wider social value that High House, for example, has successfully delivered, was at a very modest cost. Nevertheless, integrating projects within wider regeneration

plans now appears a comparatively rare occurrence.

Faced with the decline of high street retail and the growing obsolescence of multi-level city centre car parks, the offering of the visionary and innovative Tŷ Pawb project may, for the foreseeable future, offer a more valuable template for central urban economic regeneration. This appropriation of an existing building in context delivers congregational, cultural and social activities along with employment opportunities and economic regeneration more widely.

ART FORMS

Grants awarded to Theatre, the largest by type, represented 22.2% of the overall award numbers *(fig. 12.10 & 12.11)*. In a health pandemic where airborne infection, particularly in confined spaces occupied by large numbers, has been shown to be an issue — by 2020 the prognosis for many performance and exhibition formats had become dire. The cultural offers of digital media that was previously amongst the least popular (<3%) may now be best placed to respond *(fig. 12.11)*.

This is almost the opposite of what has been developing in grant awards over the period. As with digital media, art forms and activities taking place externally, particularly those in the warmer seasons where natural ventilation may be a benefit in curtailing viral infections, may also be considered more resilient *(fig.15.1)*.

Of the case studies six (54%) provide significant facilities for studios or workshops, within dedicated or mixed use facilities *(fig. 11.4)*. Mixed venues currently account for nearly 17% of all the data set *(fig.12.11)*. By nature these facilities tend to have more separate users confined in individually ventilated spaces while the functional mixes can mutually support and cross fertilise each other. They should also be considered more resilient and better capable of adaptation to emerging requirements, than many top ranked single use facilities.

Data for the proportion of external activity is unrecorded, but gathering this in the future within applications and awards could be of value in better determining the resilience of award funding. In the foreseeable future more consideration to funding digital media, external and mixed use arts facilities might also be prioritised.

BUILDING TYPES COMMISSIONED

Investment in arts buildings is contributing positively towards curating and enabling the preservation, conservation, restoration and refurbishment of the nation's historic building stock.

62.5% of all projects over the period were works to existing buildings *(fig. 12.12 & 12.13)*. Only 16.9% of all projects surveyed between 2013-2018 were either new buildings or were in the larger part new *(fig.12.13)*. This represents a strategic shift from the decade immediately following the introduction of National Lottery arts funding.

Ellen: "To see nurses crying with marks and sores on their faces, that was really hard"

The 9 case study projects *(fig.11.5)* and 62.5% of all the projects, that cover works to existing buildings, demonstrate possible future strategies.

In terms of climate changing carbon emissions, the reuse of existing buildings contributes little impact relative to new buildings, because the embodied energy is already embedded and the CO2 emissions arising from new construction have been expended historically. For this reason, re-appropriating existing buildings is generally far more sustainable than building new ones. Because a very high proportion of arts buildings reuse existing structures, strategically this sector can already be seen to be addressing the climate crisis - and probably better than other sectors.

In many instances, buildings that are being reused appear more possible to redevelop in phases, while maintaining some functionality. RAM, Wilton's Music Hall, Aberdeen Art Gallery, the Theatre Royal Glasgow and Oriel Myrddin Gallery are case studies which all example this, to varying extents. Development programmes that can offer this flexibility are also better placed, potentially, to address economic restraints which may follow the Covid-19 pandemic and Brexit.

Current approaches, by the types of arts buildings being commissioned, can be seen to offer significant benefits and lessons for the future, relative to other sectors. The high proportion of work in this sector being done on reusing existing buildings, relative to new building, should be welcome, although clearly to address the climate crisis, far more action forward is still needed.

As climate crisis influences and the effects of the pandemic and Brexit impact, proportionately more curation of existing assets by the arts sector might be anticipated. Because of the advantages offered for sustainability and for the phasing of project programmes, works focusing on existing assets could be better targeted in policy and guidance.

THE COMPETITIVE PRINCIPLE

There are many significant contradictions in how UK cultural buildings arise - not least is the competitive principle underpinning their procurement. Public projects are acquired through rigorously regulated and commercially complex competitive processes that are founded on a belief in the cultural and creative benefits these principles may deliver. Founded on the 'de facto' economic benefits of competition, a belief system that largely goes without being questioned, competitive selection gives rise to inherent tensions and inconsistencies, with certain complexity and particular issues arising.

Paradoxically (as the case studies describe), projects are most successfully delivered where clients, consultants and contractors work together collaboratively and in co-operation. This requires the successful alignment of empathies and inter-personal negotiations (requiring a level of skill and professionalism by all parties) — and these are quite opposite attributes in character to what might be described as competitive. Is competitive selection the best route for actually achieving these outcomes in all circumstances? The Wilton's Music Hall and RAM case studies suggest not (Chapters 1 & 2). The pandemic also suggests the principles of collaboration and co-operation should be considered of greater importance. In reforming procurement processes and practices these principles should be given fuller consideration — rather than the singular principle of competition.

Four individual projects alone account for 53.3% of London's total project costs, 24.2% of the UK total, and more than the combined total for Scotland, Wales and N. Ireland (fig. 12.6). As access to resources for these projects has been better than others, whether intended or otherwise, these projects have had a significant competitive advantage.

From a project's inception the capacity to establish and progress initiatives which aren't top down, but instigated by smaller/ emerging arts organisations, is not equivalent.

This might, for instance, be the case for those seeking to instigate new cultural offerings with pro-active participatory community engagement, where historically an important part might have been contributed by human capital (pejoratively 'sweat capital').

UK Community Architecture is a type of engagement which was prevalent before adoption of procurement regulations. This enabled architects to help initiatives in their communities from inception on a 'pro bono' basis and offered opportunity for paid service continuation through to completion, where proposals were sustained by policy. Opportunities to sustain and build new initiatives has however been diminished, because upon receipt of public funds appointments are required to be publicly tendered against criteria that frequently precludes those already engaged within the process. In this process a stakeholding and representative thread also becomes lost. To provide greater resilience and more flexibility consideration should be given, proportionately, to ensuring stakeholders are better incentivised to pro-actively participate in supporting small new provisions forward, to allow a new generation of initiatives to emerge.

Following a projects inception sufficient initial kick-start investment is now more frequently required for establishment financing and through developmental, planning and award pre-application stages to completion of construction. This is available to established organisations enjoying existing financial support which, along with a recognised bedrock of stakeholder support, supports progression. Competitive principles currently preclude rewarding the human capital invested by stakeholding participants while it can also preclude their further engagement.

The full impacts of the multiple skews in the competitive systems may not be fully evident currently, but the four London cases clearly indicate that larger metropolitan schemes, with significant establishment backing, benefit. The total 24.2% of UK arts capital investment on these projects may, after the pandemic, appear less viable and resilient. They have also advanced, potentially, at the expense of wider social values including the ability for new arts initiatives to emerge.

PROJECT VALUES

In project management a modelled balance in the relationships between time, cost and quality is frequently an objective. Yet, overall, any idea that there is a measurable or balanced correlation that can be applied across all the case studies, in this way, is not factually evident — something else is happening in this cohort and other values would appear to be in play (fig. 11.2, 11.7-11.9).

From the case studies of arts projects, it is possible to appraise relationships between quality, in terms of £m^2, time and project costs. When the overall reported project programmes are considered against cost this sample evidences little relationship. Due to their protracted timescales, 4-5 of the 9 completed projects do not fit any apparent consistent relationship *(fig. 11.8 & 11.9)*. While the delivery programmes for the Wyeside Arts Centre and the Oriel Mydridden Gallery, two projects currently in progression, are also becoming extended. The same lack of a consistent relationship was found between quality and time, and between quality and cost.

In project management time, cost and quality have been held to be the significant parameters determining a project procurement value' and programming. Yet time-scales show no predictable consistency, are extremely fluid and might be thought to be determined more by the cultural context. Meanwhile the lower cost projects are achieving apparently very high quality.

A lesson from this study is that adherence to traditional project management parameters holds little value. Clearly factors that are external to the equated construction time, cost, and quality such as the staging of funding approvals and grant awards, along with political, cultural and social factors are having some significant impacts. By avoiding the current standard methodology better project management might be achieved through addressing the context, accounting for other values and material factors, to ensure the value parameters are better nuanced.

EMBODIED ENERGY

The findings on embodied energy in this report when taken as a measure of sustainability are a surprisingly pervasive indicator that the procurement of arts buildings is, likely, significantly outperforming other sectors.

For a considerable time national arts organisation have had a commendable focus on environmental awareness sustained by a range of initiatives and requirements. For example all ACW projects require BREEAM sustainability certification. ACE working for example with Julie's Bicycle who have been pushing an environmental agenda over ten years, introduced environmental reporting policy as part of their funding from 2012.[2]

The LETI (London Energy Transformation Initiative) 2020 reports identify, for example, that for achieving sustainable outcomes and carbon emissions reductions targets the requirements for embodied energy should be given equivalence in project management values, to the traditional axioms of time, cost and quality.[3] In the case study cohort,

when embodied energy savings that arise from re-using a building are given equivalent consideration, as a key attribute of sustainable value, a different overall picture of project management values begins to emerge across this cohort. Alongside the traditional axioms, a better relational balance in values is then revealed – and shows alignment with the LETI recommendations.

The extent of environmental awareness shown by the sector and arts funding organisations are clearly showing impacts. The best value procurement found in this report also backs up the LETI recommendations and suggests that sustainability be a factor given equivalent value, at least, as the traditional axioms in project management. In this respect the arts sector offers lessons on how best to respond to the climate crisis that should be welcomed more widely across all industry.

IMMEASURABLE VALUES

As Wilton's Music Hall exemplifies, the case study projects are also labours of love and craft brought to fruition with immeasurable values sustained by clients and delivered by the dedication and professionalism of architects, such as Tim Ronalds. The values being upheld are beyond any easy definition and can not be ascribed to any existing quantifiable measures nor, apparently, any current sustainable or social value definitions or criteria.

Those who commission should consider carefully how best they construct their methods of selection so they are open to attract similar values.

TENDER PORTALS

In the context of the digital infrastructure supporting arts procurement, the use of Contracts Finder, the national procurement portal for England, is particularly poor given the number of English notices issued relative to Scotland and Wales *(fig. 12.16)*.

To ensure access and the transparency of notices is robust, reliable digital infrastructure is necessary. In England the predominance of multiple and privately contracted regional procurement hubs and other services providing notifications constrains access and has reduced transparency.

Although it is a requirement that information is freely available, still with different points of access, interfaces, logins and attributes for buying and selling applied to each portal access remains slow and poor. Contracts Finder was established to provide a more effective single national procurement portal for England. Since its establishment there has been little to encourage its uptake and use, unlike in Scotland and Wales, a lack of Government investment and so its functionality has been materially undermined, reducing accessibility, transparency and efficiency. This national infrastructure service is failing to serve the nation.

On 31 December 2020, following Brexit, 'Find a Tender' became the national portal, to replace OJEU — however the beta site, at Jan 2021, remained woeful by comparison.

Going forward from Brexit, the lack of an equivalently effective replacement of similar utility and capacity as OJEU by a single national UK digital procurement portal, is a concern. Realistically a portal with use that is mandated, with the capacity and facility to replace a plethora of private portals, that easily offers user friendly access, data interrogation, customised search functionality and feeds should be sought. For transparency this is critical.

TRANSPARENCY

A significant deficit in the number of award notices being issued relative to Contract Notices was identified in 'Public Construction Procurement Trends 2009-2014'. It was found, then, that in the wider construction sector only 70% of contract notices were concluded with an award notice.[4]

In this publication, transparency can be seen to have reduced further *(fig. 12.17)*. The lower proportion of award notice being issued from this new data is below that found more widely in the UK between 2009-2014. At that stage a trend over the years towards a diminishing proportion of award notices being issued relative to contract notices was highlighted. These new more recent findings align with that trend.[5]

Award Notices are public notifications of the conclusion of proceedings and provide information necessary for market transparency. This offers for example, public scrutiny feedback and capacity to evaluate procedures and processes, bid ranges and values (against estimates), the numbers bidding and who they are, and are a regulatory requirement. Without such transparency accountability,

regulatory compliance and the ability to identify aberrances (including corruption) can not be upheld. The trend this report confirms is therefore of significant concern.

Public procurement procedures are established to ensure accountability to the principles of fairness, transparency and value. But if no award notices reporting their conclusion are subsequently published the procedures have no basis. Government, authorities, procurement hubs and/or funding organisations should in the public interest act to remedy the current deficit. As a mandatory pre-requisite for obtaining funding public organisation should stipulate that award notices must be issued, to ensure accountability and transparency, and address the potential for corruption.

THE PROCUREMENT BRIEF

For clients a procurements specification and briefing are the single most important documents for describing a projects content.

The established parameters of a project, its context and requirements need to be considerately described, carefully, unambiguously, and succinctly. The opportunity available should be summarised clearly and early because it is important that suppliers have sufficient information to make an informed decision on whether or not they wish to bid. Where break clauses and unconfirmed funding is involved, these will need to be addressed. Poor descriptions and too much information can often be counterproductive to attracting high quality bids. Where a framework is to be established the distinction between the framework award stage and subsequent call off should be logical and clear.

PROCUREMENT PROCEDURAL ROUTES

Of the seven basic procedures available for the procurement of architectural services only two typically are being used in this UK sector. There were no recorded design contests, competitive procedures with negotiation, competitive dialogue, or innovation partnership procurement procedures for all the projects over the period *(fig. 12.14 & 12.15)*.

The Giants Causeway *(Chapter 10)* is, therefore, now highly unusual because, in this sector between 2013-18, a Design Contest competitive procedure does not appear again *(fig. 12.14 & 12.15)*. Relative to continental Europe, the UK is exceptional in having such a dearth

— particularly given the versatility and opportunities that design contest procedures offer for delivering access, innovation and architectural quality for the cultural sector.[6]

The 69.6% of restricted procedures reported in this sector in the period, is less than the 81% reported nationally overall, while in these findings 25% are open procedures versus 12% in the 2009-14 Trends report (2014).[7] This indicates that the sector is using more open procedures than the country as a whole, and fewer restricted procedures. But, in the context across all construction, where the UK's preponderant use of restricted procedures, and those leading to framework appointments and selection process where a bid price and companies scale are given licence to skew other considerations, this remains in need of far more attention.

Restricted procedures leading to a framework award provides value where there is a programme of work to be done by call off, over an anticipated period for broad all-purpose construction. Frameworks typically add a further tier of procedural process, are 'generic' vis 'project specific' awards, and restrict participation and competition further. For individual cultural facilities having one off commissions, which are the type most prevalent in the arts sector, frameworks are not a recommended procurement approach. As is evident from the data and case studies this generally appears to be widely understood in arts commissioning, and far more so than in other UK sectors.[8]

The importance of ensuring the right vision and that the right lead consultant is employed at the outset through a rigorous and apropriate procedural process that offers stakeholder continuity to completion can't be underestimated.

In the Aberdeen Art Gallerys' case Hoskins were responsible for the management and co-ordination of a full sub-consultant design team for the prolonged duration *(Chapter 6)*. There are many attributes and values that are offered by such uniquely ascribed and project specific service appointments. These can't for example be replicated over such a period with appointments off frameworks, used commonly in other sectors *(fig. 12.14 & 12.15)*.

The arts sector is using a better distribution of procedures, relative to the industry as a whole, and this is to be welcomed. This offers better access and a diversity of approaches appropriate for individual procurements. But, in the context of cultural commissions, far more flexibility could be shown, particularly by greater use of design contests and competitive procedures with negotiation as these offer significant benefits and may be more appropriate.

RESTRICTED PROCEDURES: PQQs & SSQs

The importance of the early SSQ/PQQ requirements in opening up or shutting down the access by smaller practices to participation in a procurement has been widely highlighted. Requirements should be appropriate to the scale of the project but also allow as inclusive an approach as possible. As outlined in the Edinburgh Printmakers case study, the practice, Page \ Park, carefully weigh up the pros and cons before submitting a PQQ, as almost all practices do. And there were concerns that the PQQ requirements would preclude from eligibility less well established practices *(Chapter 7)*.

Evidence of a specific number of similar previous projects, of an established working relationship across the design team, practice turnover, and insurance can create barriers. These are not proven in reducing risk or ensuring a quality outcome. Such barriers reduce the 'pool' of architects who are commissioned for arts and cultural buildings - which 'de facto' reduces competition.

When appointing teams or consortia of consultants, evidence of previous working relationships between the design team bidding and their experience can also preclude making new working relationships through a process, that might, specifically for any one project, be the most appropriate.

The arts sector could still be more innovative and considerate of their own ethos, and less risk averse, when framing questions, because as the Edinburgh Printmakers case study states

"Somewhat perversely for arts buildings procurement, this process appears to demonstrate a level of risk aversion which frequently contradicts the very nature and ethos of the Client art organisations"

Simpler and less prescriptive initial conditions that use the process to subsequently thin down submissions during bid stages are a benefit to clients because they elicit a broader range of submissions offering greater choice, and for consultants, more flexibility, less speculative investment and improved access. Funders guidance might consider incorporation of these considerations to address access and diversity.

ACCESS & INNOVATION

Many arts clients across the case studies would appear to have seen creative opportunities and flexibility from competitions, and a manifest desire for change — outweighing the appetite for risk seen in other sectors.

Four of the projects in the Case Studies were delivered by new practices *(fig.11.16 & allowing for Hoskin Architects being only 10 years old upon their award)*. From the data for 2013-2018, 88.4% of all project commissions in the sector were awarded to practices undertaking less than five commissions *(fig. 12.20 & 12.21)*. For accessibility this performance is far better than the national practices seen across all sectors.[9] In Wales and contrary to the Welsh Governments reputed policy on economic sustainability it's noted that smaller practices only undertake feasibility studies and are not getting the opportunity to be appointed for later project stages *(Chapter 12, Change of Architect ...)*. We also found no evidence recognising a distinct need to improve BAME access in construction procurement within the arts sector procurement.

With the smaller case study projects the appetite for engaging new talent is clear — and the payoff from extremely tight budgets in terms of the built quality and rigour brought to the challenges of difficult briefs, is exceptional.

This UK sector has evidentially maintained a unique level of aspirational patronage for the commissioning of new, emergent and smaller practices. Distinctively the arts sector also might appear to reveal a capacity for achieving innovative high-quality solutions from those they appoint.

The appropriateness of Walk the Plank's strategy delivered immeasurable benefits, effectively on a very tight programme and ensured success for this delightful and engaging solution *(Chapter 3)*. Yet Walk the Plank's competition promoter insightfully reflects upon how their future processes might strive for better access by offering a simpler approach with greater engagement.

Access and diversity issues are currently better focused in revenue funding by many arts organisations such as ACE, but far less so in their capital programming, and this should now be addressed. Although there is growing recognition of how much more can be done to further improve accessibility, including consideration of BAME access, this might best be sustained in capital programmes by embedding more progressive aspirations within funders guidance, along with an expectation of the standards to be expected from those who are funded.

COST / QUALITY ASSESSMENT SELECTION CRITERIA & FEES

In the consultants appointments the balance placed on qualitative values (versus the value placed on a bidders price), for all arts commissions, had 64.7% weighting quality at 70% or above in the selection processes, with only 35.3% weighted below, which appears to put the sector above the national average. However for four projects the selection assessments were made on price alone, at 100% *(fig. 12.18 & 12.19)*.

No evidence could be found of funders recommending a 70-30% quality/price split (or better) yet anecdotally Wales might appear to do so informally *(Chapter 12. Assessment and Selection ...)*. In the Arts sector the weighting given to quality for a consultant's appointments at selection is apparently better relative to the construction industry as a whole, yet appears to fall short of the practices of our major European neighbours *(fig.12.18 & 12.19, Assessment & Selection Criteria)*.

The client for the Theatre Royal Glasgow notably reports that:
> *"Upon reflection, in any future OJEU process, we would try and consider a means of assessing and balancing price versus quality to a greater extent"* *(Chapter 5)*.

As this case study considers, approaches in the UK that have become normalised need to be reflected on, and far more clearly needs to be done.

Meeting anticipated quality and how it is appropriately balanced against price has long been an issue under UK procurement procedures. For example, the building failures, across the Scottish PFI Schools programme and at Grenfell Tower, have exposed significant qualitative deficiencies publicly — although these might be seen as only the tip of an iceberg.[10] If the inquiries into these disasters fail to precipitate sufficient reforms within procurement, then the crisis in UK construction quality will persist. If consultant's and contractor's awards can't evaluate or embed quality, and are inadequately balanced and inappropriately weighted, then significant deficiencies will continue.

There is nothing to preclude costs being weighted in other ways. This may be by setting a fixed price (eg. for a fee or contractors' profit), so that quality (and social value) constitutes 100% of the assessment; or by assessing bidders prices on a mean narrow average assessment. In the latter case the bidder submitting a price closest to the average of all the bid submissions, receives the highest valued assessment (and so forth), as described in the Project Compass report 'Transforming public procurement: Response to the December 2020 Government Green paper' (March 2021).[11] In this way the client achieves the most viably realistic price bid for executing the works, as appraised across the cohort of bidders, which better secures them against financial risk, possible claims and untenable undercutting.

Whilst the emphasis placed on qualitative assessments is relatively high in the arts sector compared to the rest of the UK, and should be welcomed, this could, by comparable international standards, still be significantly bettered. This can be achieved by also using 100% qualitative assessment or price scoring by the mean narrow average method, and guidance should be provided that flags up the benefits of these alternative methods.

For smaller contracts it is preferable to reveal the fee budget. Although there are arguments in favour and against revealing the budget and how best value might be achieved. For design services if the budget is known it will be easier for the client to compare the bidders like for like. It also can provide a clearer indication of the resources bidders propose to provide them and the quality. This is a fairer and more transparent approach.

For bidders this provides them with greater clarity, a more realistic allocation of days/fees — or to decide not to tender on that occasion.

Where the budget is not revealed then the brief needs to be clear and precise with sufficient detail, in order for the design team to provide an accurately costed quote. How change is addressed should also be anticipated.

When a project has multiple future stages, the client should break down how a bidder allocates cost and resource into stages of the project. When a project includes sub-consultants under the lead consultant, the client should also structure how bidders complete their cost and resource allocation across different disciplines, so that an assessment of the relative allocation can be made.

WORK STAGE FRAGMENTATION

Aspects of a particularly challenging procurement process are questioned at Tŷ Pawb *(Chapter 8)*. This raises issues about the consistency of consultancy services, critical for achieving a 'Golden Thread', and the time, cost, and quality along with the morale of stakeholders and end users. Matters surrounding the appointment of architects at different RIBA work stages and subsequent novation of the architects on completion of RIBA Stage 3 to the main contractor created problems. It even appears the novation under this Design and Build Contract had to be hard fought for!

Upon the architects employment being transferred over to the main contractors, two of the stage 2-3 consultancy teams changed. Design and Build contracts transfer responsibilities for a projects design and the quality of its execution to a main contractor. When an architect is novated they become a sub-contractor to the main contractor, holding no direct contractual responsibility to the client for ensuring quality and value - and those who pay the piper call the tune.

Six case study projects highlight the risks arising with architects being called upon to be re-appointed for different RIBA work stages during a project's progression *(Chapter 1, 2, 5, 7, 8 & 9)*. From the 2013-2018 project notice records, 39.2% show projects having multiple and staged appointments over a projects programme of those which could be verified, with each new commissioning cycle incurring uncertainties, costs, delays and disruption, and frequently a change of architect *(fig. 12.22 & 12.23)*.

It should be apparent that this time and cost might be better spent on the projects themselves. To achieve best value consistency of delivery is one way of ensuring a 'golden thread' can be maintained in the quality and standard of work. Trying to achieve this, however, can be undermined by the processes adopted, as is so well described at Tŷ Pawb.

Design principles agreed during the early design stages should not be lost after RIBA Stage 3, during technical design or later, and a clear strategy should be put into place to ensure control over the design is to be maintained through the later stages of design and construction. Clients can seek to minimise risks to design quality by contracting the same design team all the way through the RIBA Work Stages, and that design development is completed before a contractor is appointed.

A presumption by clients towards maintaining consistency should be the norm. Projects can be better managed more simply by using standard terms for a consultant's appointment at the outset allowing break clauses at project stages, if works do not proceed for whatever reason, and allowing for changes in the progression, and/or if the commissioner is not satisfied with the standard of work delivered under the appointment *(Chapter 14. Change of architect between stages)*.

When using a Design and Build or Partnering process, this developing the design, including key architectural details, to RIBA Stage 4A after which the design consultancies should either be novated to the contractor or retained by the client with a watching brief can be a means to address this.

Arts funding organisations would be advised to address this in their guidance to commissioners, to improve efficiencies, effectiveness and qualitative standards, with a presumption to making delivery more effective and consistent.

HONORARIUMS

It is evident that the two case study projects offering the most reasonable honorariums notably attracted a disproportionately large number of submissions, relative to all others. For the Giant's Causeway the £24k total value of these honorariums amounted to roughly 0.31% of the project cost yet attracted 201 entries. The Theatre Royal Glasgow had total honorariums of £10k amounting to roughly 0.05% of the project cost and attracted 107 expressions of interest and 49 subsequent submissions. The difference becomes particularly significant when such a large and otherwise prestigious project as Aberdeen Art Gallery, which otherwise would seem

an apparently very attractive competition, acquired only 19 entries — it had no honorarium *(fig. 11.15)*.

The level of engagement stimulated by honorariums in also evident by the example of the open competition held for the Whitworth Art Gallery Manchester which had total honorariums of £25k, where five second stage submissions each received £5k, received 139 submissions. This project furthermore was assessed on quality at 100% *(fig.12.18 Chapter 12. Competition Programmers; Assessment and Selection Criteria)*

To attract wide engagement that can deliver the best value, clients who wish to draw architects to their bidding processes so they receive the widest choice through any competition should be more aware of the real impact honorariums have on the numbers willing to submit. This is not at all surprising as it enshrines a client's commitment to both the project and the architects.

PROCUREMENT COSTS

For project commissions close to threshold values procurement costs can amount to anything between 18%-29% as the aggregated economic costs incurred by the commissioning authorities and those bidding. While estimates show that roughly 25% of these costs are borne by the authorities and 75% by those bidding in effect the economic cost of three procurements can amount to roughly that of the cost of a project. For the specific commissioning of architecture however the figures have evidentially been higher.

With Lottery receipts declining it is particularly important that more thought should be given to how valuable resources are directed towards the project outcomes to sustain future projects, and not the procedural processes. Arts Council Wales and others might through governance, practices and guidance, consider how they might achieve this better.

CONSULTANT & PROJECT INSURANCE

The issue of insurance is raised in conclusion, although this has not otherwise been explored in the preceding data or research. It is flagged up for clients, commissioners and consultants because, over the preparation of this publication, the situation has changed significantly. For consultants, requirements for Professional Indemnity (PI) insurance in all events, have commonly borne little relationship to the value of work sought and have been a major constraint historically on access and participation, particularly by newer and smaller practices in competitive bidding. But recent and very significant inflation in construction insurance has arisen. This has been mainly attributable to the findings from inquiries into the Grenfell disaster and the insurance industries response to their risks - but also because of pandemic related claims. The order of increase in premiums now impacts upon site, consultant's insurances and business viabilities, which clients should be increasingly mindful of.

Integrated Project Insurance (IPI) and Single Project Insurance (SPI) can be an alternative to the existing PI model that also promotes better and more collaborative team practices (Glossary). However no record of their use in any public arts projects, or options for their incorporation into procurements has been found in our records.

The level and type of insurance cover does not have to be specific within any bid invitation, and the insurance does not have to be in place until the assignation of the contract, under PCR2015. In any bidder invitation insurance can be indicative of the level sought across a range of values and provide for the use of different models of insurance cover, such as IPI or SPI. Providing for insurance options this way enables selection of the most viable, effective and appropriate insurance for the project context, offering the necessary risk cover and by using a model agreed by all parties. This may provide the best way of ensuring viability, efficiency, and effectiveness while sustaining access.

In the light of the current crisis the need for further measures may also be required. It currently appears that Government may need to step in to secure the industry to effectively provide insurance of last resort or as a guarantor,.

Where PI insurance is sought it should always be set at an appropriate level as required to ensure that micro and SMEs (MSME) practices can tender. The GLA's ADUP (Architecture Design and Urbanism Panel) Framework Agreement provides a better practice example of appropriate insurance levels as follows:
- Professional Indemnity Insurance £2m
- Employer's (Compulsory) Liability Insurance £5m
- Public Liability Insurance £10m

IMPACT OF COVID-19

Aspects of the changing context is described in responses received from some of the case study contributors:

"However the cultural sector is uniquely placed to help the government's 'build back better' agenda and cultural activity is increasingly regarded as critical to the revitalisation of our urban centres. The health and wellbeing aspects of cultural engagement have also come to the fore in this challenging period. So although funding might be tight, we are seeing opportunities emerging ... in the wider cultural sector there are many concerns over the impact of COVID-19 on freelancers on whom so much of the cultural sector rely. Large scale recovery funds have focused on building based organisations rather than supporting those who make the work and bring activity into our cultural buildings ...There is an interesting dichotomy emerging ... we are seeing opportunities ... that will rely heavily on an understanding of a particular place and people"
Nicola Walls, Page \ Park Architects.

"It is unlikely that we will reopen until the Autumn (2021) and ... some social distancing of audiences is anticipated (with) ... a socially distanced orchestra in a modestly sized orchestra pit. And, we are working on modifying the airflow through the theatre to ensure we have sufficient air changes per hour to meet CIBSE requirements - for orchestra and ... audiences ... other covid mitigations will include temperature checks, staggered entry times, paperless ticketing, and quite possibly masks during performances ... restrictions on service and delivery income streams will possibly negatively impact on the overall profitability of each theatre.
Alex Reedijk, Scottish Opera.

"Whilst the double whammy of Covid and Brexit has hit the arts sector hard, this is a Client base that is used to operating creatively within a context of scarcity. Over a decade of austerity leading to funding cuts in the arts and diminished capital funding has not prevented these organisations finding innovative and joyful ways to contribute to and engage with their communities, though it has unavoidably led to less financial investment in their people and buildings, no doubt building up future problems for the sector."

.... The drive towards "Covid-secure" or "Covid-resilient" buildings is in danger of leaving several priorities behind in its wake — quality factors such as appropriateness, delightfulness, and end user / audience experience; value for money; the environmental and social values of projects. These are the foundations upon which arts construction projects are built and we supersede them at our own risk."

Luke Cooper and Sylvia Hebden,
Architecture Emporium and
Through & Around.

" ...We hope that clients will be brave and understand — and advocate for, to their funders and partners — the value of the 'hidden' costs needed to make buildings low-carbon, efficient and practical to operate. This requires a shift in narratives and a good start would be to see this reflected in procurement — less emphasis on the visual seduction of the image, and more on approach, process, research, evaluation."

Hana Loftus, HAT Projects

Arts and culture was one of the first sectors of the economy to be hit by Covid-19. Closure of arts and cultural buildings due to the pandemic will continue to have a significant impact on all organisations and the artists and cultural workers employed. Few organisations have sufficient reserves to address the current crisis to secure cultural assets forward.

The DCMS, the devolved nations' governments and funding bodies have all distributed £1.57bn of Culture Recovery Funding (grants and loans) across the sector, in addition to some direct funding of organisations.

The arts funding bodies have used their existing reserves and repurposed funding streams to create emergency response packages for organisations and artists. Much of this funding has gone to support the capital projects currently in development, especially those with funding shortfalls, cost increases and some landmark projects (e.g. The Mac in Belfast (£0.4m), The Factory in Manchester (£21m), the National Library of Wales and Amgueddfa Cymru — National Museum Wales (£6.2m), Eden Court in Inverness (£0.5m). Plus stability and renewal funding towards making facilities suitable for post Covid use.

The situation continues to change rapidly in the arts and cultural sector, as everywhere else.

(See Appendix H — for detailed Covid 19 information tracked and described to March 2021, along with the case study contributors full texts)

References

1   The London Assembly's budget and performance committee findings reported in: ' 'Olympic Park could become 'costly disaster', mayor of London warned' Z. Garner-Purkis, W. Ing AJ. 21 January 2021. www.architectsjournal.co.uk/news/ olympic-park-could-become-costly-disaster-mayor-of-london- warned#comment-10230 (accessed 21 January 2021

2   Julie's Bicycle www.juliesbicycle.com (accessed 18 November 2020)

3   LETI (London Energy Transformation Initiative) Climate Emergency Design Guide: How new buildings can meet UK climate change targets and LETI Embodied Carbon Primer Supplementary guidance to the Climate Emergency Design Guide. Jan. 2020 London Energy Transformation Initiative. www.leti.london (accessed 18 November 2020)

4   Ibid Public Construction Procurement Trends 2009-2014 pp.10-11

5   Ibid Public Construction Procurement Trends 2009-2014 pp.10-11

6   Menteth, W., O'Carroll, O., Curtis, R., Sawyer, B. Public Construction Procurement Trends 2009-2014. Project Compass CIC. Dec 2014. pp. 24-27 ISBN (Print): 9780993148101.   projectcompass.co.uk/wp-content/ uploads/2019/10/Project_Compass_CIC_Procurement_ Trends_2009-2014.pdf (accessed 28 May 2020)

7   ibid. Public Construction Procurement Trends 2014 pp. 24-27

8   ibid. Public Construction Procurement Trends 2014 pp. 38-39

9   ibid. Public Construction Procurement Trends 2014 pp. 52-59.

10   Report of the Independent Inquiry into the Construction of Edinburgh Schools. Feb 2017 chaired by Prof. John Cole www.ciob.org/media/113/download (accessed 28 May 2020)

*   Cole, J., Building standards compliance and enforcement review: report. Report for the Scottish Government. June 2018. www.gov.scot/publications/ report-review-compliance-enforcement/ (accessed 28 May 2020)*

*   Hackitt,J., Independent Review of Building Regulations and Fire Safety: final report. HCLG May 2018. ISBN 978-1-5286-0293-8. assets.publishing.service.gov.uk/ government/uploads/system/uploads/attachment_data/ file/707785/Building_a_Safer_Future_-_web.pdf (accessed 28 May 2020)*

11   Menteth, W., Curtis, R. Transforming public procurement: Response to the December 2020 Government Green paper. Project Compass CIC & The London Practice Forum. March 2021 projectcompass.co.uk/wp-content/ uploads/2021/03/PCompass_LPF-Green-Paper-Response_ Final-r3-210308.pdf (accessed 21 March 2021)

methodology

Contributors' Biographies

Chris Coleman–Smith
Hoskins Architects, Scotland

Chris Coleman–Smith, B.A (hons), Dip. Arch, MA, is a director at Hoskins Architects, an award-winning architectural practice with studios in Berlin and Glasgow. He is a University of Sheffield graduate who qualified as an architect in 1996 before moving to Glasgow and joining Hoskins Architects in 2000, where he became a Director in 2008.

Chris has a directors role on competition submissions alongside his input into the practices strategy and development. At Hoskins Architects Chris has designed and managed a range of projects working with high-profile clients in the public and private sectors, large multi-disciplinary design teams and multiple projects.

Having completed the V&A Architecture for All Gallery in 2004, Chris directed the hugely successful redevelopment of the National Museum of Scotland, winning the RIAS Andrew Doolan Best Building in Scotland Award in 2011, and 'Rockvilla' for the National Theatre of Scotland which won an RIBA national award in 2017.

Chris is currently the director overseeing the Scottish National Gallery, Edinburgh; the redevelopment of Aberdeen Art Gallery; mixed-use developments at West Register Street, Edinburgh and George Street, Glasgow; Strawberry Field visitor Centre, Liverpool; and the redevelopment of Perth Museum and Art Gallery.

Luke Cooper
Architectural Emporium Ltd., England

Luke is an owner and Director of Architectural Emporium Ltd. Qualifying in 2007, he has gained a wealth of experience across almost all sectors of the architectural profession through various senior roles across the North West. His in-depth involvement in the feasibility, design and management of cultural, commercial, health-care, and industrial projects gives him a unique ability to apply skills from different building types to an individual scheme.

Architectural Emporium are gaining a growing reputation for producing high quality, well considered projects, particularly in the arts and community sectors, where they apply an extremely collaborative approach to design. Their client list now includes major cultural organisations such as Liverpool's Royal Court, The Royal Liverpool Philharmonic, Islington Mill Arts Club, Bluecoat and Walk the Plank to name a few.

Sarah Featherstone
Featherstone Young Architects, England and Wales

Sarah Featherstone BA Hons Dip Arch (UCL) ARB is an architect and Director of Featherstone Young Architects. She has designed projects in the housing, community, cultural, education and commercial sectors. In 2008 she was awarded The Atkins Inspire Outstanding Achiever in Architecture in recognition of her contribution to both practice and education. She studied architecture at Kingston University, The Architectural Association and the Bartlett, UCL. Sarah teaches at Central St Martins and has been a visiting critic at various UK architecture schools. Sarah was one of the youngest members first recruited to the CABE National Design Review Panel and has been an External Examiner at a number of Universities including her current post at Oxford Brookes.

She was a RIBA President's Research Awards Assessor for 4 years, a RIBA Awards Judge, is currently a Civic Trust Award assessor and is a member of the Islington Design Review panel.

Sylvia Hebden
Through and
Around, England

Sylvia Hebden has undertaken built environment project management work for the last decade, is founding director at Through & Around and was Project Manager for the new headquarters for Walk the Plank.

Sylvia worked for three years for the Royal Institute of British Architects on their Places Matter! Design Review service followed by five years as the client-side project coordinator on the Stirling prize-winning Everyman Theatre in Liverpool. She moved on to establish Through and Around a project management practice that specialises in working with UK arts and community sector clients and supporting them to develop quality buildings.

Brian Heron
Ian Ritchie Architects, England

Brian Heron was the Project Architect for the Royal Academy of Music's new Theatre and new Recital Hall. The project received a RIBA National Award 2018 and was named both 'RIBA London Building of the Year 2018' and 'AJ Retrofit of the Year 2018'. Leading the team at Ian Ritchie Architects post-planning from April 2014 through to completion in January 2018, Brian was the main contact between the Client, Design Team and Contractor as well as undertaking the role of Contract Administrator on this £20m project.

In recognition of his contribution to the project, he was made an Honorary Associate of the Royal Academy of Music in April 2018.

Hana Loftus
HAT Projects, England

Hana is co-director of the award-winning Essex-based architecture and planning practice HAT Projects, which she co-founded in 2007. She also leads community engagement and communications at the Greater Cambridge Shared Planning Service, where she is responsible for developing and realising large-scale consultations on strategic plans and policy including extensive digital engagement.

Hana leads HAT Projects' work on strategy, masterplanning, community enabling, housing and workspace. Her experience includes providing community capacity building support for the GLA's Crowdfund London initiative and leading HAT Projects' work for Tendring District Council at Jaywick Sands, one of the most deprived wards in the UK, bringing together a wide range of stakeholders to create a holistic regeneration strategy. She has led the design and delivery of built projects including affordable workspace, cultural buildings and heritage projects. She has a particular interest in rural issues and has led the development of co-created design guidance SPDs with village communities as well as rural housing and workspace projects.

Hana is active in her local community as well as for national initiatives: a trustee of Roman River Music and the Creative Colchester Board; a panel member for Design South East's design review panel and a frequent contributor to journals and publications.

Walter Menteth
Walter Menteth Architects and Project Compass CIC, England

Walter Menteth RIBA, FRIAS is an architect, planner, writer and educator, director of Walter Menteth Architects, Project Compass CIC, Trustee of the North Southwark Environment Trust and Regeneration partnership manager at the London Borough of Enfield.

His practice has received various architectural awards and been nominated for the EU Mies van de Rohe award. He studied architecture at Nottingham, Southbank, and Louvain la Neuve. He has been a visiting critic, external examiner and lecturer at various UK architecture schools, a senior lecturer at the Portsmouth School of Architecture and a member of the Cabinet Office SME Panel.

He holds the inaugural 2015 RIBA President's Medal for Research and an RIBA President's Award for Practice-located Research for his work on procurement reform. Walter has won and

judged architectural competitions, has written extensively on the subject, and also contributes research in climate change, on flooding and rising sea level resilience planning and design.

Angus Morrogh-Ryan
De Matos Ryan Architects, England

Angus Morrogh-Ryan MA (Cantab) Dip Arch RIBA graduated from the University of Cambridge where he received a first class degree and went on to an exchange scholarship with the GSD at Harvard and a postgraduate diploma. He qualified as an architect in 1998.

He has a particular interest in education, arts and community projects. A creative designer with a good eye for detail, he is experienced at taking care of clients and making them feel excited and comfortable about their projects. His long standing experience of building sites has given him a good practical attitude towards trades and construction.

Angus is an Associate Advisor to Arts Council of Wales on the Arts Building Resilience programme, an assessor to Arts Council of Wales for projects including Ucheldre Arts Centre, Holyhead, and Powys Dance, and is a special architecture advisor for a major masterplan in Wola, Warsaw. He is a member of the awards jury

for the INSIDE World Festival of Interiors.

Alex Reedijk
Scottish Opera, Scotland

Alex Reedijk FRC joined Scottish Opera as General Director in February 2006, following four years at the helm of The NBR New Zealand Opera. Prior to that he was Executive Director of the New Zealand International Festival of the Arts.

Having worked for many opera companies and festivals across the world, including Scottish Opera, Wexford Festival Opera and the original Garsington Opera, he became New Zealand Festival's Deputy Executive Director with particular responsibility for the Edinburgh Military Tattoo, which made its first highly successful visit out of Edinburgh to Wellington in 2000.

Over his 13 years at Scottish Opera the company has flourished, bringing opera performances to over 45 communities across Scotland every year. There has also been an array of new initiatives for young people, and for people living with Dementia, including the world's first Dementia Friendly opera performances in 2016. He has also worked closely in partnership with Music Director Stuart Stratford to sustain and develop a very strong commitment to both

20th century opera and new commissions.

In November 2011, Alex was awarded a Fellowship of the Royal Conservatoire of Scotland. Alex is currently Vice Chairman of Citizens Theatre, and Chairman of Beacon Arts Centre in Greenock.

Ian Ritchie
Ian Ritchie Architects, England

Ian Ritchie CBE RA is director of Ian Ritchie Architects. Founded in 1981, it is one of the world's leading practices, with a longstanding and consistent reputation for delivering innovative, environmentally ethical designs using cutting edge materials and techniques. The practice has won over 100 national and international awards. In 1981 he also co-founded the design engineering firm Rice Francis Ritchie (RFR) in Paris.

Ian is a Royal Academician and elected member of Berlin's Akademie der Künste. He is Honorary Visiting Professor of Architecture Liverpool University; Fellow of the Society of Façade Engineering; and Emeritus Commissioner CABE. He advises the Backstage Trust. Recently He has been advisor to The Ove Arup Foundation, the Director of the Centre for Urban Science and Progress NYU, and to the President of Columbia University on the

Manhattanville masterplan. He was made an Honorary Fellow of the Royal Academy of Music in July 2018.

He has chaired many international juries including RIBA Stirling Prize, the RIAS Doolan Award, Berlin Art Prize, Czech Architecture Grand Prix Jury and the French government's 'Nouveaux Jeunes Albums'. He continues to lecture globally, has written several books, including poetry, and Ian's art is held in several international galleries and museums.

Jim Roberts
Fourth Street, England

Jim Roberts is a director of Fourth Street, a boutique management consultancy practice specialising in placemaking and business planning for cultural destination developments. He has over 20 years of consulting experience, advising on a broad range of projects throughout the UK and internationally in Europe, the Middle East and Asia.

Jim brings commercial rigor and financial discipline to the creative process, ensuring that business plans are anchored in sound commercial principles. His advice tends to be front-loaded in projects when key decisions need to be taken and the strategic direction nailed down. In doing this, he often shapes and authors design briefs and is regularly called

upon to support the client in managing design team and architectural competitions. Jim graduated in Management Science from Loughborough University.

Tim Ronalds
Tim Ronalds Architects, England

Tim Ronalds established Tim Ronalds Architects. In 1982, combining practice in its early years with teaching at the Architectural Association and at Harvard. A series of small projects, including Jackson's Lane and Hampstead Poolhouse, formed part of the Four British Architects exhibition at the 9H Gallery in 1990 and brought early recognition to the practice.

The practice has grown in size and its work is now focussed on performing arts and education projects, many with social agendas. Notable award-winning arts projects include the Landmark, Ilfracombe, Chequer Mead, Watford Music Centre, Circus Space, Sevenoaks Performing Arts Centre and the Colyer-Fergusson Building for the University of Kent. Several projects have involved historic buildings including Hackney Empire Theatre, Circus Space, King's Theatre, Southsea, Regent Street Cinema, and most recently The Malthouse in Canterbury. Wilton's Music Hall, the conservation of a unique Grade II* listed

Victorian Music Hall, introduced the idea of 'arrested decay' as an approach to building conservation.

Bridget Sawyers
Bridget Sawyers Ltd. and Project Compass CIC, England

Bridget Sawyers BA (Arch), Dip Arch, MA Urb Des, ARB, RSA is a director of Project Compass CIC and Bridget Sawyers Ltd. She was previously Chief Executive of the Architecture Centre Network, Head of Regions at CABE, Senior Architecture Officer at Arts Council England and a Capital Assessor for Arts Councils England and Wales and Creative Scotland – all with a focus on improving design quality.

She has sat on a number of local and regional design review panels, the National Panel of the Civic Trust Awards, and been involved in appointing design teams and artists for numerous projects.

Since 2001 Bridget has run a cultural and public art consultancy supporting design excellence through integration of art, public realm, and architecture. Current projects include the delivery of Tideway's public art programme in London and public art strategy development for Brighton and Hove Council and public art delivery for Translink in Belfast.

Cathy Stewart
Cathy Stewart Associates, England

Cathy was previously Director at Pascall + Watson and Director for Education at Woods Bagot, PRP and NBBJ. She has been a design team leader for the new British Library, for large multidisciplinary teams in both the aviation and higher education sectors and Chair for Women in Property.

She has worked as a framework manager to BAA, Manchester Airport, Imperial College, University of London and the University of Sussex.

Cathy is a qualified architect, running a practice supporting clients and end-users through building project processes. She has an MSc in Coaching and Behavioural Change, and coaches people in the property and construction industry with a specific focus on improving gender diversity and well-being in the workplace.

She was awarded 'CBI/ Lloyds TSB First Women's Award' in 2006 and 'Women in the City, Woman of Achievement Award' in 2010. In 2007 Cathy was recognised by Her Majesty the Queen as 'One of the Top 200 Women to Impact Business and Industry'.

Nicola Walls
Page \ Park Architects, Scotland

Nicola is a practicing architect, director with Page \ Park Architects and a director of the Tron Theatre, Glasgow. Her professional involvement in arts buildings mirrors her personal interests and, as Head of the Arts and Culture team, Nicola is actively involved in producing memorable spaces for people to engage with creative and cultural activities.

Page\Park's key arts projects include The Lighthouse (Scotland's Centre of Design and Architecture), the Scottish National Portrait Gallery, Eden Court Theatre in Inverness and Edinburgh Printmakers Castlemill Works. Page \ Park has recently opened a studio in Leeds to support a growing of portfolio of work outside Scotland, including in the cultural sector the redevelopment of Leeds Playhouse and the expansion of the foyers at the Symphony Hall, Birmingham. She balances her high-level oversight of large-scale redevelopment projects with a drive to help arts organisations realise their ambitions for change.

Research Methodology

APPROACH

The data used in the quantitative analysis of arts buildings in this publication has been gathered for the period January 2013 - November 2018 inclusive.

Upon commencement recipients of arts funding were identified as the source for accessing and collecting data. This provided a basis to identify arts capital projects developed and delivered in the United Kingdom during this period, to establish for example how that commissioning was undertaken and which architect was commissioned for the projects.

On this basis a quantitative dataset was constructed derived from funding awards for arts capital projects in England, Scotland, Wales and Northern Ireland for the period. This unique data comprises 502 entries with information on 421 projects.

The data research for the funding information was accessed through a desktop study searching the funding bodies and Government websites records for awards given in the period.

Awards below £25,000 were excluded as these were considered unlikely to include capital works.

Note the following were omitted from the research where funding was apparently exclusively or predominantly for:

- Heritage townscape initiatives
- Church repairs, heritage landscapes and general repairs, scheduled national monuments and castles
- Cultural hubs, creative workspace, makerspace and shared workshops, incubator hubs and community spaces, and creative enterprises
- Public art, bridges, visitor centres, and gardens.

DATA COLLECTION

Stage 1: the annual reports and Lottery Funding reports — in additional to regular reporting of funding decisions by the main arts funding bodies — were reviewed, and the grant information was collated.

The primary bodies who provide public funding for capital arts projects are:
Arts Council England
Scottish Arts Council / Creative Scotland
Arts Council of Wales
Arts Council of Northern Ireland
National Heritage Lottery Fund

Other main capital funding bodies, trusts and Government bodies records interrogated were:
Greater London Authority / Mayor's Office
Historic England
Historic Scotland
Museums and Galleries Scotland
Wolfson Foundation
Garfield Weston Foundation
Foyle Foundation
DCMS
Gulbenkian
Northern Cultural Regeneration Fund

The Grantnav.threesixtygiving.org website was also cross referenced.

GrantNav is 360Giving's search-engine for grants data. It is a free-to-use platform that brings together open, comparable grants data that is published by funders in the 360Giving Data Standard. GrantNav enables the search, explore and download of the data about where funding goes and how much is given across billions of pounds of grants, for causes and locations across the UK. The National Lottery funding distributed by the Arts Councils of England, Wales and Northern Ireland and Creative Scotland is not included on this database.

Stage 2: a desktop review was carried out for the capital awards granted.

The first phase of retrieving information was from each arts funding body. This was accessed from the funding bodies' public records, available on government websites. Information recorded for each award was classified and referenced by:
Value of the award given
Which funding 'round' of Funding organisations
Title of the project
Benefactors
Stage of the funding (Stage One or Two)
Value of the project
Appointed architect.

The information available varied in the level of detail and thus a second phase was required to retrieve further information through different internet routes.

Further systematic reviews were carried out in the following order:
    Benefactor's websites
    Local Authority Planning department websites
    Architect's and designer's websites
    Various media websites.

Stage 3: to establish how each project architect was commissioned.

There was limited information available through the funding bodies of the tender process for each project identified. Searches were made of the main procurement portals including Public Contracts Scotland and Sell2Wales, the Project Compass Sesame database, OJEU and ContractsFinder.

An additional search was undertaken for below threshold awards on ContractsFinder using key words such as museum, theatre, and gallery.

Stage 4: additional information recorded.

During the research any additional information uncovered that the authors found of interest was also collated to furnish further insights on the project history, its development, and delivery.

An important element of the study is also to understand what guidance is given to the organisations when they apply for or receive funding regarding the appointment of the architect and design team, and explore if there are any historical commissioning patterns, so where available, this information was also gathered.

GENERAL FINDINGS ON THE AVAILABLE DATA

Public Contracts.
- **OJEU and below** — award notices are rarely published
- **Award notices** — when these are provided they may be at a much later date. For example for Paisley Museum the award notice was published two years after the award was made.
- **CPV codes** — Tend to be incorrectly applied making searches difficult
- **Classifications** — Arts and cultural capital projects tend to be inconsistently classified, often under leisure or education, again making searches difficult.

In public contracts over this period these factors impacting the lack of transparency remain significant and are consistent with the wider construction industry findings by Project Compass evident over the period 2009 - 14.[1]

It was noted that the identity of the commissioned architect was often omitted from websites and other media. This accounts for the number of commissions where the designer has not been identified.

Where possible, information and projects supported by other funding bodies (including for example private funding and Section 106's) has been included. This additional research is not exhaustive and might have been expanded had resources permitted. This may have offered greater comprehension and substantiation in the conclusions, establishing a higher validity of the procurement identified.

DATA SOURCES

Arts Council England. Large Capital fund — successful applicants Tuesday 27 June 2017

www.artscouncil.org.uk/sites/default/files/download-file/170627_Large%20Capital_successful.pdf

Arts Council England. Successful applicants: Large Capital grants Stage 1, 07 Jan 2016
www.artscouncil.org.uk/fund/large-capital-grants?page=2

Arts Council England. Capital Programme Large Grants Stage 1, round 5 spreadsheet, July 2017
www.artscouncil.org.uk/fund/large-capital-grants?page=2

Arts Council of Northern Ireland Lottery Distribution Account 2012-13. ISBN: 9780102986228 London: The Stationary Office. 4 November 2013. © Crown copyright 2013

Arts Council of Northern Ireland Lottery Distribution Account 2013-14. ISBN: 9781910305218. Her Majesty's Stationary Office. 17 December 2015. © Crown copyright 2015

Arts Council of Northern Ireland Lottery Distribution Account 2014-15. ISBN: 9781910305485. Her Majesty's Stationary Office. 17 December 2015. © Crown copyright 2015

Arts Council of Northern Ireland Lottery Distribution Account 2015-16. ISBN: 9781910305645. Her Majesty's Stationary Office. 9 January 2017. © Crown copyright 2017

Arts Council of Northern Ireland Lottery Distribution Account 2017-18. ISBN: 978-1-5286-0650-9. Her Majesty's Stationary Office. 19 December 2018. © Crown copyright 2018

ACNI Awards 2010-17. Crystal Decisions.

www.artscouncil-ni.org/images/uploads/funding-documents/ACNI-awards-2010-17.pdf

Arts Council of Wales Lottery Distribution Account 2016-17. ISBN: 978-1-910305-73-7. Her Majesty's Stationary Office. 20 July 2017. © Crown copyright 2017

Arts Council of Wales Lottery Distribution Account 2017-18. ISBN: 978-1-5286-0655-4. Her Majesty's Stationary Office. 23 July 2018. © Crown copyright 2018

Creative Scotland Annual Review 2015-16. December 2016 © 2016 Creative Scotland. www.creativescotland.com/__data/assets/pdf_file/0009/37296/Creative-Scotland-Annual-Review-2015-16-FINAL.pdf (2)

360Giving Standard search in GrantNav grantnav.threesixtygiving.org/funders. grantnav.threesixtygiving.org

Notices database search Contracts Finder, CPV code 71000000 www.contractsfinder.service.gov.uk/Search/Results

Got Lottery database, an independent website listing all published lottery funding awards. Data is sourced directly from the Department of Culture, Media and Sport. gotlottery.uk/

Heritage Lottery Fund, Board decisions and minutes. Papers from 2014-18 covering London and South, Midlands and East, North, Northern Ireland, Scotland and Wales. www.heritagefund.org.uk/about/decisions?page=4

Historic England. Buildings, monuments and designed landscapes, grants given 2004-15

historicengland.org.uk/content/docs/grants/historic-buildings-monument-and-designed-landscapes-grants-given-2004-15-pdf/

Historic Scotland. Grants awarded 2015-16 www.historicenvironment.scot/media/4195/grants-awarded-2015-16.pdf

Historic Scotland. Grants awarded 2016-17 www.historicenvironment.scot/media/4196/grants-awarded-2016-17.pdf

Museums and Galleries Scotland. Grants awarded 2015-16 www.museumsgalleriesscotland.org.uk/media/1224/grants-awarded-2015-16.pdf

Museums and Galleries Scotland. Grants awarded 2016-17 www.museumsgalleriesscotland.org.uk/media/1555/mgs-grants-awarded-2016-17.pdf

Museums and Galleries Scotland. Grants awarded 2017-18 www.museumsgalleriesscotland.org.uk/media/1554/mgs-grants-awarded-2017-18.pdf

Museums + Heritage Advisor News. Dec 2018. advisor.museumsandheritage.com/news/museums-galleries-scotland-releases-466k-funds-15-projects/

Museums & Galleries Scotland, July 2018. www.museumsgalleriesscotland.org.uk/stories/14-museums-to-benefit-from-over-550k-of-mgs-funding/

Project Compass, Sesame, Directory of Procuring Bodies projectcompass.co.uk/index.php/sesame/procuring-bodies/

Project Compass, Sesame, Directory of Winning organisations projectcompass.co.uk/index.php/sesame/winning-organisations/

Sell2wales Tender Portal www.sell2wales.gov.wales/Search/search_mainpage.aspx

Public Contracts Scotland www.publiccontractsscotland.gov.uk/search/search_mainpage.aspx

A Department for Digital, Culture, Media & Sport, Art Council England awards and recipients, search criteria 02/04/2014 to 18/09/2014 www.lottery.culture.gov.uk/?v=results accessed 30/07/19

Department for Digital, Culture, Media & Sport. Arts Council England awards and recipients, search criteria 23/09/2014 to 16/03/2015 www.lottery.culture.gov.uk/?v=results accessed 30/07/19

Department for Digital, Culture, Media & Sport Arts Council England awards and recipients, search criteria 27/03/2015 to 18/01/2018 www.lottery.culture.gov.uk/?v=results accessed 25/07/19

Department for Digital, Culture, Media & Sport Arts Council England awards and recipients, search criteria 30/04/2014 to 18/01/2018 www.lottery.culture.gov.uk/?v=results accessed 25/07/19

Arts Council England. Successful applicants: Small Capital Grants programme Rounds 3 and 4 www.artscouncil.org.uk/capital-small-grants#section-6 accessed 09/09/19

Arts Council England. Successful applicants: Small Capital Grants programme Round 5 www.artscouncil.org.uk/capital-small-grants#-section-6 accessed 09/09/19

Arts Council England. Successful applicants: Small Capital Grants programme Round 6 www.artscouncil.org.uk/capital-small-grants#-section-6 accessed 09/09/19

Arts Council England. Successful applicants: Large Capital Grants Stage 1, Round 5 www.artscouncil.org.uk/capital-small-grants#section-6 accessed 09/09/19

RESEARCH LIMITATIONS

The investigation is based on desktop research and case studies. Not all the funding award data from Arts Council England and Scottish Arts Council / Creative Scotland was available. This includes the first two rounds of Arts Council England's Small Scale Capital Programme – these awards totalled £9,628,173 for round 1 and £10,265,263 for round 2. Awards from rounds 5, 6 and 7 have been included.

With any data for research purposes it is important to recognise limitations and potential credibility sabotage. It is implicit in such a methodology that the data will be influenced by the authors' subjective interpretation during the coding process. The authors are cognisant of other significant contributing factors:
• Variations in the quality and depth of the available data
• The information gathered is internet based
• It is recognised that the sponsor might create a bias from the perspective of the process and limitation on funding awards throughout the UK
• The sample size was relatively small

Reference:

1 Menteth W., O'Carroll O., Curtis R., Sawyers B. Public Construction Procurement Trends 2009-2014. Project Compass Dec. 2014. ISBN978-0-9931481-0-1 https://projectcompass.co.uk/index.php/compass/publications (accessed 28 June 2020

Glossary

Competition language can be confusing. To define and ascribe common meaning this Project Compass glossary has been mapped to the legal definitions found within Directive 2014/24/EU from which the UK Public Contracts Regulations have been transposed.

This mapping is intended to provide a unified language model for understanding architectural competitions and design contests more widely and allowing international comparison of processes and performance.

(References given to Directive 2014/24/EU below are expressed in short-form as e.g. EU Law Art 82. References given to the Public Contract Regulations are given to the Public Contract regulations 2015 [PCR2015] for England)

AGGREGATION

Adding together the value of separate contracts for the same supply service.

APPROVED LIST

The historic term for a list approved by a local authority or similar, of potential contractors, suppliers or service providers who have met pre-set criteria (a preferred supplier list). A framework panel is the contemporary equivalent.

ARTS & CULTURAL BUILDINGS

Are defined in this book as being: buildings used for the production, performing and exhibiting of art and heritage

AWARD

In a public competition, an award is what is announced in a 'contract award notice', EU Law Annex V Part D. An 'award' is not a term applied to a design contest, where the 'result' is announced within a separate notice that is specific to a 'design contest'. Upon publication of such an award, a project commission may not arise, and further stages may need to be engaged, for example in the case of 'lots' in a 'framework', an award may only offer access to future commissioning opportunities.

BEST VALUE

Arrangements to secure continuous improvement of an Authority's functions, in relation to a combination of economy, efficiency and effectiveness as required by the Local Government Act 1999; the relationship between worth and cost.

CALL-OFF CONTRACT

Individual contracts issued under a framework agreement, used for supplying a specific quantity of goods or services over a given time period. Delivery is either made via a delivery schedule or by separate 'call-off' orders placed against the contract. Similar to a framework agreement except that it is a legally binding contract with the supplier to purchase goods and services.

COMMISSION

In architecture a contract when instructions are assigned on agreed terms between an architect and/or team and a client, to enter into the design/production of a project (see: award, result).

COMPETITION

In general this covers all selection procedures in which parties compete. But competition is a confusing term. The two most important distinctions between the main competition types are how, in principle, they are selected and whether mainly for:

1. The best plan / project design solution – *'design solution'*
2. Suitable parties or teams – *'design team'*

Under EU Law the public competition procedural types are described by: EU Law Title 11.Art 26 (1) for procedures under EU Law Art 27,28,28,30,31 & 32 by "a call for competition published in accordance with" the Directive. EU Law Title 1.Art 2 (21) & Title 111.Art 78-82 defines Design Contests distinctively and are "put out to competition". www.ojeu.eu/Directives.aspx

COMPETITIVE DIALOGUE

A procedures for procurement under the EU Directives, with its own distinct methodology which permits discussion of different options prepared by bidders before the client chooses a particular solution.

CONTRACTING AUTHORITY

Typically means the organisation who will make the award which may lead to a commission. Under EU Law Art 2.1[1] a contracting authority means, "the state, regional or local authorities or bodies covered by public law or associations formed by one or more (of them)".

CONTRACT AWARD NOTICE (CAN)

Notice of an award of a contract published in the Official Journal of the European Union (OJEU), or on Contracts in fulfilment of the requirements of EU public procurement directives. They are intended to announce the results of a tender procedure with the names of those who have won the award and the contract value and numbers bidding.

CONTEST NOTICE

This is a type of public notice specifically for a public design contest, which above EU thresholds is required to be published in OJEU, under EU Law Art. 79 [1] and Annex V Part E. Some countries with their own national portals also require that a distinct notice is issue when advertising public design contests below thresholds.

CONTRACT NOTICE (CN)

A notice that is publicly advertised calling for bid submissions. In public contracts above EU Thresholds these are published on OJEU. Private websites, and National portals, such as Contracts Finder, may also publish these notices as well as those below threshold values.

CONTRACT VALUE

The total monetary value of a contract over its full duration.

CPV CODES

CPV (Common Procurement Vocabulary) codes have been developed by the European Union specifically for public procurement by standardising the classification of goods and services for the benefit of publishing authorities and suppliers. The purpose is to help procurement personnel to classify their contract notices consistently and correctly, to help suppliers find the notices which are of interest to them, and sustain transparency.

DESIGN COMPETITION

A design competition may cover any public or private competition above or below thresholds in which there is a drawn design submission that forms part of a competitive assessment and a selection process made, at any or all stages.

DESIGN CONTEST

A public procedure which enables the contracting authority to acquire — mainly in the fields of town and country planning, and architecture — a plan or design selected by a jury after being put out to competition with or without the award of prizes (World Trade Organisation General Procurement Agreement Art XV 1[j]). There are specific minimum requirements for peer review and anonymity (EU Law. Art. 2[21] & 78). In WTO & EU Law the word 'contest' has a unique meaning that does not occur else-where in any unrelated articles. A contracting authority shall organise Design Contests only within the terms described under EU Law Art. 80 [1]. For a private competition or competition below threshold held in any other circumstance a design contest is required to have at least the same minimum requirements that provide equivalent anonymous adjudication by peer review.

DESIGN QUALITY

There is no set definition for what constitutes good, quality design. However, for a discussion of the topic please see The Value of Good Design CABE www.design-council.org.uk/sites/default/files/asset/document/the-value-of-good-design.pdf and RIBA's 'Good Design — it all adds up' (2011)

EU PROCUREMENT THRESHOLDS

EU Procurement Thresholds (Applying from Jan 2018): www.ojeu.eu/Thresholds.aspx

Central Govt:

Supply/services/design contracts £118,133
Works contracts £4,551,413

Other contracting authorities:

Supply/services/design contracts £181,302
Works contracts £4,551,413

Small lots:

Supply/services/design contracts £65,630
Works contracts £820,370

EXPRESSION OF INTEREST (EOI)

Any competitor who responds to a call for competition 'expresses interest' by making a submission. An expression of interest (EOI) may be a short and simple document requiring illustration that does not include core compliance requirements sought under EU Law for some competition procedures, and may be used for assessment and selection of a shortlist. A Pre-Qualification Questionnaire (PQQ) is a term which has particular requirements from Directive 2014/24/EU and Annex V Part C which includes 11[c] &/or 15, and for this reason is more specific than an EOI.

FRAMEWORK AGREEMENT

An agreement with preferred suppliers which sets out terms and conditions under which specific 'call-offs' (for individual contracts) can be made throughout the term of the agreement. This arrangement between one or more Buyers and one or more Suppliers establishes the terms (such as price and quality) under which the Supplier may enter into future contracts with the Buyer. Framework agreements create no obligation on the Buyer to actually buy anything. Buyers invite potential suppliers to put themselves forward for the framework and choose the one(s) most able to do the work. This allows agreed specifications, delivery terms, prices, and terms and conditions of contract without the need to use a full tender process each time. Once the framework is set up, individual contracts are made throughout the period of the agreement, which typically is up to a maximum of 4 years. If there's more than one suitable Supplier on the framework, a 'mini-competition' may be held to decide who gets the contract.

INTEGRATED PROJECT INSURANCE (IPI)

This is project specific insurance that collectively insurs the client and all other partners in a buildings production. It includes all insurable liabilities of the contractor, consultants and client, including professional liabilities, and remains in place for the contractual laibility period under a single policy. It can be used as part of the IPI Alliance model which establishes principles on all parties.

ITT

Invitation to Tender. This is normally the 2nd stage in a restricted procedure.

LOT

Term used when a single notice calling for bids includes a batch of independently described award categories.

MINI COMPETITION

The process by which suppliers within the selected lot are invited to tender, typically when called off a framework.

MOST ECONOMICALLY ADVANTAGEOUS TENDER (MEAT)

The tender that will bring the greatest benefit to the Client having taken a number of factors into consideration, including quality and price.

NATIONAL PORTFOLIO ORGANISATIONS

Organisations of strategic importance with which the Arts Council England has long-term, multi-year funding agreements. The Arts Council has entered into four-year funding agreements with 829 National Portfolio Organisations commencing in 2018-19.

NEGOTIATED PROCEDURE

A procedure for procurement under the EU Directives, with its own distinct methodology under which the client after issue of a notice negotiates with bidders (at least three) who meet their criteria. The negotiations may take one or more progressive negotiation stages. Unlike other Northern European nations it is infrequently used in the UK.

OJEU

Official Journal of the European Union. The S-series of OJEU contains invitations to tender. www.ojeu.eu. From 31st Dec. 2020 following Brexit, UK contract notices are required to be published on 'Find a Tender'.

ONE-OFF PURCHASES

Used for short-term agreements to supply goods and services to meet an individual requirement.

OPEN PROCEDURE

One of the procedures for procurement under the EU Directives, under which all eligible applicants are invited to tender. It can be organised in one or more stages. For awards above EU thresholds the regulations state that in both open and restricted procedures, 'Any economic operator may submit' EU Law Art 27[1] & Art 28 [1], however a restricted procedure has more specifically defined and structured and criteria, under Annex V Part C 11-18, that require a second stage.

PQQ

A pre-qualification questionnaire (PQQ) is a list of questions relating to criteria that a supplier must meet when called upon to do so, when initially applying for a contract. Typically this first stage submission is followed by an ITT. A PQQ is a term which is now largely obsolete. When the format and structure became standardised they became known as an 'SSQ' (see below), on issue in 2016 of Procurement Policy Note 8/16.

QUALITY

A level of fitness for purpose which is specified for or achieved by the service, work or product.

RESTRICTED PROCEDURE

One of the procedures for procurement under the EU Directives, under which only eligible applicants who meet the client's criteria are invited to tender in a two-stage (or more) procurement process. (also known as two stage selective tendering).

SERVICES

Services provided to the client by an external service provider (an individual or a company). Those that have a value exceeding the current thresholds defined by the EU rules will be subject to the European tendering requirements.

SINGLE PROJECT INSURANCE (SPI)

This is project-specific insurance in the name of the owner/client which normally operates on an aggregate basis and lasts for a specific time period (often 5 or 10 years), and covers the work of all the professionals engaged on the project under a single policy. Also known as SPPI single project professional indemnity. It can be extended to cover the professional liabilities of the contractor and sub-contractors.

SOCIAL VALUE

Where the achievement of value for money on a whole life basis generates benefits not only to the organisation procuring, but also to society and the economy whilst minimising damage to the environment, over and above the direct purchasing of goods, services and outcomes.'

Chris White, the MP behind the Public Services (Social Value) Act 2012 Act, explains: -"We mean 'value' not in its narrow [financial] sense but in its true sense – recognising the importance of social, environmental and economic well-being across our communities and in our lives".

SSQ (or SQ)

Standard Selection Questionnaire for suppliers. A standard format question set with guidance . It has designated parts, to meet regulatory compliance and minimum thresholds that a bidder is required to meet to be considered for a subsequent ITT bid stage. An SSQ submission is typically the 1st stage in a restricted procedure. SSQs now replace PQQs in public contracts following their issued in 2016 as a replacement of the PQQ (see above).

VALUE FOR MONEY

The provision of the right goods and services from the right source, of the right quality, at the right time, delivered to the right place and through the right process, judged on whole-life costs and not simply initial costs.

WORKS:

Building, construction and engineering related works. Those that have a value exceeding the current thresholds defined by the EU rules will be subject to the European tendering requirements.

WORK STAGE FRAGMENTATION

Traditionally architects were appointed to carry a project through on behalf of a client from inception to completion, sustaining through the continuity of their engagement a relationship providing a golden thread for the responsibility, vision and quality of work. Increasingly however architects are being appointed only for particular RIBA work stages in a projects production, with new appointments procured upon conclusion of those stages. In other UK sectors it has become increasingly common, for example, to appoint a high-profile architect to achieve planning permission, and then appoint a different architect to detail the building design and see it through to completion. The diminished value and qualitative standards arising, considered against those publicly projected and anticipated, have become a growing concern. The discontinuity of appointments across RIBA stages is referred to in this publication as work stage fragmentation. It can have significant impacts on project costs, time, quality and values.

Index

Image credits